ANTÓNIO COSTA PINTO

SALAZAR'S DICTATORSHIP AND EUROPEAN FASCISM

Problems of Interpretation

SOCIAL SCIENCE MONOGRAPHS, BOULDER
DISTRIBUTED BY COLUMBIA UNIVERSITY PRESS, NEW YORK
1995

This volume was published
with the support of the
Camões Institute/Portugal

Copyright 1995 by Antonio Costa Pinto
ISBN 0-88033-968-3
Library of Congress Catalog Card Number 94-65458

Printed in the United States of America

Contents

List of Tables and Graphs

PREFACE and ACKNOWLEDGMENTS

For students of radical right-wing movements and the political regimes associated with them, Salazar's "New State" provides one of the most interesting opportunities for analysis of the wide spectrum of authoritarian solutions to the crisis of democracy that sprang up after World War I. A small country with a vast colonial empire, Portugal was to experience the longest-surviving right-wing dictatorship in twentieth century Europe.

Sharing many of the crisis conditions that triggered the fall of most of the democratic regimes during the period between the two world wars, the "New State" that Salazar succeeded in establishing on the heels of an unstable military dictatorship was to serve as a model to a significant segment of the radical Right in the 1930s. This was especially true in Eastern and Southern Europe, but was also the case of reactionary movements like the *Action Française* and of a significant segment of the intelligentsia associated with European corporatism and traditionalist social Catholicism, in such countries as Ireland, Austria, France, and Italy. For many conservatives, Salazar's regime provided a role model, thanks to its capacity to avoid the most aggressive and radical aspects of fascism, while integrating and deriving inspiration from some of the institutions created by it. It was precisely this characteristic which aroused the admiration of well-known intellectuals and political theorists like Mihaïl Manoïlesco and others in Western and Eastern Europe. Establishing itself with practically no interference from the world powers and managing to avoid involvement in World War II, the Portuguese dictatorship finally succumbed in 1974, riddled with wounds from the last European colonial war.

The aim of this work is to identify and analyze the links between Salazarism and European fascism. The first two chapters are an analytical summary of the interpretations of Salazarism and its origins, both in the context of the debate on European fascism and, in a more general manner, in the context of the authoritarian regimes of the twentieth century.

In the first chapter, I focus on interpretations of Salazar's regime, produced by political scientists, from the 1960s to the end of the 1980s. I have chosen this particular period because of the more systematic study of fascism undertaken by historians initiated in the early sixties. Although the main interpretative bases are contemporary with the political and social phenomena in question, it was in the sixties that genuine historical research on the subject was launched. This research not only reevaluated the theories arising from the political struggle but also gave rise to some new ones. It could even be said without causing great controversy that it was during this period that the "interpretative market" was created, which still operates today. Considering the importance, as well as the overlap between periods and fields of research, of history and political science, both shall be followed.

The second chapter concentrates on the evolution of Portuguese historiography on the subject. Before the transition to democracy in 1974, the few available studies on the Portuguese authoritarian experience were published by international scholars or Portuguese academics in exile and therefore suffer from the lack of access to most of the primary sources. When, towards the end of the 1970s, Portuguese scholars came into contact with international research on fascism, the debate was animated. Most of the works on the subject, regardless of their ideological/theoretical perspective (including Marxism), tended not to consider Salazar and his regime as one of the "fascisms". To some Portuguese historians, on the other hand, this exclusion of the "New State" from the "family" was seen as a clear case of ill will, probably resulting from ignorance. One could read a stack of books on European fascism and fail to find one single reference to Portugal. Or, if any were to be found, they would could come under the separate heading of "authoritarian regimes." Empirical ignorance certainly played a role in this but the main problem was theoretical. In recent years, however, the old ideological cleavages inherited from the opposition to Salazarism have abated considerably among the Portuguese academic community as new empirical research undermined myths following the accelerated phase of politicization in the seventies.

The remaining chapters summarize some of my research on authoritarianism and fascism in Portugal. In the third chapter, I analyze the fall of the Portuguese Republic with the military coup of 1926, the emergence of the radical right, and the lesser role played by fascism in the fall of liberalism. The central aim of this chapter is to establish which type of crisis led to the fall of the Portuguese liberal republic and to compare it to the transition processes that brought Fascism to power.

The fourth and last chapter consists of an overview of the regime, its origins and its fundamental characteristics in comparative perspective.

***

The first two chapters of this book were originally written as an introduction to a wider study of Portuguese fascism. The first version was written at Stanford University while I was a Luso-American Development Foundation Visiting Fellow at the Center for European Studies, and served as the basis for discussion, as a "Working Paper", at the European University Institute, Florence. By happy coincidence, I am back at Stanford finishing this work as a Visiting Professor in the Department of History. The main incentive to write this book came from a course I taught in 1992-1993, a colloquium on "European Fascism: New Perspectives and New Approaches", and from the dearth of recent works in English on Salazarism and its links to European fascism.

I would like to thank a few of my colleagues and friends with whom I discussed some of the chapters in this book. They are Juan J. Linz, Stanley G. Payne and Philippe C. Schmitter in the United States. In Florence Stuart J. Woolf lent his support to this and other research studies which I developed at the European University Institute.

The Camões Institute, in Lisbon, and the Department of History of the European University Institute made a significant contribution towards the publication of this book. I also wish to thank Brad Cherry and Alexandra Barahona de Brito for the difficult task of improving my English. Professor Fischer-Galatti, to whom I own the publication of this book, has been understanding as an editor with my delays in delivery of the manuscript.

In the past few years, I have participated with other historians and political scientists on various projects directly or indirectly related to the fascist theme. Among them, I would like to single out Dirk Berg-Schlosser, Nancy Bermeo, Gerhard Botz, Roger Eatwell, Emilio Gentile, Roger Griffin, Stein U. Larsen, Leonardo Morlino and Zeev Sternhell. In Portugal, I would like to thank Manuel Braga da Cruz for his support as well as that of my friends and colleagues Pedro Tavares de Almeida, João Carlos Espada, Nuno G. Monteiro, João Serra, António Goucha Soares and Nuno Teixeira. My deepest gratitude, however, goes to Anne Cova for her contributions to this and other works, at times by long distance telephone calls (and, frequently, astronomical telephone bills) whenever our academic engagements have kept us apart.

Stanford, August 1993

Chapter I

INTERPRETATIONS OF FASCISM AND THE PORTUGUESE "NEW STATE"

From the 1950s onwards, theories of totalitarianism influenced a considerable number of studies on Fascism[1]. German National Socialism, as opposed to the Soviet model, was seen to be the regime which most resembled the totalitarian 'ideal-type', characterized by Hitler's charismatic leadership and a single party representing the regime's sole ideological source which aimed to conquer the state and which maintained social control aided by institutionalized terrorism.

According to the leading proponents of this school of thought, Italian Fascism was merely an 'imperfect totalitarianism' and the remaining dictatorships of the 30s were excluded from the research as they were seen to be too far removed from the totalitarian 'ideal-type'. While Franco's regime was mentioned occasionally in these works, its Portuguese counterpart is not even cited in footnotes.

When these theories of totalitarianism were first tested by empirical research in the 1960s and the first historical works on the subject emerged, the primary concern was to circumscribe the use of the Fascist label which was, at the time, being used indiscriminately on every continent to characterize right-wing dictatorships. Even then, only marginal references to the Portuguese "New State"

---

[1] See H. Arendt, *The Origins of Totalitarianism*, (New York: 1951) and Carl J. Friedrich and Zbigniew K. Brzezinski, *Totalitarian Dictatorship and Autocracy* (Cambridge: 1956).

were made as this dual task of conceptual classification and historical research was undertaken. The reason for this omission is fairly obvious; reacting against the abusive use of the term throughout the 1960s, historians attempted to define both what was unique and innovative about syncretic European Fascist movements as well as the factors responsible for its rise in the aftermath of the First World War. These movements represented something new and unexpected in the European inter-war context and they were not mere vestiges of ideological and party political manifestations of the anti-liberal movements of the nineteenth century.

Subsequent research on the Fascist movements sought to shed light on their capacity to mobilize and find a place for themselves in the context of the social crisis precipitated by the First World War, on their ability to captivate large sectors of the electorate and on the strategies, be they revolutionary, counter-revolutionary or electoral, that these new political groupings used to subvert the liberal order with success, in the cases of Germany and Italy, and unsuccessfully in the other European countries where they emerged. It is worth pointing out that the explanations proffered for the above, in the analysis of these issues in a variety of notable studies such as Renzo de Felice's work on Mussolini and Ernst Nolte's comparative studies of Fascism, did not apply in the Portuguese case where there had been no significant Fascist movement and where a classic military coup had overthrown the Republican regime in 1926.

One of the keys to the success of this anti-democratic mobilization lay in the themes employed by Fascist propaganda, based on a syncretic and extremely fluid ideology which brought together elements from a variety of sources. The Fascism of the 1920s claimed to be anti-capitalist, made caricatures of the bourgeois plutocrat with his cigar and Jewish features, armed itself with nationalist mythology to combat "Red" internationalism, and differentiated itself from the traditional Catholic and monarchic conservatism of the end of the nineteenth century. Notably, many of the agents of this new ideological synthesis came from a wide variety of backgrounds. Mussolini had been associated with the Socialist Party and the National Socialist elite could not be said to have risen from the ranks of the conservative parties. One encountered a broad mix of Sorelian Syndicalists with Marxist roots, Futurists exalting the virtues of industrial society and war, intellectuals who were critical of "corrupted liberalism" and "political parties" as well as war veterans covered with medals.

The great majority of the participants in the historiographical debate ignored the Portuguese case as they associated the ideological origins of the Salazar regime almost exclusively with the traditional Catholic conservatism which had emerged at the end of the 19th century and which showed none of the distinguishing features which characterized fascism and which distinguished the latter from pre-existing counter-revolutionary thought. One should not conclude that this exclusion stemmed from a desire to defend or from an ideological association with the regime which was overthrown on April 25th, 1974. Portugal was excluded even from studies undertaken in the 60s and early 70s which sought to define the nature of Fascism from a Marxist perspective. Searching through the works of Nicos Poulantzas, one finds not a single mention of Portugal. The same is true of other studies, such as those of the Hungarian academic, Mihaely Vajda and of Roger Bourderon, to mention but a few of those most oft-quoted at the time.

The first collective study of Fascism which included an analysis of the Salazar regime, not merely out of editorial convenience but, more importantly, for theoretical reasons, was published by Stuart Woolf in 1968[2]. The contribution on Portugal was written by Herminio Martins. The authors' concern was to pinpoint the elements common to all European right-wing dictatorships of the inter-war period. Nonetheless, even as they wrote about these regimes, the experts were still reluctant to include the Portuguese case. According to most historians, Salazarism did not display the characteristics which distinguished Fascism from classic dictatorships. It lacked a charismatic leadership, a single party which mobilized the masses, an expansionist, war-like ideology and a tendency towards totalitarianism. Doubts remained as to whether Portuguese post-war society possessed the structural characteristics

[2] S. J. Woolf (Edited by), *European Fascism*, (London: 1968).

conducive to the emergence of fascism and which provided the basis for its capacity to attract social groups which, up to then, had traditionally voted for democratic and even socialist parties, namely; rapid industrialization, the 'massification' of political life, the onset of economic crisis and downward social mobility. Moreover, both Germany and Italy had an important factor in common absent in the Portuguese case: a very recent political unification. Portugal was an old nation with no such problems so that the 'New State' tended to be compared instead with the Dolfuss regime in Austria or the Eastern European dictatorships. From the early 1960s onwards, however, new research on dictatorships outside Europe led to the creation of a new 'ideal-type', that of the "authoritarian regime", which went on to influence historians' work on Fascism, particularly when dealing with the problems of 'classification' and 'typology'. Portugal, Spain and the other above-mentioned regimes tended thereafter to be included in this latter category.

1.1 SALAZARISM AND THE FIRST STUDIES ON FASCISM

THE "EXCLUSION" OF THE "NEW STATE"

The 1960s saw the emergence of the most significant interpretations of Fascism. Notably, given Portugal's inclusion in the interpretative debate, references to the country were scarce[3]. The main concern of initial historical works on fascism was to place the debate in a proper historical context by testing contemporary theories in the light of new empirical research. Some of the most important studies undertaken in this period were Eugen Weber's work

[3] For a general introduction, Renzo De Felice, *Le Interpretazione del Fascismo* (Bari: 1969) and *Il Fascismo. Le interpretazioni dei contemporanei e degli storici*, (Bari: 1970); Stanley G. Payne, *Fascism. Comparison and Definition*, (Madison: 1980). On National Socialism see Pierre Ayçoberry, *La Question Nazie. Les interprétations du National Socialisme.1922-1975*, (Paris: 1979) and Ian Kershow, *The Nazi Dictatorship. Problems of Interpretation*, 2nd. Ed., (London: 1989).

on the *Action Française* as well as his first general volume, the trilogy by Nolte and the special issue of the *Journal of Contemporary History* edited by George L. Mosse and Walter Laqueur in 1966[4]. Renzo de Felice's first volume of his monumental biography of Mussolini was also published in Italy, causing a considerable controversy[5]. Several years earlier, Stanley Payne had published the first monograph on the Spanish Falange[6].

Unlike Weber and Mosse who were primarily concerned with the revolutionary aspects of the fascist movements, Nolte focused on what he considered to be the French version of fascism, the *Action Française*, thus coming closer to a consideration of the Portuguese case. When it came to defining regimes, however, Nolte employed a fairly restrictive defining criterion: In his view, "if the mere suppression of parties and freedom of the press were considered sufficient criterion for fascism", all the dictatorships of the period between the two World Wars would be included; they lacked, however, a much more distinguishing characteristic: "popular support and a potential single party."[7] This intuitive half-truth was repeated systematically in almost all contemporary international historical work to justify the exclusion of the Portuguese case from the Fascist fold.

Strangely, given his attitude towards the *Historikerstreit* at the end of the 1980s, Nolte was actually the historian most likely to take the Portuguese regime into account, since all the other scholars of the period tended to stress precisely those elements which were not present in Portugal or others of minor social or political weight[8]. Nonetheless, his first "generic" definition of a "Fascist minimum", namely, "anti-marxism, anti-Conservatism, charismatic leadership, an armed party, and totalitarian aims", made it diffi-

---

[4] Eugen Weber, *Varieties of Fascism* (New York: 1964); Ernst Nolte, *Three Faces of Fascism* (New York: 1964) and the special issue "International Fascism" from the *Journal of Contemporary History*, edited by George L. Mosse and Walter Laqueur, in 1966.

[5] Renzo De Felice, *Mussolini. Il rivoluzionario, 1883-1920*, (Torino: 1965).

[6] Stanley G. Payne, *The Falange: A history of spanish fascism*, (Stanford: 1961).

[7] Ernst Nolte, *Op. Cit.*, pp. 3-21.

[8] AA VV, *Historikerstreit*, (München: 1987).

cult to account for the Portuguese case. This led Nolte to conclude
a few years later that "Portugal should not be (...) considered a
Fascist state."[9] At this stage, on the other hand, De Felice and Karl
Dietrich Bracher tended to deny the advantage of a general concept.

With his *Varieties of Fascism*, Eugen Weber sparked off a wave
of interpretative work which led to the production of a large quan-
tity of empirical work, mostly by North American scholars but also
in part by Europeans, which has continued to flourish to date. Primarily concerned with Fascist movements and their ideological
roots, Weber challenged the notion of their traditional conservative and reactionary roots and stressed their ideologically compos-
ite character and their borrowing from left-wing "syndicalism". He
questioned the validity of the "counter-revolutionary" model and
democratized the concept of revolution, broadening it to include
Fascism. In his words: "Under the surface, all sorts of ferments
were at work, both on the Right and on the Left"[10]. George L. Mosse
made similar comments in his introduction to *International Fascism*: "In our century two revolutionary movements have left their
mark on Europe: The various forms of Marxism and the Fascist
revolution."[11]

Although Weber questioned the rigidity of Seymour Lipset's
typology of extremist movements in his *The European Right* of
1965, he did not question the latter's classification of the Salazar
regime. While Lipset defined Fascism as a radicalism of the centre
socially based on the middle-class, he placed Salazarism in the
category of right-wing radicalism together with the Dolfuss regime
or the Maurras movement. In his view, while these tried to change
political institutions in order to preserve or restore cultural or economic institutions, centre or left-wing extremism employed political means in an attempt to bring about a social and cultural revolu-

---

[9] Ernst Nolte, *Les Mouvements Fascistes. L'Europe de 1919 à 1945*, (Paris: 1969), p. 339.

[10] George L. Mosse, "Toward a General Theory of Fascism", George L. Mosse (Edited by), *International Fascism. New Thoughts and New Approaches*, (London: 1979), p. 1.

[11] Eugen Weber, *Op. Cit.*, p. 24.

tion[12]. Although Weber reminded Lipset that Salazarism had never been a movement, he recognized that the dictator "devoted himself to what may be called a party of resistance."[13]

Other studies were written examining many and varied aspects of the ideological and cultural origins of Fascism and their relative attractions for intellectual elites. George L. Mosse, for example, carried out exhaustive research into the nationalism, racism and even the political choreography of these movements, thus introducing the "nationalization of the masses" question[14]. The abovementioned authors basically took on board the themes of cultural history for the first time; most of the subsequent historical research undertaken by scholars such as A. James Gregor, Emilio Gentile and Zeev Sternhell pursued similar lines of enquiry[15]. Despite the fact that the methodological and theoretical perspectives of these authors, particularly as they applied to their work on ideological origins, were valid for the Portuguese case, their line of enquiry did not make Portugal appear particularly interesting not only because of its peripheral character but above all due to its esoteric nature stemming from the predominance of the traditionalist Catholic element. The Portuguese case simply did not seem to present any special or challenging questions.

The emergence of this new, empirically based line of enquiry permitted a greater understanding of the social bases and political strategies of these movements. Some works drew attention to the diverse nature of the phenomenon and to the vast differences be-

[12] Seymour M. Lipset, *Political Man: the social basis of politics*, (New York: 1959).

[13] Eugen Weber, "Introduction" in Hans Rogger and Eugen Weber (Edited by), *The European Right. An historical profile* (Berkeley: 1965), p. 14.

[14] George L. Mosse, *The Crisis of German Ideology: Intellectual origins of the third Reich*, (New York: 1964); *Masses and Man. Nationalist and fascist perceptions of reality*, (New York: 1980); *The Nationalization of the Masses,* (New York: 1975); *Sexuality and Nationalism*, (New York: 1985).

[15] Particularly A. James Gregor, *The Ideology of Fascism. The Rationale of Totalitarianism*, (New York: 1969) and *The Fascist Persuasion in Radical Politics*, (Princeton: 1974); Emilio Gentile, *Le Origini dell'Ideologia Fascista*, (Bari: 1975) and Zeev Sternhell, *La Droite Révolutionnaire. Les origines françaises du fascisme.1885-1914*, (Paris: 1978).

tween the societies in which these movements flourished. The movements born in Eastern Europe such as the Romanian Iron Guard are a case in point[16]. That the Portuguese case was ignored stemmed neither from what one might call a 'lack of research clout', nor from a reluctance to focus of an overly narrow subject; academics continued to catalogue even the most insignificant of related details. Rather, as stated by F. L. Carstein in one of the first general studies on the subject, "The Dictatorships of Portugal and of the various Eastern European countries were not established by the advance and ultimate triumph of Fascist parties; rather, they represent a much more old-fashioned and conservative type of Dictatorship similar to those which had existed in the Iberian Peninsula - and elsewhere - in earlier decades. Although these Dictatorships were influenced by the rise of Fascism in Italy and Germany and reveal certain Fascist traits, their history has been omitted here because it differs in vital points from that of the Fascist movements in other European countries."[17]

DEFINITION OF AN "IDEAL TYPE" OF "AUTHORITARIAN REGIME"

In 1964, Juan Linz, examining Francoism in Spain, developed the concept of the "authoritarian regime" which was to become very influential in the historiography of European Fascism as it gave substance to the differences noted and described by historians between the Nazi and Fascist regimes on the one hand, and the remaining contemporary dictatorships on the other[18]. Up to then,

[16] Eugen Weber, "The man of archangel", *Journal of Contemporary History*, 1 (April 1966), pp. 101-126 and Peter Sugar (Edited by), *Native Fascism in the Successor States. 1918-1945*, (Santa Barbara: 1971).

[17] F. L. Carstein, *The Rise of Fascism*, (Berkeley: 1967), p. 7-8.

[18] Juan Linz, "An Authoritarian Regime: Spain", in Erik Allardt and Yrjö Littunen (Edited by), *Cleavages, Ideologies and Party Systems*, (Helsinki: 1964). This article was later republished in several collective works. I have used the version published by Erik Allardt and Stein Rokkan (Edited by), *Mass Politics. Studies in Political Sociology*, (New York: 1970), pp. 251-283. The same author later developed his typology in "Totalitarian and Authoritarian Regimes" in F.

the latter group of regimes had tended to be included in a third set, poised between the democratic and the totalitarian regime type. As early as 1958, Raymond Aron had, for example, referred to "this third group of regimes", "based neither on electoral nor on revolutionary legitimacy", a group in which he placed Salazarism, Francoism and the Vichy regime in its first phase[19]. Linz considered these regimes to be different from their totalitarian counterparts and observed that the authoritarian distinction was useful to understand the different ways in which they solved the basic problems common to all political regimes: maintaining control and acquiring legitimacy; recruiting elites; articulating and cohering interest groups; decision-making and establishing relationships with various institutional bodies, from the Armed Forces to religious institutions[20].

According to Linz's definition, authoritarian regimes were "political systems, with limited, not responsible, political pluralism: without an elaborate and guiding ideology (but with distinctive mentalities); without intensive or extensive political mobilization (except at some points in their development); and in which a leader (or occasionally a small group) exercises power within formally ill-defined limits but actually quite predictable ones."[21] It is worth examining this definition and accentuating the distinctive characteristics which differentiate these regimes from their totalitarian cousins, particularly as "authoritarianism" will be referred to at several points along this discussion to analyze the work of other authors and to further the development of the debate at hand.

"Limited pluralism" is understood to mean the survival of heterogenous interest groups and political or religious associations among others in the form of varying groups, as opposed to the "strong domination, if not monopoly, imposed by the totalitarian

---

Greenstein and N. Polsby (Edited by), *Handbook of Political Science*, (Reading, Mas.: 1975), vol. 3, pp. 175-411.

[19] Raymond Aron, *Sociologie des Sociétés Industrielles. Esquisse d'une théorie des régimes politiques* (Paris: 1958), p. 50.

[20] Juan Linz, "An Authoritarian Regime...", p. 255.

[21] *Idem,* p. 255.

party after conquering power; (...)" found in the fascist context[22]. In Linz's view, unlike the strong ideological component and all the concomitant utopian baggage which characterizes totalitarianism, *authoritarian regimes do not have a guiding ideology at their disposal* which is codified and instrumental. Linz prefers to refer to "mentalities" when examining the cases of Portugal, Spain, Austria and France. At the same time, however, given the well-defined presence of "social Catholicism" he wonders whether one might not use the concept of ideology in these cases anyway. Another distinctive characteristic is the absence of "extensive and intensive political mobilization of the population" by the regime after its consolidation. Political militancy is weak and participation in the regime's organizations such as the single party or the paramilitary groups is very limited. He notes that in some phases of its development the regimes themselves encourage de-politicization.

In these cases, the single party, if it exists, plays a much more limited role. It does not fulfill the functions usually ascribed to a totalitarian party: it does not monopolize access to power, it is not the ideological depository and nor does it attempt to conquer the state. Generally speaking, its organization is diffuse and bureaucratic, it is merely one of the various institutions of the regime, and it is not particularly prominent, often being created after the take-over of power and agglomerating diverging tendencies and interests. To quote Max Weber, the nature of authoritarian regimes is also more diffuse, representing a "mixture of legal, charismatic and traditional authority."[23]

This definition was later developed by research in political science, above all by Latin American specialists, and had a considerable impact on the comparative historiography of Fascism. This debate has continued to the present and can be found invariably in all classifications of the regimes of the inter-war period[24]. One should also not forget that a large part of the research on contemporary Portugal was produced by the above-mentioned specialists

[22] *Idem*, p. 256.

[23] *Idem*, p. 269.

[24] For an analysis of the use of this definition by Spanish historians see, Javier Tusell, *La Dictadura de Franco*, (Madrid: 1988), pp. 86-110.

and, in some cases, its experience was compared to that of Latin America.

From this point onwards, the Portuguese "New State" was cited as a variation of authoritarianism in almost all the works which modern political science bases itself upon[25]. Although the Portuguese case was not the object of leading research until the 1970s, references to it became increasingly frequent when classifying party systems, and when giving examples of military intervention and of the crisis and fall of liberal democratic regimes[26]. Many of these references, aside from those based on a rather superficial analysis, err due to what, for want of a better term, can be called a lack of sensitivity to the time factor, particularly important in the Portuguese case when one considers the great longevity of the regime. The following consideration of the role of the single party provides an example of this. In *Authoritarian Politics in Modern Society*, Clement H. Moore recognized that the "Fascist model influenced the Dictator's search for legitimacy, but the party was even less autonomous than the Falange. Salazar continued to rely primarily upon the conservative groups that put him in power. As a result, legitimacy, or what there is of it, rests on other grounds"[27]. Although true this, taken in and of itself, may lead one to underestimate the role of the National Union in the institutionalization of the regime after the military dictatorship. The same may be said of Giovanni Sartori who, when presenting a tripartite totalitarian, authoritarian and pragmatic classification of single party regimes in his *Parties and Party Systems*, places "pre-1974 Portugal" in the third "pragmatic" category[28].

The dichotomy between totalitarianism and authoritarianism persisted in the field of political history among those who did not

[25] Gabriel A. Almond and G. B. Powell, *Comparative Politics. A Developmental Approach*, (Boston: 1966).
[26] Juan J. Linz and Alfred Stepan (Edited by), *The Breakdown of Democratic Regimes,* (Baltimore: 1978).
[27] Clement H. Moore, "The Single Party as Source of Legitimacy" in Samuel P. Huntington and Clement H. Moore (Edited by), *Authoritarian Politics in Modern Society*, (New York: 1970), p. 52.
[28] Giovanni Sartori, *Parties and Party Systems-A framework for analysis* (Cambridge: 1976), p. 224.

deny the value of comparative regime studies. From the end of the 1960s onwards, criticisms of this dichotomy multiplied. Some authors simply rejected the dichotomy, particularly its totalitarian dimension but others, the majority perhaps, placed these concepts in a more accurate historical context and 'periodized' their application in the analysis of the German and Italian regimes[29]. Generally speaking, however, this dichotomy was taken on board by all non-Marxist and even some Marxist historians in their comparative efforts[30]. As noted by Stanley Payne, Italian Fascism was a difficult case given that, in the light of this dichotomy, the totalitarian component of the regime was relatively unsuccessful. Nonetheless, the debate continued and, when referring to the fall of the regime, Guiseppi di Palma spoke of a dual totalitarian/authoritarian legacy[31].

The generally less comparative French political historiography took a similar view. The Réné Rémond school based itself on a fairly narrow concept of Fascism[32]. According to Rémond, "Fascism is a very different phenomenon from the classic right-wing regimes", and he uses the Portuguese regime to illustrate this difference. Even when he reviewed his classic work on the 1950s, Rémond still maintained that it was "obvious that Salazar's Portugal does not belong to the category of Fascism. The "New State" of the Portuguese dictator, owing to its strictly clerical nature, its typically reactionary politics, was closer to Metternich's Austria

[29] For a summary of some of these critiques at the end of the 1970s see, Ernst A. Menze (Edited by), *Totalitarianism Reconsidered*, (Port Washington: 1981). Of especial interest are those of K. D. Bracher and of Hans Mommsen ("The concept of totalitarianism dictatorship versus the comparative theory of fascism"). The latter rejects its use.

[30] Karl Dietrich Bracher, *Controversias de Historia Contemporanea sobre Fascismo, Totalitarismo y Democracia*, (Barcelona: 1983); Karl Dietrich Bracher and Leo Valiani (A Cura Di), *Fascismo e Nazional Socialismo*, (Bologna: 1986), as an example of the recent historians' insistent use of the concept of totalitarianism.

[31] See Giuseppe Di Palma, "Italy: Is There a Legacy and Is It Fascist ?" in John H. Herz (Edited by), *From Dictatorship to Democracy. Coping with the Legacy of Authoritarianism and Totalitarianism*, (Westport: 1982), pp. 107-134.

[32] René Rémond, *La Droite en France*, (Paris: 1954).

and the reactionary principalities of the 19th century than to Mussolini's Italy[33]. Thus the model persisted and gathered strength in academic studies as the debate on the central and peripheral cases evolved.

FASCISM AND THE SOCIOLOGY OF MODERNIZATION

The theories produced by the sociology of modernization may have led to the emergence of more appropriate and inspiring models from which to analyze the Portuguese case and which helped to integrate it into the general theory of Fascism[34]. This was to be noted several years later by Portuguese researchers just as the model came under attack from various quarters and its leading proponents were starting to abandon the approach.

The new variable of "stages of development", industrialization and the conflicts inherent in the transition to industrial capitalism were introduced into the analysis of political systems. As Organski wrote: "It seems clear that the study of Fascist political systems is best approached from an inter-disciplinary point of view, for it is necessary to explore the complex and ramified linkages among three different patterns of change: economic development, social mobilization, and political mobilization. No nation develops in such a fashion that all regions and all aspects of national life keep in step with all the rest"[35].

Noteworthy among the various sociologists who focused on this issue and dealt with the subject of Fascism are Barrington Moore Jr., Gino Germani and Organski[36]. The latter is the most important insofar as our topic is concerned. His model first sets out three patterns characterizing the period preceding the Fascist take-over

[33] René Rémond, *Les Droites en France*, (Paris: 1982), p. 202.
[34] David Apter, *The Politics of Modernization*, (Chicago: 1965) and A. F. K. Organski, *The Stages of Political Development* (New York: 1965).
[35] A.F.K. Organski, "Fascism and modernization", in S. J. Woolf (Edited by), *The Nature of Fascism,* (New York: 1968), p. 20.
[36] Barrington Moore Jr., *Social Origins of Dictatorship and Democracy: Lord and Peasant in the Making of the Modern World* (Boston: 1966).

of power: (1) clear economic growth; (2) large scale social mobilization with a considerable component of rural to city migration; (3) massive and rapid political mobilization, particularly before the Fascists rise to power. A first conflict emerges between the modern and the traditional sectors, based on the former's tendency to expand at the expense of the latter, leading to the development of an increasingly dual economy and society in which context the political system becomes the main, though insufficient, link between the two poles. A second line of conflict develops between the social classes and is reflected by the "aggressive posture of the newly mobilized masses frightening the elites (and other strata)" be they traditional or modern, who respond to the threat by joining forces against it.

The point at which any given society is situated along the continuum of the above-mentioned modernization process is central to the emergence of Fascism since "compromise is the core of the political system" which Organski calls Fascist. In other words, were the modern sector to be already the more powerful of the two no compromise between it and the traditional sector would be necessary. Thus, any possibility of the phenomenon emerging in societies which are already highly industrialized or still predominantly agrarian is excluded. Fascism could therefore only develop in societies at the "turning point" in this transition process[37].

By observing how the regimes dealt with this dual conflict once installed one can better understand their function. On the one hand, political power was vigorously employed to "protect the non-modern portion from the incursions of the modern sector" through a series of measures which aim to protect the agrarian sector. On the other hand, although making concessions to and at times subsidizing the process of industrial development, its main contribution to the modern sector was to keep the industrial workers under strict control. Thus, "the modern sector may continue to grow but it must pay most of its bills"[38]. This tendency generally led to practically zero growth in the industrial sector. In short, the Fascist formula

[37] A. F. K. Organski, *Op. Cit.*, p. 30.
[38] *Idem*, p. 32.

consisted of re-enforcing the threatened traditional elites and their joint resistance with the modern elites to pressures "from below", thus permitting the modern elites to somewhat consolidate their position at the expense of a reduction in consumption.

For Organski, political mobilization under Fascism fulfills one purpose; namely, that of "disciplining the masses into an attitude of obedience in which non-participation in decision-making is taken for granted and becomes a virtue, and of further disciplining them into an attitude receptive to making sacrifices"[39]. Ideology becomes a simple "device" which the elites use to legitimize their interests and way of life. The other great analytical advantage of Organski's model lies in its dynamic approach. "Fascism", he concluded, "is part of a process of transition from limited participation to a mass system, and Fascism is a last-ditch stand by the elites, both modern and traditional, to prevent the expansion of the system over which they exercise hegemony. The attempt always fails and in some ways the Fascist system merely postpones some of the effects it seeks to prevent"[40].

Barrington Moore, whilst pursuing lines similar to Organski, was more sensitive to diversity. Nonetheless, he also caused confusion by including Nazi Germany in his analysis. As far as Gino Germani is concerned, his main contribution related to the means of social mobilization in the context of the transition to political "massification"[41]. Some of this author's views were later discussed in the 1980s by Portuguese researchers and will be analyzed below.

The contribution made by the sociology of modernization left its mark on research on Fascist regimes. However, as a number of ensuing studies showed, the debate on the modernizing and anti-modernizing nature of the German and Italian regimes continued[42].

---

[39] *Idem*, p. 33.
[40] *Idem*, p. 41.
[41] Gino Germani, *Autoritarismo, Fascismo e Classi Sociali*, (Bologna: 1975).
[42] Henri A. Turner Jr., "Fascism and modernization" in Henri A. Turner Jr. (Edited by), *Reappraisals of Fascism*, (New York: 1975), pp. 117-139, for a version of Nazism as an "anti-modernizing utopia" and Italian fascism as a modernizer see A. J. Gregor, *Italian Fascism and Developmental Dictatorship* (Princeton: 1979).

From the end of the 1970s onwards, historians ceased to mention these authors and the problem of "modernization" has been excluded from more recent academic debates[43].

MARXIST CONTRIBUTIONS

Although they were sensitive to the dynamics of social change and rejected the use of merely political classifications, the models discussed above were distinct from the Marxist analyses. Organski noted that the "Marxists are wrong when they claim that Fascism is a creature of the bourgeoisie. As we have seen, syncretic systems represent an attempt by the agricultural elite to slow the pace of industrialization and to control its consequences"[44]. This distinction, however, is rather forced as it is not a foregone conclusion that these elites were in no way bourgeois.

It was, perhaps, studies informed by marxism which made the most important contributions to the contemporary analyses of Fascism and it would be redundant to review them all in their diversity[45]. The most important of these contributions were produced in the 60s and 70s. Once again, it was the thematic choice and the concentration on the role of the movements, which led to the exclusion of the Portuguese case. One cannot conclude that this exclusion resulted from a focus on the central cases of Germany and Italy, since many of these studies, developing theories on populism and Fascism referred to peripheral cases such as the Peron regime[46].

The central challenge however, was to interpret the less linear aspects of the fascist phenomenon, namely: the fact that the move-

[43] See Stanley G. Payne, "Fascismo, Modernismo, Modernização", *Penélope*, 11, Lisboa, 1993, pp. 85-102.

[44] A. F. Organski, *The Stages of Political Development...*, p. 155.

[45] Almost all the interpretative works include them. For a detailed anthology of the analyses of the period between the two World Wars see David Beetham, *Marxists in Face of Fascism*, (Manchester: 1983).

[46] As will be seen below, I do not mean that the subject of populism was not important to the analysis of the crisis of liberalism in Portugal, the dictatorship of Sidónio Pais being the most obvious example.

ment was a popular, middle-class one; its representing a relative break with the traditional elites; the relative autonomy of the political from the economic spheres; and, most notably in the German case, the importance of the ideological factor, a factor which none of the Marxist analyses of the 1930s (or any of the others, for that matter) had in any way anticipated. It was, for example, important to understand how and why there had been "one social order in which Hitler [had been] unable to rise above the rank of corporal and fifteen years later another in which he [became] the central figure in a process of reconstruction of power"[47]. Among the leading Marxist authors of this period were Nicos Poulantzas and Mihaely Vajda[48].

Vajda's hypothesis is introduced in the very first paragraph of his study: "The definitive nature of Fascist dictatorship is that it sprang from a 'mass movement' and, as a capitalistic form of rule, depended on this movement for support. It was the leaders and participants of the movement, not the bourgeois politicians, who assumed the power functions of the dictatorship (...) There is a widespread view that every anti-democratic form of capitalist rule after the First World War must be regarded as Fascist, and so one might expect it necessary to prove that the Italian and German dictatorships were characterized by different traits from those of all other dictatorships at the time, in order subsequently to ascribe any importance at all to the Fascist 'movement' itself"[49]. Vajda sticks to this assumption and set about proving it using some stimulating arguments.

According to Otto Bauer and Clara Zetkin there were traits which the Fascist regimes and the other dictatorships evidently had in common; nonetheless, anything but a clear distinction between the two was rejected. Thus, in Vajda's view, Francoism was seen to

[47] Jules Monnerot, *Sociologie de la Révolution: mythologies politiques du XXe siècle, marxistes-léninistes et fascistes, la nouvelle stratégie révolutionnaire*, (Paris: 1969), p. 495.
[48] Nicos Poulantzas, *Fascisme et Dictature: La Troisième Internationale face au Fascisme*, (Paris: 1970) and Mihaly Vajda, *Fascism as a Mass Movement*, (London: 1976), originally published in 1970.
[49] Mihaly Vajda, *Op. Cit.*, p. 13.

belong to another family for reasons not unlike those already mentioned above: the traditional elites were not denied the exercise of power; the radical demands of the masses were not satisfied as they were in a typically counter-revolutionary context; there was no development of an aggressive foreign policy[50]. When examined from this perspective, one can imagine what might be concluded about the case of Portugal.

The work by Nicos Poulantzas also deals with the subject under discussion. In his book on Fascism, Poulantzas concentrates on criticizing the interpretative approach of the Third International and emphasizing the petit-bourgeois nature of the movements, the relative autonomy of Fascist power from the dominant classes as well as the role of mass mobilization[51]. Poulantzas did not subscribe to the theories on totalitarianism which distinguish the German case from the Italian; he classified them together as "regimes of exception" and excluded other dictatorships such as the Spanish one. Thus, in a subsequent study on the crisis and fall of the Portuguese, Spanish and Greek authoritarian regimes, one of his initial assumptions was that the latter were not "Fascist in the strict sense of the word"[52].

The influence of these authors over the general and even Marxist historiography of Fascism was limited[53]. Basically, these scholars were more preoccupied with understanding the phenomenon as a phase in the history of capitalist development and although they did not go into the peripheral cases, they tended to defend the existence of a "generic Fascism". This is the case of German Marxist historiography, of which the work of Reinhard Kühnl may be considered an example, and above all of Italian Marxist historiography. However, although they based their work on the same as-

[50] *Idem*, p. 14-15.

[51] Nicos Poulantzas, *Op. Cit*, pp. 237-258 and 331-356.

[52] *Idem, La Crise des Dictatures*, (Paris: 1975). I have used the English version, (London: 1976), p. 9.

[53] For a critique of Poulantzas' analytical work from the point of view of Marxist historiography, see Jane Caplan, "Theories of Fascism: Nicos Poulantzas As Historian", in Michael N. Dobkowski and Isidor Wallimann (Edited By), *Radical Perspectives on the Rise of Fascism in Germany, 1919-1945*, (New York: 1989), pp. 128-149.

sumption, several studies reevaluated the importance of ideology and its role in political action.[54] British Marxist historiography distinguished itself from the ordinary economism still dominant in this field precisely on the subject of German Nazism. Tim Mason's contribution to *The Nature of Fascism,* an important contribution to this new approach, was notably entitled "The Primacy of Politics"[55]. "The existence of an autonomous political sphere with its own self-determining laws goes generally unrecognized by Marxist historians..." According to Mason, this appears to be the case of the Nazi regime: "...both domestic and foreign policy of the National Socialist government became, from 1936 onwards, increasingly independent of the influence of economic ruling classes and even, in some essential aspects, ran contrary to their interests. This relationship is, however, unique in the history of modern bourgeois society and its governments; it is precisely this that must be explained."[56]

In general, it is this relationship that the more innovative sector of Marxist historiography sets out to examine. Tim Mason thus cited many examples in which "an ideologically determined policy triumphed over economic calculation"[57].

BETWEEN "CLERICO-CORPORATISM" AND "CLERICO-FASCISM"

In 1967, several of the abovementioned authors participated in a series of seminars in Reading.[58] The reports on the debates reveal an interesting fact: Although research advanced overwhelmingly up until the 1980s, the interpretative debate remained essentially unchanged. There was an evident lack of interdisciplinary

[54] See Roger Bourderon, *Le Fascisme. Idéologie et pratiques (essai d'analyse comparée),* (Paris: 1979).

[55] T. W. Mason, "The primacy of politics - political and economics in National Socialist Germany" in S. J. Woolf, *Op. Cit.,* pp. 165-195.

[56] *Idem,* p. 167.

[57] *Idem,* p. 192.

[58] These meetings gave rise to the works already mentioned above, edited by Stuart Woolf.

communication, with historians contesting the applicability of the models proposed by the sociologists and political scientists. Differences emerged between the proponents of a "generic Fascism" as a form of regime and the proponents of more restrictive criteria. Moreover, the relative weight of political, ideological, and economic factors came to the fore.[59]

Some of the authors, basing their classification on various specific aspects of the Dolfuss and Salazarist dictatorships and placing particular emphasis on the corporatism of both regimes, and the role played by the Catholic Church under them, began to define the latter as "clerico-fascist", "clerico-corporatist" or "semi-fascist". In this writer's opinion these definitions made as a rule by historians, completely confused the issues since the analytical dimension of these concepts was very limited and they made no attempt to distinguish the experience of these cases with that of others. Charles F. Delzell, for example, characterized the Portuguese regime as "semi-fascist", "clerico-corporatist" and "authoritarian" - all in the space of one page[60]. And Henri Michel, to give another example, used the term "clerico-fascist" when writing about Portugal and Austria[61]. Neither of the above contributed anything new to what had been said previously as both emphasized features with which one was already familiar.

1.2 SALAZARISM IN RECENT INTERNATIONAL RESEARCH

Generally speaking, more recent historiography on Fascism did not change its position on the Salazar regime significantly. On the one hand, reflecting the general evolution of research methods in the various fields, there was a tendency towards increasing methodological diversity as well as empirically-based research less concerned with the testing of general models. On the other hand, with

[59] S. J. Woolf, *Op. Cit.*, pp. 51-61, 104-115, 196-202 and 245-252.
[60] Charles F. Delzell, *Mediterranean Fascism. 1919-1945*, (New York: 1970), p. 331.
[61] Henri Michel, *Les Fascismes*, (Paris: 1977), p. 90-91.

the obvious exception of the Iberian Peninsula where both regimes survived until the 70s, Fascism was gradually abandoned by sociology and political science and left to historians. The number of general and comparative works decreased but monographic studies proliferated: literally hundreds of these, undertaken from every perspective and employing all methods of analysis ranging from the ideological to the social, political, and economic, using local historical, oral and biographical perspectives, appeared on the most diverse aspects of Fascism.

As observed by Geoff Eley, the accumulation of more recent research "seems to have compromised the explanatory potential of the old theorizations"[62]. Nonetheless, whether one wishes to accept or challenge them, the old theories are still primary points of reference because, despite the undeniable empirical advances, no new ones have emerged to take their place. The most rewarding outcome of this mass of new research was, perhaps, the opportunity to undertake a more precise classification of movements and regimes from a comparative perspective as witnessed by the various new "descriptive and classicative" proposals which emerged in its wake. The aspects of the definition of Fascism which Eley referred to as the most complex, notably those related to social groups, the economy, political change and emergency conditions, became lost with the focus on national peculiarities[63].

It is worth examining, even if briefly, the analyses of the Portuguese case made by the national historiographies, particularly of those countries whose regimes were more susceptible to comparison with the Portuguese "New State".

---

[62] Geoff Eley, "What Produces Fascism: Preindustrial Traditions or a Crisis of the Capitalist State?" in Michael N. Dobkowski and Isidor Wallimann (Edit. by), *Op. Cit*, p. 69-70.
[63] *Idem*, p. 70.

ITALIAN HISTORIOGRAPHY ON FASCISM

Italian output on that country's Fascism, a central theme of its recent history, is so extensive that it is pointless to attempt to examine the historiography in its entirety[64].

Generally speaking then, Italian historiographical output, not renowned for it consensual nature, generated some notorious polemic rifts. It underwent its own *Historikerstreit* provoked by the famous De Felice interview of 1975, the *Intrevista Sul Fascismo*[65]. For our purposes it is important to mention that these rifts centred on the peculiarity of the Italian phenomenon. Comparisons with Nazism have been central, and it is around that issue that the controversy centered up to the 1980s[66].

Italian historians, however, have very rarely engaged in the comparative study of the two regimes. References to Portugal were also limited as the discussion centred primarily on the abovementioned rifts. In the 1970s a few studies were carried out on Portugal, but they were usually peripheral to Italian historiography on Fascism[67]. The specificities of Portugal's transition to democracy aroused some interest among Marxists in 1975. Some contributions, for instance, were made in the 1980s by Enzo Colloti, one of the authors who espoused the notion of a "generic Fascism"[68].

Reflecting this perspective, some of the studies which took the Portuguese case into consideration rejected the latter's exclusion

---

[64] As an introduction to the research in the 1960s and 1970s see, Emilio Gentile, "Fascism in Italian Historiography: In Search of an Individual Historical Identity", *Journal of Contemporary History*, Vol. 21 (1986), pp. 179-208.

[65] Renzo De Felice, *Intervista sul fascismo*, a cura di M. A. Ledeen, (Bari: 1975). For a *bilan* of his monumental biography of Mussolini see *Passato e Presente*, n° 1, Gennaio-Giugno 1982, pp. 5-30.

[66] As recently as 1988 and in the midst of the German *Historikerstreit*, certain of De Felice's interviews on "anti-fascism" and Italian democracy provoked strong reactions. See Jader Jacobelli's short collective synthesis (a cura di), *Il fascismo e gli storici oggi*, (Bari: 1988).

[67] A. Albonico, *Breve Storia del Portogallo Contemporaneo*, (Napoli: 1977) and P. Giannotti and S. Pivato, *Il Portogallo dalla Prima alla Seconda Republica (1910-1975)*, (Urbino: 1978).

[68] Even though always marking the peculiarities of Portugal's case. For an example, see Gustavo Corni, *Fascismo e Fascismi. Movimenti, Partiti e Regimi in Europa e nel mondo*, (Roma: 1989), pp. 93-98.

by noting that "Fascism - as it occurred in other central and eastern European countries -" could be arrived at by a variety of different routes. Moreover, they emphasized the similarities of the "precise and functional reaction of a particular bourgeois group to the crisis of the liberal state and the powerful advance of the popular classes"[69]. According to E. Santarelli, the author of the preceding statement, Salazarism represented the "extreme Right, non-radical but traditionalist wing of European Fascism"[70].

Enzo Colloti recognized from the outset that "Salazar's Portugal [was] perhaps the case which caused the experts the greatest difficulties in [their attempts to fit] it into the Fascist phenomenon"[71]. In his view, "These difficulties with arriving at an unequivocal definition of the Portuguese regime [arose] from the complexity of [its] ideological and institutional components as well as its social characteristics"[72]. Colotti, familiar with the position of other historians on the Salazar regime, disagreed with those who denied its Fascist character on the basis of the formal nature of its political institutions, but he did recognize that "the more specifically Fascist elements of the Portuguese Right were unable to leave their mark on the constitution of the 'New State'"[73].

To summarize, for this author "in contrast with the Italian Fascist regime but like the Austrian experience, the Portuguese regime's formation lacked a real process of mass mobilization and pseudo-revolutionarism: the regime chose to be conservative and the recruitment of its leading elite was restricted and was notable for its special emphasis on technocrats with university degrees. From this perspective, there was an attempt at creating a leading oligarchy to reach a consensus among the middle classes, with no desire to bring about any social transformation in Portugal"[74].

---

[69] Nuccio Cocco, "Salazarismo" in Nicola Tranfaglia et Alli (a cura di), *Storia d'Europa*, Vol. 3, (Firenze: 1980), p. 1039.

[70] E. Santarelli, "Il caso porthogese: radici e premesse di una rivoluzione", *Critica Marxista*, n°4, 1975, pp. 41-59, quoted by N. Cocco, *Idem*, p. 1038.

[71] Enzo Collotti, *Fascismo, Fascismi*, (Firenze: 1989), p. 117.

[72] *Idem*, p. 118

[73] *Idem*, p. 119.

[74] *Idem*, p. 121.

Which, then, are the features which led Colloti to consider that
Portugal was not a marginal phenomenon but rather one which reflected the "epigonal characteristics of Fascism"? He found there
were several: the "totalitarian" elimination of political adversar-
ies; corporatism which was instrumental in the elimination of the
autonomy of the workers' movement; and spiritual and economic
statism. There was also the important fact that when the "conservative stabilization" had failed, all the virulence of internal repression had been channelled into a long struggle which eventually
had broken up the unity of the Armed Forces[75].

Renzo De Felice took a different position. Although he had never
actually studied the Portuguese case in depth, he had no doubt that
regimes like Salazar's "should not be deemed Fascist but classic,
conservative, and authoritarian instead". Once again, his main criterion was the difference in the character of the regime's relationship with the masses[76].

HISTORIOGRAPHY ON FRANCOISM

Recent research on Francoism has not followed an appreciably
different course from that on Portugal for obvious reasons. Although
historiography on the contemporary era developed earlier than in
Portugal most of the research impetus came from sociologists and
political scientists. International research also made a decisive contribution toward the first scientific studies on the Franco regime[77].

The seminal studies by Spanish historians on Francoism were
not unlike those undertaken by the Portuguese. Juan Linz's various studies were based on Francoism upon which he based his "authoritarian ideal-type". These studies made up a large part of the
initial efforts undertaken and they were to influence a large number of subsequent topical studies. Criticism of Linz's model did

[75] *Idem*, p. 122.

[76] Renzo De Felice, "Il Fenomeno Fascista", *Storia contemporanea*, anno X, n°
4/5, Ottobre 1979, p. 624.

[77] For a debate of this research see Stanley G. Payne, "O Fascismo Espanhol
Revisitado", *Ler História*, 8 (1986), pp. 115-120.

not significantly differ from criticism related to other cases[78].

Among the most interesting of these critiques, however, were those which proposed alternative models of characterization for regimes including the "New State", such as the one presented by the sociologist, Salvador Giner. In Giner's view, Francoism as well as its Southern European counterparts -Portugal in particular- could be defined as variations on modern despotism, what he called "reactionary despotism". Giner's ideal type is different from Linz's perhaps more in outward appearance than in essence, but it does add an element which should not be ignored: the class characteristics the regime[79]. The "reactionary coalition" on which these regimes were based differed from the "middle-class" model owing to the intervention of the agrarian, industrial and financial oligarchies. Due to its syncretic nature, this "coalition" which accompanied the development of the new regimes promoted the distancing of the political system from the totalitarian regime model. Giner also attempts to relate the syncretic nature of these regimes with their longevity in the case of the Southern European periphery[80].

A second problem with Linz's definition with obvious implications for Portugal is the time factor. Manuel Ramirez stated that it was impossible for a single conceptualization to encapsulate a regime that had lasted as long as Franco's. He put forward three different classsifications to characterize the three stages of the dictatorship. Of most interest for the present study, he defined the first as totalitarian and considered it to be a form of Fascism[81].

Nearly all of the empirical work refers back to the primary cases of the Fascist experience, Germany and Italy. Javier Tusell alone

[78] See the critique of Juan Martínez Alier, "Notas sobre el Franquismo", *Papers: Revista de Sociologia*, 8 (1978), pp. 27-51.

[79] See Salvador Giner, Eduardo Sevilla-Guzmán and Manuel Pérez Yruela, "Despotismo Moderno Y Dominación de Classe. Para uma sociologia del régimen franquista", *Papers: Revista de Sociologia*, 8 (1978), pp. 103-141.

[80] Salvador Giner, "Political Economy, Legitimation, and the State in Southern Europe" in Philippe C. Schmitter Et Alli (Edited By), *Transitions From Authoritarian Rule. Southern Europe* (Baltimore and London: 1986), p. 24.

[81] M. Ramirez defined three phases: totalitarian (1939-45); empirico-conservative (1945-60); "tecno-pragmatic (1960-75). See Manuel Ramirez, *España.1939-1975. Régimen Político e Ideologia* (Barcelona: 1978), pp. 23-35.

mentioned the "New State" in a more recent comparative study in which the whole of this bibliography is analyzed. Tusell dedicates an entire chapter to the comparison between Salazarism and Francoism, placing the Portuguese regime at one end of the "regime-type" spectrum and Francoism at the centre "between the two extremes of totalitarianism and authoritarianism represented by the regimes of Mussolini and Salazar"[82]. Tusell is also quite aware of the different periods in the regimes' development and for him, they were very similar after 1945 when Franco's regime approached Catholic corporatism and the Falangist components became secondary. Up until then, while Francoism drew closer to Fascism, Portugal remained closer to the authoritarian ideal. For Tusell, the different periods were much clearer in Spain than in Portugal. Their longevity, however, made them members of the same political family, that of "non-totalitarian conservative dictatorships"[83].

FRENCH HISTORIOGRAPHY - VICHY AND SALAZAR

Ideological affinities were never as close as they were between the regimes of Salazar and Vichy. No-one looked to the Portuguese "New State" as much as sectors of the Vichy regime did. The radical right and French Fascism found at the heart of the Vichy regime have been the target of exhaustive and occasionally polemic research, some of it originating from abroad - mainly from North America and Israel - thus making a confrontation between diverse historiographical traditions possible[84]. More so than in the Italian case, any discussion on the subject requires consideration of these international studies as the latter were not mere interpretative syntheses but represented considerable empirical research contribu-

---

[82] Javier Tusell, *Op. Cit.*, p. 270. See from the same author, "El Franquismo como Dictadura", in Hipólito de la Torre (Coord.), *Portugal y España en el Cambio Político (1958-1978)*, (Mérida: 1989), pp. 47-58.

[83] *Idem*, pp. 272-304.

[84] The most important was provoked by the works of Zeev Sternhell. See António Costa Pinto, "Fascist Ideology Revisited: Zeev Sternhell and His Critics", *European History Quarterly*, Vol. 19 (1986), pp. 465-483.

tions up to the 1980s and some of them broke new ground[85]. One of the key contributions made by these studies was their assertion that Fascism in France was not merely an imported phenomenon as most French studies claimed[86]. Generally speaking, French historians from Rémond in the 1950s to date used a fairly narrow concept of Fascism. This is understandable since most of their research concentrated either on the political and ideological movements which had co-existed in France from the turn of the century or on the "fascist intellectual", a label found preferable to "intellectual Fascism". One ought to add that the individual evolution of some well-known political figures from the socialist or other left towards the most radical Fascism, less common in other countries, called for a greater conceptual clarity when dealing with the subject[87]. Typologies of authoritarian political movements, both bipartite and tripartite, were used in France more than in any other country in an attempt to isolate Fascism from radical right-wing movements along lines similar to some Anglo-Saxon trends. Strangely enough, the strongest case put forward for making no differentiation came not from France but from abroad, notably from Nolte in the 1960s and Robert Soucy and others in the 1980s[88].

The majority of academics specializing in the Vichy regime considered it to be an authoritarian regime distinct from Fascism[89]. Almost everyone seems to agree with this characterization including historians from abroad, from Robert Paxton to the most recent

[85] Eugen Weber, *Action Française*, (New York: 1961); Robert O. Paxton, *Vichy France. Old Guard and New Order* (New York: 1972). See also, John F. Sweets, "Hold that Pendulum! Redefining Fascism, Collaboration and Resistance in France", *French Historical Studies*, Vol. XV, No. 4 (Fall 1988), pp. 731-758.

[86] See Philippe Burrin, "Le Fascisme" in Jean-François Sirinelli (Sous la direction de), *Histoire des Droites en France*, Vol. I, (Paris: 1992), pp. 603-652.

[87] See Philippe Burrin, *La Dérive Fasciste. Doriot, Déat, Bergery, 1933-1945*, (Paris: 1986), with a different perspective of Zeev Sternhell, *Ni Droite ni Gauche. L'idéologie fasciste en France*, (Paris: 1983).

[88] See Robert Soucy, *French Fascism. The First Wave*, (New Haven and London: 1986).

[89] See Jean-Pierre Azéma and François Bédarida (Sous la direction de) *Vichy et les Français* (Paris: 1992).

studies. It is not surprising therefore, particularly in aid of theoretical coherence, that the comparison with Portugal should be made and that it should be in this context that Portugal is most oft-cited as an "authoritarian" variant. Notably, these references have been more mentioned than actually developed or practised.

The list of references to the "New State" begins in the 1950s but for our purposes we need only refer to Pierre Milza's most recent work. Milza not only draws attention to "the basic differences from Fascism" but also introduces the economic and social dimensions when he states that "the main aim of Salazar's dictatorship was to maintain and strengthen the power of the big agricultural landowners to the detriment of financial and industrial capital". This merely confirms "the frankly reactionary nature of the regime which tries to hold back rather than stimulate economic progress and whose main aim is to restore the traditional values of Portuguese society"[90].

The comparison may seem obvious, but it should be introduced nonetheless: as clearly stated by French historians, despite the autonomy with which Vichy was established as a political regime it was a regime of "occupation" and it did not come to power autonomously as either an ideological project or as a political project with a pre-determined social base[91]. In Portugal on the other hand, the opposite seems to have been the case as one can gather from the regime's longevity and the absence of significant external pressures. This variation directs any comparative efforts more towards the field of ideology and the "ideal-type" political regime which dominated Vichy than towards the historical conditions which brought about the fall of liberalism and the establishment of the regimes in both countries.

The sense of a shared identity among Vichy collaborators in the 1940s was felt in the profound influence of the main French radical right movement in Portugal. Maurras's *Action Française*

---

[90] Pierre Milza, *Les Fascismes*, (Paris: 1985), p. 332.
[91] António Costa Pinto, "L'Etat Nouveau" de Salazar et le Régime de Vichy", Jean-Pierre Azéma and François Bédarida (Sous la direction de), *Op. Cit.*, pp. 670-684.

was the main source of inspiration for its Portuguese counterpart, *Integralismo Lusitano.* The latter was, in turn, the most anti-democratic, ideological movement of the time. Although he came from the ranks of the social Catholic movement, the Portuguese dictator himself never concealed the existence of Maurras's influence and he supported him even in the adverse post-war climate in a rare, if not unique, gesture. On the other hand, the example of the "New State" was constantly referred to by the French radical Right throughout the 1930s[92]. This phenomenon is actually better known in France where it has been relatively well researched than it is in Portugal. René Rémond used this example to differentiate Portugal's regime from Fascism: "It is enough to see in which French circles sympathies were aroused: among the Maurrasian and the integralist extreme Right"[93].

Reiterating a widely-held opinion, Pierre Milza stated that "Vichy's closest link was with Dr. Salazar's paternalistic regime, at least if one considers the aims expressed by the two dictatorships: the restoration of the traditional institutions and elites; the re-establishment of the moral order and the spiritual leadership of the church; the rejection of modernism and industrial civilization revealing a distrust of Fascist totalitarianism, its ideological outcome, and of liberalism and Marxist socialism. The divergence from the Portuguese case, however, was quite clear on two points. On the one hand, the Vichy experience unfolded in an established industrial country and the regressive route it invited its followers to take stemmed much from an utopian ideal. On the other hand, Vichy's ruling elite was much less homogenous that the one that from the early 30s onwards ruled the destiny of the "New State". Thus, right from the start, a hiatus was established between the ultra-reactionary hard-core and the other power-mongers[94]. A similar thesis was held by North American historians such as Robert Paxton and even by some French political scientists and historians

---

[92] See Pierre Rivas, "La réception de Salazar dans la littérature française", communication au Colloque "Salazar et L'Estado Novo", E.H.E.S.S., Paris, 10-12 Mai 1993.

[93] René Rémond, *Op. Cit*, p. 202.

[94] Pierre Milza, *Le Fascisme Français. Passé et Présent.* (Paris: 1987), p. 230.

who wrote about the Portuguese regime[95]. In his conclusions, Jacques Georgel wondered: "Was Salazarism Fascism? The question has been debated. The preceeding pages, to my mind, justify the answer 'no' (...) If by Fascism we mean an ordinary dictatorship, then Salazarism was in fact Fascism; but from the scientific point of view, this assimilation is of no interest. If one wished to take the term 'Fascism' as a precise definition, one must go further"[96].

AUSTRIAN HISTORIOGRAPHY

Dolfuss's dictatorship has always been mentioned, both in Portuguese and international research, as being comparable to Salazar's. Some common elements are instantly recognizable: the importance of Catholicism and corporatism or the creation of the regime "from above". Austrian researchers do not seem to have made similar comparisons but the international academic community, however, felt the comparison to be apt, particularly those who considered "clerical fascism" to be a working category.

Austria has a special place in the history of Fascism and it is unique in that it experienced two dictatorships, one right after the other. The authoritarianism vs. totalitarianism debate in this case does not appear to have been a merely academic question. Certainly not for those who lived under both these regimes. Although Austrian Nazism has sometimes been considered to be a foreign phenomenon resulting from "occupation", an argument used more for reasons of political or international convenience than anything else, the native character of both experiences is assumed by modern Austrian historiography and the comparison is therefore legitimate.

---

[95] See Robert O. Paxton, "A França de Vichy sob uma Perspectiva Comparativa", *in* AAVV, *O Estado Novo. Das Origens ao Fim da Autarcia*, Vol. I, (Lisboa: 1987), pp. 49-58.

[96] Jacques Georgel, *Le Salazarisme. Histoire et Bilan, 1926-1974*, (Paris: 1981), p. 301. See also, Jacques Marcadé, *Le Portugal au XX Siècle, 1910-1985*, (Paris: 1988).

For our purposes, the central point of interest is the Dolfuss-Schuschnigg regime (1933-1938), defined by its opponents at the time as "Austro-Fascism". The debate on its characterization uses the same theoretical references as those applied in the case of the Iberian Peninsula. Whilst for some the definition is appropriate for others, like Gerhard Botz, Dolfuss's dictatorship "did not have the essential traits of a true Fascist regime; nor was it simply a corporatist state in the sense of Catholic social doctrine. Observed at its height in 1934, it was not much more than a traditional dictatorship, established 'from above', an authoritarian state with a Fascist veneer and a corporatist patina. From the point of view of the classification of political regimes, the basis for the definition "Austro-Fascism" seems questionable"[97].

For both historical and theoretical reasons, most attempts at comparison were made with Italy owing to Italian Fascist political and financial involvement in Austria stemming from a strategic rivalry with Nazi Germany and which merged with support for the Austrian Fascist movements and the establishment of the Dolfuss regime itself. Moreover, given that Austria was not a highly industrialized country and that it had an important agricultural sector, its economy, society and the cultural importance of Catholicism were factors which highlighted the similarities with the Italian case[98].

For comparative purposes, several factors seem to bring Dolfuss's and Salazar's regimes closer together but some difficulties arise nonetheless. Some are of a historical nature and derive from the different conditions relating to the creation of the "Na-

[97] See Gerhard Botz, "Fascismo e Autoritarismo in Austria. Heimwehr, nazionalsocialismo e "austrofascismo", in Roberto Cazzola and Gian Enrico Rusconi (A cura di), *Il "Caso Austria". Dall'"Anschluss" all'èra Waldheim*, (Torino: 1988), p. 48., *Krisenzonen einer Demokratie. Gewalt, Streit und Konfliktunterdrückung in Österreich seit 1918*, (Frankfurt: 1987), pp. 211-236. As an introduction to the several interpretations see John Rath and Carolyn W. Schum, "The Dolfuss-Schuschnigg Regime: Fascist or Authoritarian ?", in Stein U. Larsen et alli (Edited By), *Who Were the Fascists. Social Roots of European Fascism* (Bergen: 1980), pp. 249-256.
[98] For a similar effort from Italian historiography see Enzo Collotti, *Op. Cit.*, (Firenze: 1989), pp. 91-103.

tional State" and from outside interference in the overthrow of liberalism. There are other endogenous differences such as the way in which the two regimes were formed and broke with democratic rule. The similarities which are worth studying are found in the workings of formal apparatus of the political system, in the latter's ideological legitimation and in the central importance of the Catholic church under both dictatorships.

The importance of the Catholic church was decisive, both in the overthrow of democracy and in the ideologies of each regime, particularly their corporatist nature. Both dictatorships were created "from above", had single parties with similar vocations and origins and showed the same distrust of domestic Fascist movements, particularly in the case of Austria where they had a greater social and political weight. "From above" ought to be qualified since while in Portugal a clear break with the liberal order was made, in Austria it was one of the political "camps" with a party representation still under democratic rule which "fascistized" the regime. These and other issues have not yet been the subject of a comparative study but in the 1980s the predominant classifications invariably placed Austria 'close' to Salazar's regime, virtually placing it them in the same "family".

THE EASTERN EUROPEAN DICTATORSHIPS

The Eastern European dictatorships present similar and perhaps more serious problems of comparative analysis and characterization than those posed by the cases of Portugal and Austria. It would be pointless to attempt a historiographical summary here. Part of the bibliography cited on the inter-war dictatorial regimes was based, perhaps in excess, on the academic work of Western and exiled specialists. A whole series of pioneering works were written by North American and Western European social scientists[99].

---

[99] See some works as the already quoted of Peter Sugar or Joseph Rothschild, *East Central Europe between the Two World Wars*, (Seattle: 1974) and Anthony Polonsky, *The Little Dictators. The History of Eastern Europe since 1918*, (London and Boston: 1975).

The idea of the existence of a powerful political blockade against research into the subject or of the impact of ideological factors on the study of these regimes was not mere exaggeration up to the recent breakdown of the barriers. It was at the end of the 1960s that a body of empirical and comparative research began to emerge evincing both a variety of interpretations as well as vast national differences but part of this research often failed to appear in the international debate[100]. Most of the authors who left their mark on interpretative debates in the West were discussed, the authoritarianism-Fascism duo was accepted by many of them, the concept of totalitarianism was used, the limitations of some Marxist models were re-stated regarding, for example, the relationship between the social, economic structure and the established authoritarian systems. Upon reading studies on Fascism written by historians from Eastern Europe in the 1970s and 1980s one encounters the same problems and conceptual doubts as those already found in the other above-mentioned research[101].

Momentarily putting aside the debate on the legitimacy of grouping together in one category the very different sets of political and economic conditions found in these countries, it is nonetheless a fact that most of dictatorships in this part of Europe, from the small Baltic states to the Balkans, had very similar characteristics[102]. Moreover, their inclusion in a classification of European Fascism does not appear to be controversial. Whatever one's attitude to the application of the concept, these regimes will always remain closer to their counterparts at the other end of Europe and to Austria than to Nazism and Italian Fascism. If one excludes the short period of

[100] See *Fäsismus a Europa. Fascism and Europe*, 2 vol., (Prague: 1969-1970). For a example of this effort from Polish historiography *vide*, Janusz Zarnowski (Editor), *Dictatorships in East-Central Europe. 1918-1939*, Polish Historical Library n° 4, (Wroclaw: 1983).
[101] Janus Zarnowski, "Authoritarian Systems in Central and South-Eastern Europe (1918-1939). Analogies and Differences" and Franciszek Ryska, "European Fascism. Divergences and Similarities. Prospects of Comparative Research" in Janus Zarnowski (Editor), *Op. Cit.*, pp. 9-26 and 223-246.
[102] See Joseph Held, (Edited by), *The Columbia History of Eastern Europe in The Twentieth Century*, (New York: 1992), particularly the introduction by Stephen Fischer-Galati.

Iron Guard rule in Romania (albeit shared rule), none of the other Fascist movements in this region came to power[103].

It is particularly important to clarify the Fascist-authoritarian problem in these cases. This is so because of the undeniably real and frequent presence of native Fascist movements in the region carrying more political weight than their Iberian counterparts and because of the greater or lesser repression used by the budding authoritarian powers themselves. The balance between regime-Fascist movements was also affected by the growing influence of Germany and Italy[104].

Despite each country's peculiar characteristics, some common elements brought most of the regimes together. All of these regimes were on the under-developed periphery of industrialized Europe and the greater part of their populations still worked in the agricultural sector. All of them made attempts to establish democratic rule. All of them were based on traditional elite power and they were largely born out of an anti-democratic elite response to democratization and social change. As stated by Zarnowski, they were "a new form of power of (sic) the old ruling classes and circles, and were not governments by a new Fascist elite of the type produced by mass Fascist organizations in Italy and Germany"[105]. The means they used to overthrow the liberal order was the classic military coup[106]. Given the overlapping existence of native Fascist movements, research tended to draw attention to the differences

---

[103] See Stephen Fischer-Galati, *Twentieth Century Rumania,* (New York: 1992) and Radu Ioanid, *The Sword of the Archangel. Fascist Ideology in Rumania*, (Boulder: 1990).

[104] About the relations between the two fascist regimes and the movements and regimes of Eastern Europe see Jerzy W. Borejsza, *Il Fascismo e L'Europa Orientale. Dalla propaganda all'aggressione*, (Roma-Bari: 1981).

[105] Janus Zarnowski, " Authoritarian Systems...", p. 11.

[106] Metaxas's "New State" could also be included given that it shared many of the caracteristics of those dictatorships that do not "correspond to either the Italian Fascist or the nazi models, althought it borrowed certain elements from both". See John V. Kofas, *Authoritarianism in Greece. The Metaxas regime*, (Boulder: 1983).

between the social bases of the regimes and those of the movements[107].

There were a wide variety of forms of government ranging from the more institutionalized dictatorships such as those found in the Baltic nations to others based on limited pluralism such as Hungary or Poland up to 1935. Smetona's Lithuania, for example, was much closer to its western counterparts; it was more like the Portuguese "New State" than Pilsudski's regime in Poland which, unlike Salazar's, did not completely eliminate the opposition. An element common to all of these regimes was the creation of parties supporting the regime "from above", similar in type, bases and functions to their counterparts in the Iberian Peninsula.

For the purpose of comparison one should consider a few elements specific to this part of Europe. One of these is the "national question" - different in this region from other areas, and its related problems of national minorities and the re-establishment of the "National State". Another element is the issue of the international influence resulting from the power struggle after the Versailles Treaty.

When examining the nature of these regimes, national historiographies pose the questions with which we are already familiar from our literature; they do not bear repeating. Suffice it to say that Franciszek Ryska suggested in his conclusions that one should go back to basics stating that the initial assumption "there is no Fascism without Fascists" should guide subsequent research[108]. References to the "New State" are few and far between and, although they are constantly cited as being the most similar, there has been as yet no work which systematically compares these regimes and those of the Iberian Peninsula[109].

---

[107] We exclude the changes provoked by German occupation or by its inspiration, from the late 1930s on.

[108] Franciszek Ryszka, " European Fascism...", p. 245.

[109] For some elements of comparison between Portugal and Rumania, see Philippe C. Schmitter, "Reflections on Manoilescu and the political consequences of delayed-dependent development on the periphery of Western Europe", Kenneth Jowitt (Editor), *Social Change in Rumania, 1860-1940*, (Berkeley: 1972), pp. 117-139.

SYNTHESES AND GENERAL INTERPRETATIONS

The majority of the general works produced in the 1980s also reflected the Fascist-Authoritarian dichotomy. One can quote two examples of this from different historiographical traditions. There is Stephen J. Lee who in *The European Dictatorships* placed the "New State" among the type of dictatorships that were "fundamentally non-Fascist"[110]. And from the French historiography one has Pierre Milza's *Les Fascismes* which echoes the same opinion only providing greater detail[111]. In 1986 Stuart Woolf restated the similarities and the differences between the Iberian and the German and Italian regimes, differences also applicable to the Eastern European cases, and concluded that "finally, the main distinguishing characteristic between the authoritarian and Fascist regimes in Europe between the two World Wars was the relative absence, in the former, of plans for aggressive expansion and also a realistic hostility to the danger posed by the Fascist movements at home"[112].

In a comparative essay, Juan Linz pinpoints four types of situations of breakdown or of overthrow of liberal regimes. Linz sticks to the idea that the Fascist component is absent from the former process. In a chapter comparing Salazarism and Francoism, however, he proposed that the former was closer to the Italian "ideal-type". In effect, "we could argue that the regime created by Salazar was more coherent ideologically, organizationally, continuous with its elite recruitment and over time than the Franco regime with its more easily distinguishable phases and twists in policy"[113].

Over the last few years some new analytical perspectives have been proposed with regard to Fascism. In *The Nature of Fascism* Roger Griffin put forward a new classification for movements and regimes that went beyond a mere re-focussing of the ideological

[110] Stephen J. Lee, *The European Dictatorships. 1918-1945*, (London: 1988), pp. 107-134.

[111] Pierre Milza, *Op. Cit.*, p. 332.

[112] Stuart Woolf, "Movimenti e regimi di tipo fascista in Europa", in Nicola Tranfaglia and Massimo Firpo (a cura di), *La Storia. I grandi problemi dal Medioevo all'Età Contemporanea*, Vol. 9, (Torino: 1986), p. 325.

[113] Juan Linz, *Fascism, Breakdown of Democracy, Authoritarian and Totalitarian Regimes: Coincidences and Distinctions*, Mimeo.

dimension of a new "ideal-type"[114]. Salazarism was nonetheless included in the "para-fascist" regime definition along with others abovementioned. These regimes were defined by Griffin as dictatorships which were compelled to adopt some of the devices of the "era of the masses", namely a "facade of popular legitimation". He recognized the fact that Salazarism had experimented with "Fascizing elements" but cited the case of the elimination of Rolão Preto's fascist clique to illustrate the "fundamental conflict between para-fascism and the real thing"[115].

SALAZARISM: A SOUTHERN EUROPEAN MODEL

It is worth noting that there is a comparative dimension which although more widely employed by political scientists than by historians, is now finding some favour among historical researchers. But for the occasional exception, the use of the concept of "Southern Europe" as a unit of comparison and analysis pertinent to the contemporary history of nations like Portugal, Spain, Italy and Greece has been very infrequent[116]. It was only from the 1960s onwards and with the transition processes which led to democracy in the 1970s in particular, that the Southern European concept gained momentum. It focused on both the common context of "underdevelopment" or "economic backwardness" examined by economic and social historians, and on the common framework of the analysis of political instability during the protracted periods of transition to democracy in the 70s. Its retroactive use, however, is difficult considering the absence of unifying agents such as the Austro-Hungarian Empire or the Communist experience throughout the second half of the 20th century in the case of Central and Eastern Europe. The inclusion of a country such as Italy whose economic and political development throughout the course of this century

---

[114] Roger Griffin, *The Nature of Fascism*, (London: 1991).
[115] *Idem*, pp. 122-123.
[116] See Stanley G. Payne, 'The concept of "Southern Europe" and political development', *Mediterranean Historical Review*, 1, 1986, pp. 100-115.

has, at times, deviated significantly from the other Southern European cases, is problematic.

During the 70s and 80s, however, a number of political scientists and historians attempted to prove that "the paralellisms of recent decades are not new phenomena and that our four nations [Portugal, Spain, Italy, and Greece] have followed a common pattern of historical development which justifies grouping them together under the regional concept of Southern Europe"[117]. More political scientists than historians have engaged in this type of comparative analysis since the latter have been more reluctant to overcome the barrier which the concept of "Nation-State" represents as a unit of analysis. A variation on the same theme which occurred almost exclusively in the realms of sociology and political science was the broadening of the scope of comparative study to include Latin America based on the same cluster of characteristics used to explain Southern Europe's uniqueness.

Howard Wiarda whose works on Portugal will be discussed at various points in the course of this study, summed up some of the recurring factors subsequently taken up by other authors[118]. Of these factors, the leading one was "a continuing and comparatively high degree of corporatism, patrimonialism, and organic statism"[119]. A "pivotal" role was assumed by the State and the very processes of political change during that period took place "under State auspices and control". These changes, even then they lean towards more "pluralist" and "liberal" models, "continue to take place within an organicist, patrimonialist, corporatist, and bureaucratic-statism framework and does not necessarily imply a transition to a fully 'laissez-faire' society and polity"[120].

---

[117] Edward Malefakis, "The socioeconomic and Historical Context", in N. P. Diamandouros, R. Gunther and H. J. Puhle, *The Consolidation of Democracy in Southern Europe* (Forthcoming).

[118] Howard Wiarda, "From Corporatism to Neo-Syndicalism: The State, Organized Labor, and the Changing Industrial Relation Systems of Southern Europe", Monographs on Europe, Center For European Studies, Harvard University, 1981.

[119] *idem*, p. 62.

[120] *Idem*, p. 63.

The persistance of these elements which have also prevailed, even if in somewhat different form, in 20th century Latin America, encouraged the proliferation of comparative studies between the two regions. These works are pertinent to the study of authoritarianism and right-wing dictatorships like Salazarism[121]. The presence of a selective, oligarchic liberalism, the emergence of populism during the transition to the "era of the masses", recurring military intervention in politics, and the establishment of dictatorships which sought to legitimize themselves through corporatism, were elements shared by the two different regions from the beginning of the 20th century onwards. In the sphere of authoritarian regimes, characteristics such as the presence of single parties with limited power, catering to special interests and the strong presence of the bureaucracy and the State, led to the "bureaucratic-authoritarianism" label for Latin America which fit some of the dictatorships of Southern Europe, Salazarism among them. Interestingly enough, some Southern European dictatorships had more in common with Latin American dictatorships than with Italian Fascism.

During the 1980s a number of comparative studies on Southern Europe's transition to democracy included chapters on relevant historical and cultural conditions that led to political change[122]. In one of these studies, historian Edward Makefakis suggested some of the factors essential for the comparative study of the democratic crises, the Fascist regimes and dictatorships of Southern Europe. For him, the key was to be found in the "intermediacy" of Southern Europe in terms of the stage at which it found itself in the transition toward an industrial society - between the Western European model and the rural societies to the East.

In brief, Malefakis explains how the "modern political movements arose earlier, but were unable to establish their hegemony",

[121] See Guillermo O'Donnell, *Modernization and Bureaucratic Authoritarianism: Studies in South American Politics*, (Berkeley: 1973) and James Malloy, Ed., *Authoritarianism and Corporatism in Latin America*, (Pittsburg: 1977).

[122] See Salvador Giner, "Political Economy, Legitimation, and the State in Southern Europe", *cit.*

and how powerful institutions, like the Church, the Armed Forces, associations and interest groups linked to sectors of the oligarchy, were instrumental in setting the Southern European nations on a course which did not follow the Western European pattern[123]. His analysis is not appreciably different from that of Nicos Mouzelis as the latter emphasizes the problems of societies which have experienced an "early parliamentarianism and late industrialization"[124]. Even though "capitalism was accepted as [the] primary mode of economic organization... its legitimacy was always questioned"[125]. It was this "economic dualism" which left a harsh imprint on Southern Europe's social and political reality.

As indicated by a number of abovementioned authors, the search for a specifically Southern European trend with respect to Fascism is not without problems[126]. Indeed, the definition of dictatorships such as those of Primo de Rivera or Salazar as the Southern European "norm" is contradicted by the evolution of Italian Fascism. Comparisons are risky whenever the attempt is made to include the Italian dictatorship as a paradigm for this part of Europe. Malefakis, for example, acknowledging the differences ("if only because of Mussolini and the Fascist party"), considers the latter to be superficial and not actual throughout the 1920s[127]. The evolution of Mussolini's regime in the 30s, on the other hand, clearly signalled a distancing from regimes like Salazar's and Metaxas', thus bringing one back to the question posed initially in the works analyzed above. It is not surprising then that the first students of the Portuguese case, most of them coming from a Latin American research background, approached Portugal searching for corporatism, "social Catholicism", colonialism and the role of the military. A considerable number of these students concentrated on

---

[123]   Edward Malefakis, "The socioeconomic and Historical Context", in N. P. Diamandouros, R. Gunther and H. J. Puhle (Edited By), *Op. Cit.*

[124]   See Nicos Mouzelis, *Politics in the Semi-Periphery. Early Parliamentarism and Late Industrialization in the Balkans and Latin America*, (London: 1986).

[125]   Edward Malefakis "The Socioeconomic....", *Cit.*

[126]   *Idem.*

[127]   *Idem.*

the last two of the above questions as the colonial war dragged on, presaging the political mobilization of those who had overthrown the parliamentary republic in the 1920s.

Chapter II

PORTUGUESE RESEARCH ON SALAZARISM

The "New State's proximity in time makes it a particularly fertile area of research for political scientists, historians, sociologists whose approaches borrow from the traditions in each others' disciplines. It was only in the 1970s, however, that the study of 20th century Portugal began to take off, having been relegated until then to the periphery. Its inclusion in university curricula is recent, specialization in the subject is rare and links with international historiography still tenuous[1].

The transition to democracy in Portugal gave rise to the gradual institutionalization of national studies on the 20th century, particularly those which focused on the "New State". The natural euphoria of a "revolutionary" transition expressed in the "denunciations" were followed by the first serious social science studies. Many of the latter were subsequently translated and used as a basis for this new field of research abroad. Two conferences held in the 1980s on the subject outlined the research undertaken up to then, revealing the quantitative and qualitative progress which had taken place in the field[2].

[1] Manuel Braga da Cruz and Manuel de Lucena "Introdução ao desenvolvimento da ciência política nas universidades portuguesas", *Revista de Ciência Política*, Lisboa, 2ª semestre de 1985, nª 2, pp. 5-41; João B. Serra, "Os Estudos sobre o Século XX na Historiografia Portuguesa do Pós-Guerra", *Penélope* nº 5, 1991, pp. 111-147; António Costa Pinto, *O Salazarismo e o Fascismo Europeu. Problemas de interpretação nas ciências sociais*, (Lisbon: 1992).

[2] See AA. VV. *O Fascismo em Portugal*, (Lisboa: 1982) and AA.VV, *O Estado Novo - Das origens ao fim da autarcia, 1926-1959*, 2 Vol., (Lisboa: 1987).

Although research into Salazar's regime became progressively less politicized, it naturally reflected existing ideological rifts, particularly those of the various opposition factions. Some of the differences stemmed from the extreme left's objections to the Communist Party's interpretation of the role of the regime with regard to the development of capitalism in Portugal; others from the liberal opposition's views on the equally obstructive role of the "New State". These early differences, stemming directly from the internal disputes among the nation's cultural elite were, in fact, quickly toned down. They will not be fully addressed in this chapter so as to focus more effectively on the relationship between the "New State" and Fascism.

2.1 GENERIC INTERPRETATIONS

Stanley G. Payne referred to the newly emerging research on Portuguese authoritarianism in his bibliographical study of 1980[3]. Stuart Woolf's work of 1968 included a contribution on the "New State". Herminio Martins was systematically quoted by historians, although he does not go into detail on the characterization of the regime. An unpublished article of the 1970s by Martins on the crisis and overthrow of the liberal republican regime had a more limited circulation, but was nonetheless referred to in later years in several works[4].

The first empirical studies on the "New State" appeared between 1968 and 1974 giving rise to a number of new interpretations on the nature of the regime. These works generally originated in the fields of political science and sociology and their authors, most of them North American, tended to be either specialists on Latin America or Portuguese exiles working in similar fields. Some pioneering studies on the First Republic of a more academic nature were written during the same period, dealing with the question of

---

[3] See Stanley G. Payne, *Op. Cit.*, pp. 157-160. See also his "Fascism and Right Authoritarianism in the Iberian World: the last Twenty Years", *Journal of Contemporary History*, vol. 21(1986), pp. 163-177.

[4] Namely by Juan Linz and Philippe Schmitter, See infra.

the origins of authoritarianism for the first time. A. H. Oliveira Marques, a Portuguese historian who taught in the United States, was not only responsible for most of these studies, but also wrote the first history of Portugal which included an introduction to the Salazar regime[5]. Some authors attempted to put forward a generic interpretation of the nature of the "New State" and of the crisis of the Portuguese liberal regime, although they tended to focus on these issues only partially.

THE FALL OF LIBERALISM AND THE "NEW STATE"

In his "The Breakdown of the Portuguese Democratic Republic", Herminio Martins put forward a "non-deterministic" model to explain the fall of the First Republic. Adopting a comparative perspective, he emphasized the possible "margins of choice" available to the political elites of the time[6]. He stressed the relative "life expectancy" of the republican regime compared to the European average in the first half of the 20th century. The Republic was described as precocious in its "de-stabilization" of relations with the Catholic Church, (immediately following the French case) due to the role played by anti-clericalism, which Martins calls the lowest common denominator of the republican movement. Certain structural economic and social elements in the country, notably the distribution of the economically active population (60% in the primary sector), the level of urbanization (10.5%) and the level of illiteracy (70%), did not aid the formation of a "political culture" easily adaptable to republican ideals. Despite an underdeveloped

---

[5] See A. H. de Oliveira Marques, "Revolution and Counterrevolution in Portugal. Problems of Portuguese history, 1900-1930", *Studien über die Revolution*, (Berlin: 1969), pp. 403-418; "the Portuguese 1920s: a general survey", paper presented to the V ISSA Annual Conference, Nottingham, 1972, published latter in *Revista de História Económica e Social*, n° 1, Janeiro-Junho 1978, pp. 87-103; *History of Portugal*, Vol. II - *From Empire to Corporate State*, (New York and London: 1973).

[6] See "The Breakdown of the Portuguese Democratic Republic", Mimio., Seventh World Congress of Sociology, Varna, 1970, p. 3. Most of the papers presented at this session, organised by Stein Rokkan and by Juan Linz, produced the collective work *The Breakdown of Democratic Regimes,* quoted above.

economy and the concentration of 60% of the economically active population in the agrarian sector, no "peasant" or "agrarian" parties emerged in Portugal as they did in Northern and Eastern Europe.

In spite of the patterns of political violence and social conflict which preceded the war, it was Portugal's entry into the First World War and the resultant crisis that precipitated the turning point in the life of the Republic. Thus, Herminio Martins singles out the Sidonio Pais dictatorship as Europe's first experiment in corporatist and charismatic dictatorship. With the emergence of a "mass society" with the sudden entry of the previously unassimilated masses into urban, industrial life, as well as the rise of "political bargaining" with a weak working class seeking a degree of economic equity through the threat of violence, Lisbon was very much like Barcelona as far as levels of social violence are concerned and not far below the average in other liberal democracies in the decade's final years. There were some differences on the Right. In Portugal, the counterpart of the *Action Française* did not create Camelots but it did gain an increasing ideological influence within the Army.

Hermínio Martins gives an account of the conditions prevailing immediately before the coup of May 28, 1926: Order was being restored in the social arena; economic figures indicated neither stagnation nor relapse; in the political arena there was continuing instability; relations with the Army, almost always poor, deteriorated after the war and the "entente of monarchists and right-wing republican officers which had been essayed in 1917-1918 was tried again with more determination and persistence"[7].

In his article on the "New State", Herminio Martins does not actually go into the problem of "interpretations" but, in addition to providing an overall view of the origins and development of the regime, he discusses some of the analytical models of that period[8]. He stresses that the three requisites of Fascism represented in Por-

[7] *Idem*, p. 20.
[8] Included in the work of Stuart Woolf quoted above, this article was not included in the 2nd edition (London: 1981). I have used the American edition, (New York: 1969), pp. 302-336.

tugal by National Syndicalism were not embodied in the Salazar regime: The "leadership is not charismatic in the usual sense associated with historic Fascist regimes, political support is not mobilized on a large scale, and the mechanism of political recruitment and succession have not been elaborated"[9]. Nonetheless, by 1936 Herminio Martins sees a "new level of 'fascistization' of the regime, or at least a stage of political development going beyond the traditionalistic, conventionally authoritarian, Christian corporatist policy which was perhaps the initial 'plan' of the regime, and which is the dominant international stereotype"[10]. Even though the "organization complex" thus created underwent certain changes, the truth is that it survived and "cannot simply be regarded as a temporary aberration (...)"[11].

In the case of Portugal the question of the origins of the "New State" and of Fascism became confused with the wider crisis of clientelist liberalism. Two themes tended to become confused when examining, along classic international research lines, the history of the "surrender" of liberal culture and the rising popularity of anti-democratic alternatives among intellectual elites: The political and ideological origins of the authoritarian regime and its leader were confused with the political and ideological agents of the overthrow of liberalism in 1926.

As it happened, in the Portuguese case the two phases in the transition to authoritarianism were quite distinct such that some of the most important agents involved in the fall of liberalism later played a secondary role in modelling the "New State". The absence of a Fascist party which could have somehow dominated or led the transition process contributed to the lack of definition.

Initial research efforts focussed precisely on finding the causes of and accounting for this "absence". For Manuel Villaverde Cabral, were one to place greater emphasis on the form of the State and its structures and less on its "choreographic" aspect, the Portuguese regime would be one of the "most perfect varieties (...) of Fas-

[9] *Op. Cit.*, p. 332.
[10] *Idem*, p. 322.
[11] *Idem, ibidem.*

cism"[12]. According to Cabral, the first question that needs to be posed is "did Portuguese authoritarianism arise exclusively from the peculiarities of Portuguese society and its political system or was it part of a larger international trend?" In Cabral's view, although Portugal had not seen a "straightforward Fascist movement, it did experience throughout most of the first quarter of the 20th century a protracted period of social and political mass conflict during which the Portuguese liberal system was placed under extremely severe pressures (...)". In his opinion "these increasingly anti-liberal, anti-democratic and anti-socialist organized pressures, although not unified into a single mass movement, were, so to speak, functional equivalents of a Fascist movement insofar as they performed all the roles normally assigned to Fascist parties"[13]. The basic reasons for the absence of a Fascist party "from the reaction of the petit bourgeoisie to the failure of the parliamentary state" were above all "the contamination from the start of the right wing dictatorial reaction by the monarchic element on the one hand, and by the Catholic element on the other, either jointly or separately"[14].

Several researchers in the 1980s chose to focus on the subject of the crisis of the republican regime. They put forward a number of explanatory hypotheses ranging from Sternhell's intellectual argument against the liberal order to the models employed by modernization sociologists, particularly Organski's which saw Fascism as a "compromise" solution by the dominant classes to weather the transition to an industrial society. Although the former hypothesis was expounded in innumerable studies which will not be reviewed here, the latter was well supported from an academic point of view even if generally found in sketchier studies[15].

---

[12] See Manuel Villaverde Cabral, "Sobre o Fascismo e o seu advento em Portugal: ensaio de interpretação a pretexto de alguns livros recentes", *Análise Social*, Vol. XII(48), 1976, pp. 873-915; "O Fascismo Português numa Perspectiva Comparada" in AA.VV., *O Fascismo em Portugal*, (Lisboa:1982), pp.19-30; "Portuguese Fascism in Comparative Perspective", (paper presented at the XIIth IPSA World Congress, Rio de Janeiro, August 1982).

[13] See Manuel Villaverde Cabral, "Portuguese Fascism...", p. 3.

[14] See Manuel Villaverde Cabral, "Sobre o Fascismo...", p. 914.

[15] See José Machado Pais, *As "Forças Vivas" e a Queda do Regime Liberal*

The issue of the ideological and political origins of Salazarism is also to be found in Manuel Braga da Cruz's research on the social Catholic movement and the Catholic Centre Party of which Salazar was one of the leaders. For Braga da Cruz this was the "original mould of Salazarism both politically and ideologically" which distinguished it from the "secular" mold of European Fascism[16]. The origins of Salazar's regime corresponded more closely, in the opinion of Braga da Cruz, to the program of social Catholicism than to that of the radical right represented by Integralism, perhaps the most important ideological pressure group during the crisis of the liberal regime. The predominance of the former was evident not only at a merely ideological level but also in the actual institutions of the regime, the existence of corporatism and the single party and among the political elites themselves.

Although it was of central importance in the process of the overthrow of the liberal republic, the Integralist Portuguese version of the *Action Française* went on to play only a secondary role in the formation of the "New State" and it was also an important source of Fascist opposition.

"FASCISM WITHOUT A FASCIST MOVEMENT"

In his 1971 introduction to a thesis on the corporatist system of the "New State", Manuel Lucena put forward a comparative analysis of the regime based primarily on a political classification even though incorporating historical and sociological analyses[17]. His definition of the regime was expressed thus: "Fascism without a Fascist Movement"[18].

Republicano, Madrid, Unpublished Dissertation, 1983, and "A crise do regime liberal republicano: algumas hipóteses explicativas", AA VV, *O Estado Novo - das origens...*, pp. 129-144.

[16] See Manuel Braga da Cruz, *As Origens da Democracia Cristã e o Salazarismo*, (Lisboa: 1980), P. 19.

[17] See Manuel Lucena, *A Evolução do Sistema Corporativo Português*, Vol. I - *O Salazarismo*, (Lisboa: 1976). For a discussion of theses of some of the authors mentioned here and of his own, see his article, "Interpretações do Salazarismo: notas de leitura crítica -I", *Análise Social*, Vol. XX (83), 1984-4°, pp. 423-451.

[18] See *Op. Cit.*, p. 27.

Lucena did not accept the concept of "generic Fascism" as he considered Nazism a different category of Fascism. He concentrated on the comparison between the institutions of the Italian and Portuguese regimes and concluded that they were more alike than any other two such regimes. Contrasting the two cases with classifications which emphasize the fundamental similarities between Italian and German Fascism, Lucena denies that the latter two are related. He bases this claim precisely on the theory of totalitarianism; in his opinion, although the Italian case appears to be ideologically close to the latter model it reality it is quite distinct.

Italian Fascism and Salazarism were different in origin as each society was different; both, however, produced very similar types of States. In Portugal the single party hardly existed in reality but not only is "absence a form of existence" but its function was nonetheless carried out: it justified the absence of all other parties and prevented the crystallization of tendencies at the heart of the regime. In Italy the party had more clout and greater totalitarian tendencies but it did not go so far as to "fascistize" institutions and Italian society, so that the system became a "compromise regime in which totalitarianism was little more than a fantasy. Lucena recognized the significant differences between the two regimes. He observed they arose from the absence of a movement in the Portuguese case since the two regimes were identical in terms of state types: "Both were single-party dictatorships which put society and the state under the principle of class collaboration and were supported by an alliance of all the groups of the national bourgeoisie. In both, corporatist organizations imprisoned social classes and professional groups within their webs and monopolized their representation. Finally, both were conceived in terms of stubborn nationalism. These traits are those of Fascist states and Fascist corporatism anywhere"[19].

Political forms "do not depend strictly on their origins". There were many liberalisms without "taking the Bastille"; the same can

---

[19] See Manuel de Lucena, "The evolution of Portuguese corporatism under Salazar and Caetano" in Lawrence S. Graham and Harry M. Makler, *Contemporary Portugal. The Revolution and its Antecedents*, (Austin: 1979), p. 65-66.

be said for Fascism. The differences between Portugal and Italy may be seen in State doctrine and in the movement itself. The latter, although important, is not essential. "To the extent that Fascism is a *sui generis* political form, to the extent that it must not be confused with traditional dictatorships and yet does not overlap with either liberalism or communism, to the extent that it creates unprecedented and stable institutions (a fact with is undeniable), Portugal has a fascist regime"[20]. One should note that whilst Lucena refuses to include National Socialism in the Fascist fold, he introduces a very wide definition of Fascism which could encompass all the non-socialist dictatorships of the period. On the other hand, however, Lucena stresses that the comparison with the Italian Fascist regime works if one takes into consideration only the first phase of Mussolini's regime up to the establishment of the Rome-Berlin Axis.

THE "REGIME D'EXCEPTION" THAT BECAME THE RULE

Philippe Schmitter, who went to Portugal in 1971 to study the corporatist regime, introduces different viewpoints in some of his studies[21]. Like others who followed in his path, Schmitter's previous area of expertise was Latin America. Unlike many others, however, he neither rushed into dubious comparisons with Latin

---

[20] *Idem*, p. 71.

[21] For the purpose of this analysis, we are interested above all in some of the articles presented at various conferences from 1972 onwards and published after the fall of the regime. See Philippe C. Schmitter, "Corporatism and Public Policy in Authoritarian Portugal", *Contemporary Political Sociological Series*, Sage Professional Series, Vol. I, (London: 1975); "Liberation by *Golpe*: Retrospective Thoughts on the Demise of Authoritarian Rule in Portugal", *Armed Forces and Society*, vol. II, n°1, November 1975, pp. 5-33; "The Impact and Meaning of 'Noncompetitive, Non-Free and Insignificant' Elections in Authoritarian Portugal. 1933-74", in Guy Hermet, Richard Rose and Alain Rouquié (Edited by), *Elections Without Choice*, (London: 1978), pp. 145-168; "The 'Régime d'Exception' That Became the Rule: Forty-Eight Years of Authoritarian Domination in Portugal" in, Lawrence S. Graham and Harry Makler (Edited by), *Op. Cit.*, (Austin: 1979), pp. 2-46. I have used another version of this last article, published in Stein U. Larsen et Alli, *Op. Cit.*, (Bergen: 1980), pp. 435-466.

America and nor relegated the Iberian authoritarian regimes to a "future" conditioned by the corporatist "pattern"[22]. Later in this chapter his conclusions regarding the regime's institutions will be examined but for now his generic interpretation will be focused on.

Although Schmitter drew from the theoretical literature on "authoritarian regimes" he stressed that the latter's static approach frequently made it difficult to perceive the development of internal dynamics. The very establishment of these regimes "involved a great deal of uncertainty, experimentation, failure, coercion and violence until something like a coherent interdependent institutional pattern emerged. More important, that pattern, once established, is also subject to the inexorable law of uneven development"[23]. Part of the "secret" of the stability of the Portuguese regime was the relatively slow development of these "desynchronizing" developmental variables which were mainly the "product of a deliberate policy". Between the 1930s and the 1950s Portugal had the lowest rates of urbanization, literacy, industrialization and economic development of all the European countries[24].

After a brief incursion into the literature on the social bases and the economic and political factors which were at the basis of the authoritarian and Fascist solutions, Schmitter begins by stressing the already familiar lack of Fascist dynamics preceding the takeover of power. None of the groups worthy of note in the First Republic were directly responsible for Salazar's takeover of power. Moreover, "While it would certainly be an exaggeration to claim that Salazar created authoritarian rule in Portugal *tout seul et de toutes pièces*, the evidence suggests that he played a very personal and imperious role in both the direction of policy after 1928 and in the backing of elites after 1932. Of course, he must have accommodated his choices to the demands and "advice" of various privileged classes, conservative and reactionary political forces, as well as those entrenched institutional actors, most notably the military

[22] See his doctoral dissertation, *Interest Conflict and Political Change in Brazil*, (Stanford: 1971).
[23] See Philippe C. Schmitter, " Liberation by *Golpe*...", p. 13-14.
[24] *Idem*, p. 14.

and the church (...)", but "to an extraordinary degree Salazar could create from above the 'elite' to which he felt the [New] State could or should be held accountable"[25].

Beginning with the analysis of the composition of the Corporatist Chamber and the National Assembly representing the winning coalition in the first phase of the regime, Schmitter stresses the importance of bureaucrats and of their ties with the State (68%). On the other hand, "the gerontocratic image of the regime" in the 1960s should not allow one to forget that Salazar's rise to power symbolized the coming of a new and fairly young generation. Based on these elements, Schmitter speaks of the "Fascistization" of 1935-36 in relative terms because although it brought about a new dynamic it did not effect any change in political elites. The most distinguishing characteristics of this founding elite were its youth, its dependency on public office and its close relationship with the financial and fiscal sector of the "weak and dependent Portuguese capitalist economy".

As far as economic foundations are concerned, Schmitter wonders if it is plausible to argue that the emergence and consolidation of authoritarian domination in Portugal corresponds to imperatives of a structural nature, of a backward and dependent economy in crisis. He concludes that it does. He also points out, however, that this did not occur for the reasons most often cited. He emphasizes that Portugal was far from having exhausted the model of import substitution and that the effect of her economic dependency is of little importance, as evidenced by the reduced impact of the 1929 crisis in Portugal. Some of the problems may be included under the financial crisis of the State. The economic situation on the eve of the fall of the liberal regime seems to suggest "the relative autonomy of the political factors" since it was not "the imminence of economic collapse" that caused the authoritarian wave[26].

Schmitter was not far from Hermínio Martins' opinions with regard to the factors that led to the fall of the liberal regime and

[25] See Philippe C. Schmitter, " The Social Origins, Economic Bases...", p. 438.
[26] *Idem*, p. 454.

said that if in retrospect the transition process between military dictatorship and authoritarianism seemed calm, in reality it was very far from being so. "Armed insurrections, *pronunciamentos*, personal resignations and general strikes came from a wide variety of groups: some who had supported the 1926 coup; some who had opposed it; some who felt the measures were going too far and would destroy the nation's political life; others who felt that Salazar was not going far enough in establishing an integral, syndicalist-Fascist state."[27].

In conclusion, Schmitter stresses that, if the emergence and consolidation of Portuguese authoritarianism was not "unique" in post-war Europe, the combination of these elements and the final product was quite distinctive. It lacked or deliberately avoided what, in other experiences, was called the "Fascist minimum".

"In common with analogous Eastern European experiences, this form of conservative-bureaucratic authoritarian rule emerged in conjunction with a crisis of financial accumulation at a very early stage of capitalist development and a double crisis in the fiscal management and ideological hegemony of the liberal state. Many, if not most, of its cadres were recruited from within the state bureaucracy and the ideological apparatus of its universities. To the limited extent that mass support was involved, peasants, provincial *mesoi* and local notables on the geographic and social periphery of Portuguese society were 'mobilized' against its more cosmopolitan, secular and developed center. The absence of linguistic or ethnic minorities, the weakness of a credible communist or proletarian threat, and the *éloignement* of Portugal from great power competition all contributed to moderating if not obliterating some of the scapegoating, xenophobia, violence and other extremist *bizarreries* which characterized authoritarian movements and regimes with similar social origins, economic functions and political imperatives elsewhere in Europe."[28]

---

[27] *Idem*, p. 457.
[28] *Idem*, p. 462.

A "CENTRALIZED AND BUREAUCRATIC EMPIRE"

Lawrence Graham centered his studies on the administrative relations with the colonies and put forward a definition of the regime based on S. Eisenstadt's concept of a "centralized and bureaucratic empire"[29]. According to him, the "New State" could be classified as a contemporary version of "centralized bureaucratic control with the political struggle confined to the very same arenas, but without the institution of monarchy"[30]. Graham emphasized the importance of the state's administrative apparatus in relation to the specifically "political" institutions of Salazarism. After a purge of the elements attached to the clientelistic structure of the Republic's parties, the dictator put his trust in bureaucracy, reigned over it and used it, thus increasing the discrepancy between "the form and content" of the regime.

An example of this discrepancy was the well-known corporatist character of the regime, cultivated in the official ideology but never put into practice, which leads him to conclude that "the reality under which Portugal was ruled from 1930 down to 1974 was that of an administrative state."[31] The issue of administrative weight vis-a-vis political weight was later addressed in various studies of a more limited scope.[32]

THE EASTERN EUROPEAN DICTATORSHIPS

Although Stanley G. Payne was not directly involved in studies on Portugal, he reviewed the research and referred to the "New

[29] See Lawrence S. Graham, "Portugal: The Bureaucracy of Empire", *LADS Occasional Papers*, Series 2, N° 9, (Austin: 1973) and also "Portugal: The Decline and Collapse of an Authoritarian Order", *Contemporary Political Sociological Series,* (Beverly Hills: 1975). On this concept see S. Eisentadt, *The Political System of Empire*, (New York: 1963).

[30] See Lawrence S. Graham," Portugal:...", p. 8.

[31] *Idem*, p. 15.

[32] See Paul H. Lewis, "Salazar's Ministerial Elite, 1932-1968", *Journal of Politics*, 40, August 1978, pp. 622-647. Lewis focused attention on the predominance of technicians as opposed to politicians in Salazar's ministerial elite.

State" in several comparative works[33]. For Payne, the Portuguese regime belongs to the same category as the eastern European dictatorships of the same period, "corporative, institutionalized (...) systematically authoritarian (...) without any direct Fascist party component"[34]. Referring to Manuel Lucena's definition, Payne considers that "the very precept of a 'Fascism without a Fascist movement" indicates that we are dealing with a different phenomenon. The Salazar regime was, in fact, one of the most fully institutionalized of all the interwar authoritarian regimes (partly explaining its longevity), for its structure, partly paralleling that of Italy, was more thoroughgoing than that of the Balkans or east-European regimes." But it is here that one should search for elements of comparison, particularly with the Austrian regime of Dolfuss -Schuschnigg[35].

If one accepts the fact that Salazar's regime was not based on the "culture of Fascism" or a party of a similar nature but rather on Catholic corporatism, one finds similarities with Italian fascism only in certain characteristics of the state. In all else (origins, culture, ideology and political base) comparison shows nothing but differences[36]. In Payne's opinion it is only by using an extremely loose concept of Fascism, including "all the forms of non-communist authoritarianism", that the Portuguese regime may be considered Fascist, moreover, were that to be done, the results would be worthless and ineffectual[37]. Avoiding hasty comparisons with the more recent Latin American dictatorships, Payne writes that the model of "bureaucratic authoritarianism" used to define the latter is of some benefit when studying those of the inter-war period[38].

[33] See Stanley G. Payne, "Fascism in Western Europe" in Walter Laqueur (Edited by), *Fascism: A Reader's Guide. Analyses, Interpretations, Bibliography*, (Berkeley: 1976), pp. 295-311; *Fascism...*, pp. 157-160 and "Salazarism: "Fascism" or "bureaucratic authoritarianism" ?", AA VV, *Estudos de História de Portugal. Homenagem a A. H. Oliveira Marques*, vol. II-sécs. XVI-XX, (Lisboa: 1983), pp. 523-531.
[34] See Stanley G. Payne, *Fascism...*, p. 157.
[35] *Idem*, p. 159.
[36] Stanley G. Payne, "Salazarism...", p. 527.
[37] *Idem*, p. 530-531.
[38] See about "bureaucratic authoritarianism" in Latin America, Guillermo O'Donnell, *Op. Cit.*

FASCISM OR AUTHORITARIANISM?

While latent in most recent research, the interpretative debate on the characterization of the Portuguese regime has been dealt with only indirectly. In fact, Portuguese research has not yet experienced rifts like those caused by De Felice in Italy or by the German debate of 1986. Although there were several contributors, two authors basically reflected the two positions with regard to the Fascist/authoritarian debate. Very little was added by others in general less concerned with the problems of regime characterization.

M. V. Cabral rejected a large part of the work produced by political science, which he considered to have failed in its attempts to classify Portugal's case, and he did not find the distinction between Fascism and authoritarianism viable. Like Lucena, Cabral emphasized that the form of the State under Salazarism: "(...) after a brief period of military dictatorship, resembled the Italian regime more than any other authoritarian state of the inter-war period."[39] Cabral went back to the prespective which emphasized the differences between Italian Fascism and National Socialism. In his view as the former "comes closer to other Southern European authoritarianisms than to the German totalitarianism and to those unsuccessful totalitarian movements in other European developed countries which I will call Nazi." He also challenged the positions of international researchers, particularly targetting Stanley Payne who associated the "alleged conservative authoritarianism" in Portugal with that of Eastern Europe in general and of Horthy and Pilsudsky in particular, as the latter two never eliminated pluralism and did not develop corporatist systems comparable to those of Portugal and Italy[40].

Cabral's arguments approach Lucena's, although, as noted above, the former adopts a more "historical" approach stressing the similarities between the crisis of Portuguese liberalism and the crises preceding the Fascist wave, as well as the "Fascistizing" traits of the pro-dictatorial reaction in the post-war period. Other positions close to those mentioned above, were adopted in various

---

[39] Manuel Villaverde Cabral, "Portuguese Fascism...", p. 3.

empirical studies which will be discussed later; the latter, however, rarely dealt with the characterization of Salazarism[41].

Braga da Cruz has based his argument precisely on the classics of political science in order to build a typology of the relationship between the party and the State in the dictatorial regimes in the interwar period, aiming establishing whether the "New State" was, in fact, Fascist"[42]. Agreeing with those who distinguished Fascism from the authoritarian regimes and who emphasized the radical, modernizing character of the former, Braga da Cruz is of the opinion that the Portuguese regime was a governmental dictatorship and not, as in Fascism, a party dictatorship. "If Fascism is authoritarianism", he stressed, "not all authoritarianisms were Fascist (...) Fascism was merely one of several authoritarian nationalisms which appeared in the first quarter of the century, immediately after the war (...)"[43].

Drawing from the bibliography discussed in the first chapter of this work, Braga da Cruz proposed a party-State typology which may be summarized as follows: if the party dominates the State in National Socialism and becomes part of it in Italian Fascism, in Portugal it depends on it entirely. Salazarism was, then, as opposed to Fascism, not a party dictatorship but a governmental dictatorship[44]. The conservative authoritarianism of the Portuguese regime also differed ideologically from Fascism "as it did not draw inspiration (...) from a secular vision of the world or of life (...) and its nationalism, unlike Fascist nationalism, was a traditionalist, conservative and integrationist nationalism."[45] It was also different in its political methods: "as opposed to Fascism, it was never intended to be founded on the role of the mobilized and organized masses in

---

[40] *Idem*, p. 24.

[41] See Fernando Rosas, "Cinco pontos em torno do estudo comparado do fascismo", *Vértice*, 13, Abril de 1989, pp. 21-29.

[42] See Manuel Braga da Cruz, *O Partido* .., p. 11. *See* also his "El modelo político salazarista", Hipólito de la Torre (coord.), *Portugal y España en el cambio político (1958-1978)*, (Mérida: 1989), pp. 37-45.

[43] *Idem*, p. 30.

[44] See my review in, *Annales ESC*, mai-juin 1988, n°3, pp. 691-693.

[45] See Manuel Braga da Cruz, *O Partido...*, p. 256.

a single party nor on the totalitarianism of the State's power (...) It was, rather, an authoritarianism of extremely traditional domination and markedly paternalistic exercise of political power."[46] A similar position was endorsed by foreign political scientists who, although more interested in the transition to democracy in the 1970s, analyzed Salazar's regime nonetheless. The latter studies generally consisted of syntheses, usually as an introduction to the study of the democratic regime established in 1974, and were based on the literature cited above. In the opinion of Thomas C. Bruneau, "the most accurate term for conveying the sense of what the Salazar regime was and how it operated is a conservative and authoritarian regime of personal rulership."[47] Along Lawrence Graham's lines, both Bruneau and Walter Opello emphasized the bureaucratic nature of the regime whose "linkages with the broader civil society were essentially administrative not political in character"[48]. It was also in studies on the fall of Salazarism that Manuel de Lucena refined his definition of the 1970s starting with the distinction between Fascism and Nazism and insisting on the similarity between the Italian and Portuguese regimes[49].

One final problem regarding the characterization of the regime lies in the division of its life into different periods. Salazarism and Francoism were the only authoritarian regimes of the "Fascist Era" that survived 1945 and carried on into the 1970s. This, as we have seen above, led some Spanish authors to consider the possibility of several characterizations of the regimes according to phases.

This possibility was not considered in the case of Portugal. In order to characterize the regime as fascist Cabral focused on the interwar period[50]. Everyone else, however, suggested unique char-

---

[46] *Idem*, p. 256-57.

[47] See Thomas C. Bruneau, *Politics and Nationhood. Post-revolutionary Portugal*, (New York: 1984), p. 18.

[48] See Walter C. Opello Jr., *Portugal's Political Development. A comparative approach*, (Boulder: 1985), p. 61.

[49] See his "Post-fascisme? Néo-corporatisme? Ou quoi? (réflexions sur la chute du régime salazariste et sur ce qui s'en est suivi)", paper presented to the Conference "Modern Europe after Fascism", Bergen, June 27-29 1985.

[50] See Manuel Villaverde Cabral, " Portuguese Fascism...", p. 2.

acterizations for Salazar's regime and did not consider the different phases important for the purpose of regime definition.

2.2 OTHER CONTRIBUTIONS

Some of the authors mentioned above, most particularly the political scientists, were concerned above all with studying the possible evolution of the regime after the illness and replacement of Salazar in 1968. An analysis of what they wrote in the years immediately preceding the fall of the regime would provide one with an extremely interesting inquiry into the futurological claims of political science.

The "honeymoon" period following Marcello Caetano's emergence attracted the attention of a great deal of mostly North American political scientists. Some of them expressed great confidence in the longevity of the regime at a number of conferences in 1973[51]. Others predicted important roles for the regime's own institutions (i.e. the corporatist institutions) following a possible liberalization. They were all wrong. As Philippe C. Schmitter wrote in a rare moment of self-critique for the social sciences, "no scholarly or journalistic observer of Portugal foresaw the overthrow of Marcello Caetano, much less the rapid and complete collapse of authoritarian rule in Portugal. Quite the contrary."[52] Futurological limitations aside, a series of studies were made on a variety of the regime's institutions, meanwhile overthrown, opening the way for new empirical research[53].

---

[51] See some papers presented at the first Conference of the ICGMP, University of New Hampshire, October, 10-14, 1973.

[52] See Philippe C. Schmitter," Liberation by *Golpe*...", p. 5.

[53] Ignoring analyses centered on the 1960's, I have given preference here to those conclusions either referring directly to the regime's first phase or having an important link with it.

THE "CORPORATIST REVOLUTION"

Corporatism was the field which attracted most research[54]. This did not seem unusual since corporatism had been one of the regime propaganda's favourite themes, explaining the originality of Portuguese authoritarianism. Of all the dictatorships of the same period which proclaimed themselves corporatist, the "New State" was the most stable and, as Schmitter said, it constituted an ideal "laboratory" for analytical study. Based on extremely diverse theoretical concerns, all these studies brought to light new information on the subject. Howard Wiarda's is no doubt the most controversial of them all.

In his introduction, Wiarda analyzes the origins of Portuguese corporatism and places them in an "Iberic-Latin" historical and cultural context[55]. According to him, these societies were structurally corporatist and the Anglo-Saxon mindset very often ignored this dimension, so he proposes to adopt an anthropological "cultural relativism" in his study. Either Wiarda was swayed by the ideological output of the Integralists who, at the beginning of the 20th century, naturally attempted to "re-invent" the corporatist tradition which liberalism with its foreign ties tried to destroy, or he was highly influenced by the Latin American field from which he came[56].

All other studies on the subject quite correctly view the contemporary origin of the corporatist ideologies as authoritarian alternatives which emerged during the crisis of liberalism at the turn of the century and which in Portugal were no more "original" than those which developed in other European countries. Of all the scholars mentioned, Manuel Lucena was the most thorough and challenging[57].

---

[54] See, apart the works of Manuel Lucena and of Philippe Schmitter, Howard J. Wiarda, *Corporatism and Development. The Portuguese Experience*, (Amherst: 1977).

[55] See Howard J. Wiarda, *Op. Cit.*, pp. 2-28, and Manuel de Lucena, "Uma leitura americana do corporativismo português", *Análise Social*, vol. XVII (66), 1981-2°, pp. 415-434.

[56] *Idem*, pp. 29-54.

[57] Also the most known. I shall limit myself to a very brief summary of his ideas.

Lucena began by analyzing the place of corporatism in Salazar's political system and emphasized its secondary role among the institutions of the new regime. In opposition to the aspirations of the "Integral" corporatists in the formal apparatus, liberal representative principles were maintained in the constitution of 1933 and the compromise was not particularly favorable to the corporatist institutions which remained in a position of inferiority. The *Estatuto do Trabalho Nacional*, obviously Italian-inspired, restrained its fascist counterpart in a very Catholic way. Moreover, after the first wave of legislation in the 1930s, its structure remained incomplete and was vastly different from the original plan. After the *Sindicatos Nacionais* (National Unions) were formed under strict state control, the "corporatization" of the employers' associations was much more moderate and it served as a lever for economic intervention in certain sectors, allowing the survival of some organizations which resisted its control. It was only in the 1950s that some "Corporations" were formed. They operated, however, in a different setting and had hardly any capacity for decision-making or autonomy in contrast with the well-known "association model". Although different in many ways, Italian Fascist and Portuguese corporatism had some similar functions: namely "to tie down the workers' movement, develop national capitalism, re-inforce the state"[58].

Schmitter has no doubt as to the role of social control of the corporatist system which aimed at "disarming and rendering dependent upon state-sponsored paternalism those groups whose articulated demands might have hindered the accumulation (...) and hampered the consolidation of the political hegemony of a national bourgeoisie". He agrees with Lucena that this is only one side of the coin[59]. In effect, although the "corporatization" of the employers' sector was more flexible, it was still a particularly strong reality in some sectors and the all-powerful bodies of economic coordination ruled over a pyramid that belied the proclaimed model of "association".

---

[58] See Manuel de Lucena, *Op. Cit.*, p. 221.
[59] See Philippe C. Schmitter, "Corporatism...", p. 19.

It could be said that the primary function was the dual one; at the level of the political system the corporatist structure did not have much of an impact. The corporatist institutions played a secondary role in the constitutional apparatus and in the sphere of political decision-making but their existence is not to be scorned in terms of their effect. Schmitter put forward a counter-factual model comparing Portugal with countries that had experienced similar "starting points" like Ireland or Greece, but which had different political systems. His conclusion is that: "its fiscally orthodox and economically conservative policies and its strong insistence on the decisional autonomy of state institutions, while they inhibited long-run growth and development, did produce a distributional outcome which appeared less unequal than that of Greece (...)". On all other points the comparison is negative for the "New State"[60].

Schmitter's assumptions on the general functions of the Portuguese corporatist system were not dissimilar to those generally attributed to the single parties of authoritarian regimes: *"preemptive*, i.e. seeks to set out from above structures of associability and channels of interest representation in anticipation (...); *preventive,* i.e. attempts not to mobilize (...) but to (...) occupy a certain physical, temporal or ideational 'space', foreclosing, if not prohibiting, alternative uses of that same space; *defensive*, i.e. encourages associations to act in the protection of corporatist 'rights', privileges or exemptions granted from above, rather than in the 'aggressive' promotions of new projects or interests; *compartmental*, i. e., manages to confine potential conflicts within specialized, non-interacting decisional 'orders' (...)". Taking all these factors into consideration, he concludes that "the role and consequences of state corporatism must be assessed, not primarily in terms of what it openly and positively accomplishes, but in terms of what it surreptitiously and negatively prevents from happening."[61].

Wiarda's conclusions are considerably more complicated and controversial. His work accurately describes the evolution of the corporatist system up to 1974 but, predictably, he holds that

---

[60] *Idem*, p. 57.
[61] *Idem*, p. 58.

Portugal's "future" (from 1974 onwards) remains under the shadow of the corporatist syndrome mentioned in his introduction[62]. This critique does not invalidate the quality of many of Wiarda's hypotheses, specifically those having to do with the ideology of the Portuguese corporatists and the capacity of the corporatist system to "integrate" the old free unions.

Fatima Patriarca's study of the corporatist system's formative period in the 1930s demolishes several historiographical myths relating to the workers' movements of the 1920s. It does so by clearly proving the weakness and the organizational and ideological dispersion of organized labor in Portugal, and demonstrating the weak resistance to "corporatization"[63]. Indeed, most unions integrated themselves into the new corporatist order[64]. The most polemic conclusion arrived at in this most complex study - at least for Portuguese historiography - refers, however, to the very existence of a very real "social preoccupation" on behalf of the "New State". At least in its first few years, the "New State" tried to "take seriously" some of the corporatist social legislation, facing the declared resistance of Portuguese employers' interests.

On the other hand, Patriarca does go on to prove the clear dominance exercised by social Catholicism as the overriding ideological influence over the corporatist apparatus' elite. "The way in which Salazar and the Portuguese corporatists", it concludes, "conceive of relations the state has with the working classes, and its role in society and political action, distances itself from the conception of Italian fascism."[65]

---

[62] See his recent works about the Portuguese transition to democracy.

[63] See Fátima Patriarca, *Processo de implantação e Lógica e Dinâmica de funcionamento do Corparativismo em Portugal. Os primeiros anos do Salazarismo*, Lisbon, (Forthcoming).

[64] *Idem*, p. 281.

[65] *Idem*, p. 624.

THE CATHOLIC CHURCH AND THE "NEW STATE"

In 1973 the *Revue Française de Sciences Politiques* published a special issue on the role of religious institutions in the authoritarian regimes. It was edited by Guy Hermet and included an article on Portugal[66]. Also in 1973 other research was conducted into the subject of relations between the Church and the state from the beginning of the century up to the 1930s[67].

Both works were more than mere statements of the extreme unity, if not symbiosis, between the "religious question" and the overthrow of the liberal regime and, above all, of the ideological and political mold of the dictator. Richard Robinson stressed the importance of organizations like the CADC and the *Centro Católico* (Catholic Center) as a mold for the "New State", spawning a young group of intellectuals and politicians opposed to the growing influence of *Integralismo Lusitano* (Portuguese Integralism) the most important of the anti-liberal ideological groups on the eve of the fall of the parliamentary republic[68]. Silas Cerqueira's contribution concentrated on the role of the Church during the period of Salazarism.

The role of the Church in the regime was manifold. It was not merely a question of providing public political support on demand or of its willing efforts to lend most of her rites and symbols in the regime's service. Cerqueira referred to the Church's blessing of the anti-communist and anti-liberal crusade of the 30s, its support of the regime's Fascist-type institutions like *Mocidade Portuguesa* (Portuguese Youth, MP) and the *Legião Portuguesa* (Portuguese Legion, LP), its participation in the "electoral" campaigns after

---

[66] See Silas Cerqueira, "L'Église catholique et la dictature corporatiste portugaise", *Revue Française de Sciences Politiques*, vol. XXIII, n° 3, Juin 1973, pp. 473-513.

[67] Namely the ones of Richard Robinson. See his "The Religious Question and the Catholic Revival in Portugal, 1900-30", *Journal of Contemporary History*, 12 (1977), pp. 345-362 and Thomas C. Bruneau, "Church and State in Portugal: Crises of Cross and Sword", *Journal of Church and State*, Vol. 18, n° 3, Autumn 1976, pp. 463-490.

[68] Richard Robinson, " The Religious Question...", p. 358.

the Second World War and its defense of the colonial war in the 60s. The Church also provided a model of mobilization, synchronizing the "renewal of religious practice" and of popular "piétisme" with the new political power's role of savior, an element which is sometimes underestimated. The religious cult of Fátima and the "parapolitical" functions it fulfilled are the most obvious example[69].

The Portuguese Catholic Church not only contributed to the ideological framework of the regime but was also "one of its essential instruments, always under its political direction"[70]. To wit, the postponed concordat (planned in 1933 but only concluded in 1940) affirmed some of the basic principles of the separation of Church and State. It upheld divorce for civil marriages and established relative control of the State over the religious institution. As Hermínio Martins pointed out, "while in Spain the 1950 Concordat granted the Church virtually everything it could ask for, the 1940 Concordat did not turn Portugal into a confessional state nor did the Church receive considerable educational or financial privileges."[71].

Silas Cerqueira mentioned some core ideological Church-State elements, from corporatism to anti-liberalism and anti-communism, spread by the Church under the guidance of the regime. He wrote: "Some of these ideological themes can be found in all conservative ideologies in a normal period (...)" but here they were exaggerated and "formed a whole, a system."[72] The legitimizing functions were numerous not only at a central political level — after each crisis, above all after 1945, a corresponding declaration of support followed and it began to be more discreet only in the final phase of the regime — but also in the rural areas and small towns where a whole "logistic" apparatus provided considerable "political socialization".

The most recent research does not invalidate the above thesis. And this in spite of the obvious tensions — particularly those hav-

---

[69]   Silas Cerqueira, "L'Église Catholique...", pp. 481-490.
[70]   *Idem*, p. 504.
[71]   Herminio Martins, "Opposition in Portugal", *Government and Opposition*, Vol. 4, N°2, Spring 1969, p. 262.
[72]   Silas Cerqueira," L'Église Catholique...", p. 504.

ing to do with Salazar's having imposed certain limits on the Church's ambitions and his continuing to maintain in place numerous pieces of liberal and republican legislation. The ever successful, as Manuel Braga da Cruz has well proven, strategy of the church during the regime's formative stage was that of blocking any totalitarian tendencies and working against the "fascistizing" pressures of Rolão Preto's National Syndicalism: "The Catholic elites concentrated most particularly on the effort to form and mold the new regime within the Church's own doctrinary orientation, hoping to maintain the regime's distance from any political inclinations or state evangelistic of totalitarian social models that would collide with Catholic thought. Specifically included as such were Fascism or Nazism on the outside, and on the inside, National Syndicalism."[73].

DEVELOPMENT OR STAGNATION?

The economic policy of the "New State" is perhaps the field which has been most studied and debated by modern research[74]. Its inclusion in the relations between Fascism and Salazar's regime is not direct. For many authors Fascism never had *one* economic policy which distinguished it clearly from other political regimes. In other words, and returning to Alan Milward's question, the problem is to find out if beyond the political sphere there "was also a specific set of economic attitudes and policies which may equally aptly be labelled "Fascist?"[75].

As mentioned above, the debate on the "development" or "stagnating" role of Salazar's regime in the sphere of Portuguese capitalism was an important theme in the ideological struggle within

---

[73] , See Manuel Braga da Cruz, "As Elites Católicas nos Primórdios do Salazarismo", *Análise Social*, vol. XXVII(116-117), 1992, p. 574. See also, from the same author, "O Estado Novo e a Igreja Católica", Joel Serrão and A. H. Oliveira Marques (Dir. de), *Nova História de Portugal*, Vol. XII, pp. 201-221.

[74] See Eloy Fernandez Clemente, "A história económica de Portugal (séculos XIX e XX)", *Análise Social*, vol. XXIV(103-104), 1988 (4°, 5°), pp. 1318-1323.

[75] See Alan S. Milward, "Fascism and the Economy", in Walter Laqueur (Edited By), *Op. Cit*, p. 409.

the different political families of the opposition to the regime in the 1960s, later expressed in the academic field.

These works, which mostly put forward Marxist interpretations, placed the regime not only within the field of the development of the capitalist mode of production in Portugal but also in the field of the very political "recomposition" of the national ruling classes. They presented a whole series of observations on the class content of the dictatorship and the role of the different factions of the bourgeoisie (agrarian, commercial and industrial)[76].

The outcome of some of the measures adopted by the regime were not so controversial for they were common to all the authoritarian and Fascist regimes of the period. Namely the destruction of the trade union movement and its substitution by corporatist organizations strictly controlled by the State and the adoption of an interventionist model combined with bureaucratic control by (or by not) means of the same apparatus. More controversial however, following an analysis of the comparative weight of rural and industrial élites, and returning to Organski's theme, was the situation of rural resistance to industrial development, a key element of economic policy throughout the 1930s[77].

Nuances and lateral variations aside, two prespectives emerged. The first one expressed by Cabral claimed that the regime developed a "model of programmed stagnation" during this period as a result of the "historical compromise" on which it was based and given the political weight of the agrarian sector. Part of the "mystery" of the long life of the regime lay in this model as "the slower and more controlled the economic and social growth, the more chances there are of the inevitable effects of growth being absorbed without the model being challenged (...)"[78]. Other studies, in near agreement with Cabral's position, stressed the restrictive role of

[76] For a review of the economic policy in the thirties, See Fernando Rosas, *O Estado Novo nos anos trinta. Elementos para o estudo da natureza económica e social do salazarismo (1928-1938)*, (Lisboa: 1986), pp. 23-53.

[77] The agrarian policy of the Portuguese "New State" is the theme of a book of Fernando Oliveira Baptista, *A Política Agrária do Estado Novo*, (Porto: 1993).

[78] See Manuel Villaverde Cabral, " Sobre o fascismo...", p. 895.

the regime's industrial development, determined by the regime's ideology in the 30s, and tried to prove that "the Salazar regime, while recognizing the need for industrial development, operated to control the pace of industrialization to prevent the formation of a potentially disruptive urban proletariat (...)"[79]. Expressing a slightly different opinion some studies, in the wake of Poulantzas' work, saw in the political economy of the regime a strong, interventionist State bringing about the transition from competitive to monopolistic capitalism and the progressive "submission of the different spheres of production to big industry"[80]. On closer examination, the two positions tend to meld. Most of the authors quoted do not disagree with the synthesis put forward by Alfredo Marques on the political and social significance of the regime's economic strategy developed after May 28, 1926. According to Marques, the economic policy of the 1930s expressed a "class alliance" which he calls an "agrarian-industrial alliance (AIA)". Due to the diversity of interests represented in this AIA "and to the incapacity for leadership of all its main components, the State took on the role of guarantor of the compatibility of diverse interests and undertook a plan of action to reconcile their differences and minimize their contradictions which, however, would only be possible through the preservation of the *status quo*. This plan of action required not only the presence of the Administration but also the State's guardianship over the private economy. For this purpose, State jurisdiction was to achieve an extreme degree of autonomy in relation to the social forces with which it was closely united."[81]

Fernando Rosas developed this thesis exhaustively in a study which focussed precisely on the State's political orientation and

---

[79] See Elizabeth Leeds, "Salazar's 'Modelo Económico': The Consequences of Planned Constraint", *in* T. C. Bruneau, Victor M. P. da Rosa, and Alex Macleod (Edited By), *Portugal in Development: emigration, industrialization, the European Community*, (Ottawa: 1984), p. 13.

[80] See Joel Frederico da Silveira, "Alguns aspectos da política económica do fascismo: 1926-19330", in AA VV, *Op. Cit.*, p. 386.

[81] See Alfredo Marques, *Política Económica e Desenvolvimento Económico em Portugal (1926-1959)*, (Lisboa: 1988), p. 24.

its instruments for economic intervention (basically through the corporatist apparatus). He also deepened the interconnection between economic policy, the political system and social groups. He adoped a position between the two already mentioned. For him the "New State's" mission regarding the divided and crisis-stricken bourgeoisie was to "arbitrate" contradictory interests, "to interpret them (...) as a whole and to set forth and keep in balance their different social aims and strategies."[82] Rosas concentrated particularly on the disagreements between the agrarian and industrial sectors and rejected the idea that the economic policy of the 1930s supported only agrarian interests, since the data he presents indicates that there was "development, concentration and modernization of the industrially based sectors and of other more technologically advanced sectors (...)". He also recognized that the role of arbitrator "resulted in an economic policy which was generally contradictory, hesitant, often without any clearly discernible reason other than that of seeking the equilibrium and stability of the system even if it meant shaky overall growth, which was in fact the case"[83].

Most of this initial research into the economic policy of the "New State" reflected the positions adopted in the old Marxist debate on the role of Fascism as a response to the workers' offensive during the capitalist crisis in the imperialist phase. It was, however, toned down by some of the problems inherent in the internal debate of the Portuguese political and intellectual élites. It challenged, for example, the idealistic vision of the liberal opposition which saw the "New State" as an irrational and "medieval" regression. Although it had a different theoretical basis, this prespective was at times adopted by the Communist Party, the main clandestine opposition force to the regime. Seen outside this context of ideological struggle, the various positions adopted are not always discernible. Apart from the classical works published on the relationship between fascism and "big business", this theoretical debate was primarily dominated by Organski and Poulantzas. However, in re-

[82] See Fernando Rosas, *Op. Cit.*, p. 121.
[83] *Idem*, p. 281.

cent years there have been fewer references to Fascism, either as a concept or as a historical experience[84].

There is still a need for comparative works in the area of economic policy in the same vein as Manuel Lucena's or Braga da Cruz's studies in the political field. Although there are no comparative studies, some of the references above contributed to Milward's line of questioning and, in Portugal's case, added the problem of division into the various periods. According to Alfredo Marques, "if, in the entire period of the Portuguese dictatorship, there is a set of economic measures which reminds us in some way of the interventionism of 'paradigmatic' European dictatorships (Germany and Italy)", they were not those of the 1930s but those of the 1950s, when a strategy for "economic growth" was drawn up"[85]. He considered this strategy to have been a failure in view of the resistance of the old AIA, however, proving the AIA's strong implantation in the "Portuguese economic and social fabric."[86]

Some monographs have also pointed out the singularity of Salazar's industrial policy, namely its extreme governmental bureaucratic control and its "industrial conditioning rule" (*condicionamento industrial*). After a comparative study of the models of intervention of Francoism and Italian Fascism, one author concludes that the extreme control and conditioning of Portuguese industrial development represented a "specific national solution"[87]. In its first phase, the "New State", seen from the perspective of the inclusion of a wavering economic policy in the individualization of Fascism, appears to create some new problems.

---

[84] For this different perspective, see Jaime Reis, "The Historical Roots of Modern Portuguese economy: the first century of growth, 1850s to 1950s", Richard Herr (Ed. by), *The New Portugal. Democracy and Europe*, (Berkeley: 1992), pp. 126-148.

[85] See Alfredo Marques, *Op. Cit.*, p. 25.

[86] *Idem*, p. 26.

[87] See José Maria Brandão de Brito, *A Industrialização Portuguêsa no Pós-guerra (1948-1965), O condicionamento industrial*, (Lisboa: 1989), p. 141.

INTERNATIONAL FACTORS

International factors were not an important element in the overthrow of republican liberalism and the establishment of Salazarism. If there is anything to emphasize in this respect, it is precisely the opposite, i.e. the relative independence of internal political sectors. Unlike the authoritarian experiences of the same period in the Eastern European countries, Portugal's case was a typical example of the establishment of an authoritarian regime in a small country on the periphery of Europe without any significant intervention from the major powers and of a genuinely native character.

The central focus of Portuguese foreign policy and the main concern of the national political élites was, from the end of the 19th century onwards, the defense of the country's vast colonial heritage bequeathed by history and British interests. Britain had watched over and ensured Portuguese independence since the 17th century. There was, in fact, no change in this respect between the liberal republican regime and Salazar's "New State".

Some research into British attitudes towards the dictatorship lead us to conclude that the Foreign Office kept up with events without interfering and that it supported Salazar's rise to power[88]. This was a far cry from the time when it was the British Embassy that gave orders as it had in the 19th century, and when its approval was essential before any break, such as occurred with the revolution of 1910. During the process of transition to authoritarianism, "if anything, the pattern of British attitudes towards political events in Portugal during that period is one of expectancy", observed Cabral.[89] That there were no signs of a change in foreign policy on the part of the Portuguese contributed to this view.

[88] See Fernando Rosas, *O Salazarismo e a Aliança Luso-Britânica*, (Lisboa: 1988).

[89] See Manuel Villaverde Cabral, "Dependency and autonomy in Portuguese politics: Authoritarianism and Democracy in an International Perspective", mimeo., p. 18.

The only international event which was decisive and which had significant impact on Portuguese internal policy was the crisis of the Second Republic and the civil war that followed in neighboring Spain, as it was felt to be a genuine threat to the consolidation of the regime[90]. The repressive clamp-down and the creation of para-military organizations which until then had not been planned and were actually viewed as hostile by Salazar are usually associated with this international event. This movement has been characterized by some historians as the driving force of what they called the "Fascistization" of the regime. In fact, organizations like the Portuguese Legion (1936) were created during the Spanish Civil War and the Portuguese Youth (1936), for which plans had already been drawn up several times, suddenly came into being[91]. It was also during this period that the Fascist image became more pronounced. Once Franco's victory was assured after 1938 that image declined.

The situation in Spain dominated Portuguese foreign policy up until the turning point of World War II. At first, Salazar supported the Francoist insurrection and discreetly opened his territory to that sector while formally remaining neutral. This was later followed by more open support but without ever endangering the Anglo-Portuguese alliance. After Franco's victory and during the first phase of World War II, the main concern of the Portuguese regime was to avoid Spain's participation on the side of the Axis, given Spain's adherence to the Anti-Comintern Pact, and to maintain the neutrality of the Iberian Peninsula.

Another interesting but little studied dimension is the mistrust on the part of the "New State", both ideologically and from the international relations perspective, of German Fascism and, more

[90] See César Oliveira, *Portugal e a Segunda República de Espanha, 1931-1936*, (Lisboa: 1987); *O Salazarismo e a Guerra Civil de Espanha* (Lisboa: 1988), and Hipólito de la Torre Goméz, *La Relación Peninsular en la Antecamara de la Guerra Civil de España (1931-36)*, (Mérida: 1989).
[91] See Simon Kuin, "Mocidade Portuguesa nos Anos Trinta: a instauração de uma organização paramilitar de juventude", *Análise Social*, (Forthcoming), and Luís Nuno Rodrigues, "A Legião Portuguesa no Espectro Político Nacional (1936-1939)", *Penélope*, 11, 1993, pp. 21-36.

strangely, of Italian Fascism. Even before the convergence of Rome and Berlin, when Fascist Italy made some "internationalist" efforts in the name of "Latinity" in competition with Nazism, the regime's reaction was slight and mistrustful as one of the few studies on the subject indicates[92]. Invitations to take part in the CAUR were discreetly declined in the name of Portuguese independence and, in the field of international relations, Mussolini's colonial claims gave rise to a certain anxiety on the part of the regime which balked at the slightest attempt to change the political balance in Africa.

Portuguese historians have also shed light on another subject. They have helped clear up doubts regarding the regime's attitude towards World War II. Salazar's neutrality was genuine and not "forced". It made use of "concessions" to Britain to affirm the country's progressive autonomy while not jeopardizing its colonial heritage.[93] In this respect, Salazarism took a different position from Francoism which was closer to the Axis at least until the turn in the war, even if with some reluctance on the part of some sectors of its institutions[94].

THE MILITARY

The military was the main participant in the processes of political disruption which occurred in Portugal in the 20th century and it was they who were responsible for the beginning and the end of the "New State"[95]. They were the only institution that Salazar feared

[92] See Simon Kuin, "Fascist Italy and Salazar's Portugal, 1926-1936", *Yearbook of European Studies, 3-Italy/Europe*, (Amsterdam: 1990), pp. 101-118.

[93] See António Telo, *Portugal na Segunda Guerra*, (Lisboa: 1987); AA.VV., *Portugal na Segunda Guerra Mundial. Contributos para uma reavaliação*, (Lisboa: 1989); Fernando Rosas, *Portugal entre a Paz e a Guerra*, (Lisboa: 1990).

[94] See Paul Preston, *Las Derechas Españolas en el Siglo XX: autoritarismo, fascismo, y golpismo* (Madrid: 1986).

[95] See João B. Serra and Luís Salgado de Matos, "Intervenções Militares na Vida Política", *Análise Social*, (72-73-74), Iº vol., 1982, pp. 1165-1195. For a general introduction See Maria Carrilho, *Forças Armadas e Mudança Política em Portugal no Séc. XX. Para uma explicação sociológica do papel dos militares*, (Lisboa: 1985) and José Medeiros Ferreira, *O Comportamento Político dos Militares. Forças armadas e regimes políticos em Portugal no séc. XX,* (Lisboa: 1992).

and, indeed, it was they who made the most threatening overtures to overthrow him. The only time during the regime in which the dictatorship hung by a thread was at the beginning of the 1960s when the colonial war broke out. This was due to opposition from high-ranking military officers. It was also a dissident officer, General Humberto Delgado, who was the unifying force of the serious "electoral" shock of 1958 caused by the opposition movements. Most of the research has concentrated on the study of the military institution and its relationship with the First Republic[96]. We now know considerably more about the republicans' inability to reform the armed forces, the impact of Portugal's participation in World War I, the politicization of the army after the war and the influence of the radical right within its ranks[97]. Moreover, the essential facts of the plot behind the conspiracy which led to the *coup d'état* of 1926 were reconstructed quite accurately, even if a certain deterministic finality did dominate certain aspects of the causality established[98].

Less attention has been given to the withdrawal of the military from the political limelight with the consolidation of the authoritarian order and to the type of relationship the "New State" had with the military, which successfully "civilized" the dictatorship established in 1926. The Fascists and radical right had considerable influence over the so-called "lieutenants of the 28th of May". Those members of the military hierarchy who occupied political posts, including several prime ministers, were conservative republicans who like Vicente de Freitas or Ivens Ferraz frowned upon Salazar's strategy[99]. General Carmona, President of the Republic after 1928, was sensitive to any attempts to relegate the Armed Forces to second place and had more power in the 1930s than his weak image of the post-war period might lead one to believe.

[96] See Douglas L. Wheeler, *Republican Portugal. A Political History, 1910-1926*, (Madison: 1978).

[97] See António José Telo, *Decadência e Queda da I República Portuguesa*, I° vol, (Lisboa: 1980); Douglas L. Wheeler, *A Ditadura Militar Portuguesa, 1926-1933*, (Lisboa: 1988).

[98] See António José Telo, *Op. Cit.*, 2ª vol., (Lisboa: 1984).

[99] See César Oliveira (Prefácio e notas), *A ascensão de Salazar. Memórias de seis meses de Governo -1929- do general Ivens Ferraz*, (Lisboa: 1988).

In spite of this and of the tensions which existed in the relationship between the regime and the military institution, there seems to be no doubt that the "New State" removed the military from the political limelight, established a new type of relationship between the political powers and the Armed Forces and ensured a relatively peaceful domination over them at least until the end of World War II[100]. The corporatist compensations given to the military institution were substantial but some of them, at least as far as the immunity of members of the military before civilian courts and police was concerned, were inherited from the First Republic. Moreover, some of these reforms hit certain privileges hard[101]. The mere coincidence of the spontaneous ideology of "order" that most of the military subscribed to and the nature of the regime is not enough to explain everything. Some military privileges disappeared in 1945 and were followed by strict police control over the military institution after the attempts associated with the "democratic opposition" to overthrow the regime.

THE SINGLE PARTY

The differences between the National Union and any Fascist party are easily recognizable even when, as in Italy, the party became dependent on the State. The non-Fascist nature of Salazar's party has always been used as a point of reference when trying to define the Portuguese regime.

The National Union was a creation of Salazar's, established and organized by governmental decree. Legislation on the party was passed in the same way as legislation on the administration of the railways. The administration controlled it, let it slumber or revitalized it according to the situation at the time. The single party of

---

[100] See Douglas L. Wheeler "The Military and the Portuguese Dictatorship, 1926-1974: "The Honor of the Army", In Lawrence S. Graham and Harry M. Makler (Edited by), *Op. Cit.*, pp. 191-219 and José Medeiros Ferreira, *Op. Cit.*, pp. 175-202.

[101] See Tom Gallagher, "Fernando dos Santos Costa: guardião militar do Estado Novo 1944-1958", in AA. VV., *O Estado Novo...*, *Op. Cit.*, vol. I, pp. 199-219.

Salazarism was studied from a comparative point of view by Braga da Cruz. However, in view of the non-Fascist nature of the party and the government's influence over it, comparison with the Fascisms that came to power only emphasized the differences. A much more rewarding comparison could be made precisely with those parties which had similar origins like the regimes of the same period which created parties from above. These range from the dictatorship of Primo de Rivera in Spain (and even that of Francoism) to those of central and Eastern Europe. Indeed, seen from this point of view and considering the longevity of the Portuguese regime, the National Union makes for an extremely interesting case study of the functions of the parties which, unlike the Fascist ones, neither reached power at all nor, once created, fulfilled functions of control and monopoly of access to power or mobilization of the masses which the Fascists generally did.

Some of the National Union's fundamental functions conferring legitimation on the process of institutionalization of the "New State" were obvious, and we should not forget that Salazar's regime had its origins in the military dictatorship established in 1926, which was extremely unstable, and had a heterogeneous base of support of many political clienteles. The resistance by the republican opposition and the Fascist party (the National Syndicalists) to the creation of the National Union were indicative of its original function. Arlindo Caldeira summarized them as follows: To support the monopolization of political power by the government, to neutralize all forces likely to dispute Salazar's power, to legitimize the regime through elections, to unite the different factions and compel them to solve possible conflicts within the National Union, so as not to destabilize the regime[102].

The National Union could be compared to a field laced with mines where generally by repressive means, as in the case of the Fascists organized autonomously during the military dictatorship, those joining the regime were sent and subsequently fenced off.

---

[102] See Arlindo Manuel Caldeira, "O partido de Salazar: antecedentes, organização e funções da União Nacional (1926-34)", *Análise Social*, vol. XXII (94), 1986, p. 975.

Moreover, the army was kept away from public life. Political activity was generally off limits outside public life. It did manage to continue however since, besides the Fascists, the Catholics and Monarchists were still legally organized and exercised some power over the military.

Several of the authors already mentioned emphasized the absence of an ideological role and propaganda or mobilization of the masses on the part of the National Union — an easily discernible fact since the party all but disappeared during the 1930s. In 1945, the party came to life when, in an adverse international situation, the regime permitted the appearance of an electoral opposition under close control and it became necessary to encourage votes for the government's lists. However, even this action to ensure victory was more administrative than political as electoral marshalling even for propaganda purposes was routinely avoided and was in fact openly discouraged. The National Union was also not the exclusive channel of access to political office, from the Corporatist Chamber to Ministers and Secretaries of State who in many cases did not come from the party ranks. However, it did have some control over access to the lower echelons of the civil service where it was essential to belong to the party. As Braga da Cruz emphasizes, "its importance grew as one went from central administration to local administration."[103] The social composition of the party also distinguishes it from Fascism. The National Union had no *petit bourgeois* component typical of the Fascist parties and their "social" demagogy. Its composition consisted instead of local notables with landowners and businessmen setting up most local committees in the 1930s[104].

The provinces, where influence was exerted at a local level, constitute a promising area of research to help us better understand the role of the party. This field has, unfortunately, not received the attention it deserves. It should be kept in mind that the "New State" was not established after a democracy but after a clientelistic and

[103] See Manuel Braga da Cruz, *O Partido...*, p. 177.
[104] See Arlindo Caldeira, " O partido de Salazar...", p. 960 and Manuel Braga da Cruz, *O Partido...* p. 234.

oligarchic republic based on restricted electoral participation, with some obvious points of continuity inherited from the old constitutional monarchy of the 19th century[105]. Although it changed the rules of the game, the National Union was a central instrument in the adaptation of the local notables to the new political system[106]. It was in this area that we feel its role was most important.

In an article of 1968 on the opposition to the "New State", Hermínio Martins mentions the regime's high degree of political rationality in the field of administration of violence, opting for an "optimum of terror rather than a crude maximum (...)"[107]. The same could be said with regard to the institutional apparatus of the political system, a formal compromise between liberal and corporatist principles of representation. This instance of political compromise with the conservative republican conservatives who had supported the 1926 coup was quite evidently perverted but never abolished. As we have already indicated, the electoral principle was maintained and religiously followed within the established time limits.

The appearance of an "electoral opposition" to the regime after 1945 did not go unnoticed by researchers. Faced with the question: "why did that manifestly anti-liberal, anti-democratic regime, bother to hold even a simulacrum of elections at all?", Schmitter quite correctly detects some answers which are not valid in Portugal's case. Unlike the socialist regimes of the time, the 99% rule never existed in Portugal. Neither did "Salazar seek to use the electoral process as a mass-mobilization device", nor did the masses play a role in internal legitimation, a function they fulfilled in other more "plebiscitary" authoritarian regimes[108].

[105] For a review of political clientelism in modern Portugal, See Fernando Farelo Lopes, "Panorama de la Littérature sur le Clientélisme au Portugal", *C.E.M.O.T.I.*, n° 9, F.N.S.P., Paris, Janvier 1990, pp. 85-90.

[106] See Rui Ramos, "O Estado Novo perante os poderes periféricos: o governo de Assis Gonçalves em Vila Real (1934-39)", *Análise Social*, vol.XXII (90), 1986, pp. 109-135; António Costa Pinto, "As elites Politicas e a Consolidação do Salazarismo: O Nacional Sindicalismo e a União Nacional", *Análise Social*, vol. XXVII (116-117), 1992, pp. 575-613.

[107] See Herminio Martins, "Opposition...", p. 263.

[108] See Philippe C. Schmitter," The Impact and Meaning...", p. 146.

As noted above, one must emphasize that up to 1945 not even a dummy "opposition" was allowed during the elections, whose function was the legitimation of the regime. The subject was not broached until it began to look as if the Allies would win World War II. Of all the reasons for holding elections in the authoritarian regimes discussed in Schmitter's work, the most prosaic was, in our opinion, the only important one: "to legitimate it in the eyes of foreigners" and was therefore externally motivated[109]. All other reasons were of secondary importance.

THE OPPOSITION

The only study on the opposition to the "New State" concentrated on the period between World War II and the regime's fall in 1974[110]. Unfortunately, we know much less about the movement of resistance to the establishment of the Military Dictatorship, the consolidation of Salazarism and even about some of the old Fascist opposition.

After numerous attempts at revolution on the part of the republicans and the destruction of anarcho-syndicalism as a dominant force in the workers' movement, it was the small Communist Party which rose rapidly to the leadership of the clandestine opposition to the regime[111]. In contrast with the opposition to other regimes of the same type, Portugal did not have an important opposition in exile (it only reappeared in the 1960s)[112]. After the fall of the Spanish Republic and the dissolution of some of the movements of ex-

---

[109] *Idem*, p. 150.

[110] See Dawn Linda Raby, *Fascism and Resistance in Portugal. Communists, liberals and military dissidents in the opposition to Salazar, 1941-1974*, (Manchester: 1988).

[111] For a sociological and historical approach of the anarchist and the Portuguese working class see, João Freire, *Anarquistas e operários. Ideologia, ofícios e práticas sociais: o anarquismo e o operariado em Portugal, 1900-1940*, (Porto: 1992).

[112] See the comparative chapter of Stanley G. Payne, "La oposición a las dictaduras en la Europa occidental: una perspectiva comparativa" in Javier Tusell et alii, *La Oposición al Régimen de Franco*, 3 vols. (Madrid: 1990), pp. 51-64.

iled republicans at the end of the 1920s, it was inside the country and using all possible legal spheres of action that the opposition gradually reorganized, with some strength, to emerge in the 1940s[113]. Although it is only after 1945 that one can talk of an "electoral opposition" to Salazarism, dissidence survived in various legal publications which continued to exist in the 1930s despite strict censorship. This change in the opposition to the regime was reflected in the composition of political prisoners between 1933 and 1939. There was not only a spectacular increase in their numbers during the Spanish Civil War, clearly expressing the regime's tougher repressive measures, but they were also mainly workers and members of the Communist Party[114]. For the period which we are interested in, 1933-1945, there are few studies of the opposition movements and of the opposition movements' views on the nature of the regime[115].

SCHOOLS AND IDEOLOGY IN A "CONSERVATIVE REGIME"

In her introduction to a thesis on Salazar's school system in the 1930s which she researched mainly before 1974, Maria Filomena Mónica discussed some of the bibliography cited here. She noted the great discrepancies between this bibliography on the central cases and the analysis of Salazar's regime and concluded that "hardly anything that has been written on Fascism applies to Portugal's case"[116]. She supported the position that "the differences between Salazarism and Italian Fascism are greater than the simi-

[113] See A.H. Oliveira Marques, *A Liga de Paris e a Ditadura Militar, 1927-1928*, (Lisboa: 1976) and *A Literatura Clandestina em Portugal, 1926-1932*, 2 vols. (Lisboa: 1990-1991).
[114] See articles of José Pacheco Pereira and João Arsénio Nunes in the collective works quoted above.
[115] See Fernando Rosas, *Op. Cit.*
[116] See Maria Filomena Mónica, *Educação e Sociedade no Portugal de Salazar (A escola primária salazarista 1926-1939)*, (Lisboa: 1978), p. 98.

larities (...)". Influenced by Barrington Moore, she characterized
the regime as a "lower form of conservative modernization, particularly peaceful and dilatory, through revolution from above"[117].
In the conclusion to her work, she stressed the central role of
the Catholic Church in the socialization of schools in the "New
State", where the central values were obedience, resignation, charity
and patriotism, legitimizing a social order considered to be an "im-
mutable structure"[118]. Given the non-totalitarian character of the
regime, leaving "many areas of private life virtually free of political indoctrination", the "natural" hierarchy was enough, in most
cases, to ensure order. The "Church still fulfilled its old role of
ideological apparatus par excellence". She also suggests that in
Portugal of the 1930s, this apparatus was "more important than
the school itself"[119].

However, during its first phase the "New State" would dedicate
an almost obsessive attention to the construction of a "nationalist"
educational apparatus, submitting the latter to a thorough purge,
reinforcing ideological control over teachers, and eliminating all
traces of the old republican and liberal ideology, as well as isolat-
ing it from any international movements whatsoever[120]. Not only
did the curriculums now dress themselves in traditionalist conservative and nationalist doctrine, but the Catholic religion would also
become a central element in official instruction[121].

---

[117] *Idem*, p. 94 and 105.

[118] *Idem*, p. 345.

[119] *Idem*, p. 355-356. On the impact of the regime in rural society, See José
Cutileiro, *A Portuguese Rural Society*, (Oxford: 1971) and Joyce Firstenberg
Riegelhaupt, "Peasants and Politics in Salazar's Portugal: The Corporate State
and Village "Nonpolitics" *in*, Lawrence Graham and Harry M. Makler (Edited
by), *Op. Cit*, pp. 167-190. I have used the Portuguese version of the former,
(Lisboa: 1976).

[120] See António Nóvoa, "A "educação Nacional", Joel Serrão and A. H. Oliveira Marques (Dir. de), *Op. Cit.*, Vol. XII, pp. 455-519.

[121] *Idem*, p. 460.

***

The contributions of more recent Portuguese research are far from exhausted and we have only discussed the interpretation of the leading studies with regard to relations between Salazar's regime and European Fascism. In the last few years a large number of monographs have contributed towards an improved empirical knowledge of Salazarism. In spite of the significant absence of work on most of the regime's institutions, especially those which were most inspired by Fascism, some of the variables of the debate discussed here are not likely to be affected when those institutions do come under study.

Chapter III

FASCISM
AND THE BREAKDOWN OF
PORTUGUESE LIBERAL REPUBLIC (1910-1926)

Some historians, influenced by the research on the seizure of power by the fascist parties in Germany and Italy, raised the following question: why was it that liberalism was not overthrown by a Fascist-type party in Portugal?

It is important to point out that the question is not necessarily pertinent to the analysis of the process whereby the Portuguese republican regime went into crisis, as it would assume a deviation from a common pattern of post-war democratic crises, a deviation which was not the case, even in merely quantitative terms. In most of the cases in which liberal and democratic regimes collapsed after the First Word War, the Fascists were either minor partners in reactionary coalitions or not present at all.

Is best to start by determining the nature of the regime overthrown in 1926. *Portugal's First Republic was not a young democracy taking its first hesitant steps in the "era of the masses", as were so many others in the Europe of 1918.* It was not a product of increased popular suffrage based on mass parties, as were the Weimar Republic, the Italian post-war democratic regime, the Third Republic in France and, later, the Spanish Second Republic.

3.1 THE SOCIO-ECONOMIC CONSTRAINTS OF POLITICAL CHANGE

THE TURN OF THE CENTURY

Portugal entered the "age of the masses" without a number of upheavals which marked parallel processes of democratic regime crisis and overthrow in inter-war Europe. As an old "nation-state" whose political frontiers had remained basically unchanged since the late middle ages, demonstrating an accentuated pre-state continuity, Portugal was a kind of "ideal type" of liberal nationalist ideological model on the eve of the 20th century. "State" and "nation" got on well with each other, enjoying a significant cultural homogeneity: There were no national or ethnic-cultural minorities in Portugal and no Portuguese populations in neighboring countries; similarly, there were no religious or ethnic-linguistic minorities. Even dialects were a rarity, found only in some areas near the Spanish border. Thus, if anything stands out in the field of these historical and cultural variables, markedly present in other cases, it is their negligible presence or complete absence in Portugal[1].

Because of this, Portugal had no territorial claims in Europe. She was, in fact, within the British sphere of influence, which guaranteed her vast colonial heritage. The most important of the historical variables was Portugal's imperial, followed by colonial, nature. From the 17th century onwards, Portuguese imperial power had been complemented by her political and economic dependence on Britain. At the end of the 19th century, the liberals were confronted with the threat of the European powers against their "historic rights" in Africa, the stronghold of Portuguese colonialism since Brazil's independence in 1822.

Tensions with Britain increased dramatically in the 1880s, leading, after the British ultimatum of 1890, to the emergence of the first strong anti-British sentiments in modern public opinion[2]. The

---

[1] See António Costa Pinto and Nuno Monteiro, "Problems of National Identity in Portugal", *WerkstattGeschichte* 8 (1994), pp. 15-26.

[2] See Nuno Teixeira, *O Ultimatum Inglês. Política externa e política interna no Portugal de 1890*, (Lisboa: 1990).

British foiled Portuguese aspirations to the territories of what is now Zimbabwe, forcing her to abandon intentions to unite Angola and Mozambique by threatening to invade Portugal in 1890. This episode cemented modern Portuguese nationalism, symbolically marking what became Portugal's main foreign policy characteristic up to the 1970s, namely the defense of her colonial heritage. In fact, one could say that "the identification of the colonial empire with nationalism in Portugal provides a kind of functional equivalent to the divisive nation-state issues" found in other European societies at the time[3].

In the second half of the 19th century Portugal could be categorized as a non-industrialized country governed by a stable "oligarchic parliamentarianism". The dynamic of social and economic change did not differ much from that of other "semi-peripheral" countries which Nicos Mouzelis has defined as having an "early parliamentarism and late industrialization"[4]. Turning to the exploitation of the colonial African patrimony whilst timidly advancing out an industrializing policy based on "import-substitution", this oligarchic and clientelistic liberalism began to come apart at the turn of the century. The emergence of the republican movement which mobilized large sections of the urban middle and lower middle classes, until then "excluded" from politics, was expressive of this crisis[5].

From the beginning of the century onwards, whether in electoral or political and social mobilizational terms, the Republicans were able to provoke the erosion of the limited clientelist system of monarchic "rotativism" with a populist strategy. The Republican Party had an extremely flexible program with a great capacity to exploit themes such as nationalism, anti-clericalism, the expansion of political participation, the right to strike, and other demands

---

[3] See Hermínio Martins, "Portugal", Margaret Scotford Archer and Salvador Giner (Edited by), *Contemporary Europe: class, status and power* (London: 1971), p. 63.

[4] See Nicos P. Mouzelis, *Op. Cit.*

[5] See Pedro Tavares de Almeida, *Eleições e Caciquismo no Portugal Oitocentista (1868-1890)*, (Lisboa: 1991).

made by a feeble labour movement. On the eve of the 1910 revolution it united a political constellation which ranged from a moderate and electoralist faction to Jacobin authoritarians. This coalition included secret organizations uniting radical republicans and anarchists with a strong popular base in Lisbon, such as the "Portuguese Carbonaria", who would insert themselves into many of the party's parochial committees[6].

In October 1910 the constitutional monarchy was overthrown in Lisbon. This rapid revolution was overseen by republican members of the armed forces and aided by decisive action on the part of civilian and military members of the Carbonaria, primarily sargeants and corporals. Most military units remained neutral. Portugal would thus become one of Europe's first republics at the beginning of the 20th century.

The republican elites did carry out a timid but radical "mass nationalization", always being conscious of the social and political "siege" of the rural areas still dominating Portuguese society. These elites were the principal movers behind the creation of the national symbols and school socialization apparati that would characterize 20th century Portugal. They would also be the "sanctifiers" of the colonial empire as a central element of the Portuguese "nation's" viable identity. A new national Flag and Anthem, a new civil liturgy with its own holidays, a model of "citizen building", a populist-type political mobilization, and an accentuated "nationalization" of teaching programs accompanying the expansion of school system, characterized the 1910 rupture.

THE RURAL SIEGE

There was a significant acceleration in social and economic change between the end of the 19th century and the 1930's, with industrial development and an important urbanization movement. But it was moderate in comparison to most other west European countries. During the period under analysis, Portugal was situated

---

[6] See Douglas L. Wheeler, *Republican Portugal...* , pp. 32-47.

on the "semi-periphery of the world economy"[7]. She had a backward economy and a weak, incipient, and sparse industrial base[8]. The evolution of the structure of the economically active population gives us a more accurate picture of this backwardness. In 1911, Portugal had about 5 1/2 million inhabitants, and an economically active population of 2.545.000, 58% of these worked in agriculture, 25% in industry and 17% in the tertiary sector. By 1930 the active population in agriculture had decreased by 3%, the tertiary sector had increased by 3%, the secondary sector remaining stable[9].

At the base of the rural social pyramid were the poor peasants. In 1915, approximately 57% of agricultural landowners had very small holdings and many of the remainder owned only small pieces of land. In 1930, little had changed and one found "(...) the presence of almost one million active men, women and children who belonged to a type of activity not directly dependent on capital and whose main productive activity was scraping a living out of tiny pieces of land which they partially or totally owned"[10]. Among a few large holdings, these small ones were concentrated in the north and center of the country. These were the areas of greatest wine production. The latter was the major structuring element of capitalist relations and of interest groups connected to agriculture and commerce, - as it was not only the most important agricultural, but also overall export commodity.

Cereals and the more modern agricultural sector were in the center and south, especially north of Lisbon and in the Alentejo. The latifundio area of the Alentejo, with its very large holdings and concentration of the agricultural proletariat (around 3,8% of the active population in agriculture), grew wheat and cork. The latter was Portugal's second agricultural export. The most modern farming methods were to be found in the Ribatejo, which sup-

---

[7] See Kathleen Schwartzman, *Op cit.*

[8] See Jaime Reis, *O Atraso Economico Português numa Perspectiva Histórica*, (Lisboa: 1993).

[9] Estimate, since the 1930's census transferred to the tertiary a good part of the primary sector.

[10] See Fernando Medeiros, *A Sociedade e a Economia Portuguesa nas Orígens do Salazarismo*, (Lisboa: 1978), p. 34.

plied urban and external markets. The Portuguese emphasis on agro-exporting was based on an isolated labor force which was not monetarily remunerated. In quantitative terms, fruits, wine (mainly Port), raw cork and wool, accounted for more than half of Portuguese exports. Approximately two-thirds of colonial products were reexported, with England still being the major trade partner (22% exports and 27% imports, in 1910)[11].

In the industrial sector the active population hardly increased at all during this period. This sector requires a more detailed analysis. Of the 25% active in this sector in 1911, most were craftsmen and small owners who "use[d] family labour, at home or irregular seasonal labour"[12]. Outside the Lisbon and Oporto areas "the industrial proletariat was a "fantasy" of statistics, according to which the number of "factory owners" exceeded the number of workers and included "mill owners", carpenters, smiths, tailors, bakers, cobblers, etc[13]. In 1917, 81,2% of the "factories" counted employed only between 1 and 20 workers. Only 14% employed up to 100 and only 4,4% more than 100.

The textile and food industries absorbed the larger part of the industrial proletariat. Although scattered around the country, the largest units were either in the Lisbon and Setúbal area or in the center. The smaller, cottage-type industries were found in the north. During the war the food industries saw the increasing importance of milling and fish canning.

The metallurgic industry absorbed only 9% of the industrial proletariat and was concentrated in Lisbon. It was also during the war that one saw the development of one of the great poles of the "working class culture", connected to the growth of the chemical industry. This however did not affect the incipient, dispersed, and almost family-based nature of the Portuguese industrial sector.

[11] See Kathleen Schwartzman, *Op. Cit.*, p. 57.

[12] See António José Telo, "A busca frustada do desenvolvimento", António Reis (Edited By), *História Contemporânea de Portugal*, Vol. 3, (Lisboa: 1989), p. 127.

[13] See Paulo Guinote, "A sociedade: da agitação ao desencanto", *Idem*, pp. 189-190.

On the eve of the 1910 revolution the Portuguese upper classes were strongly dominated by a small group of rural property owners. The latter lived in the cities, either from urban or, for the most part, from rural rents, associated with an old commercial elite that placed its capital mainly abroad. Not much can be said about the middle classes due to absence of good social studies. From the 1911 Census one can place 10% of the active population (around 600,000) in the "middle classes"[14]. The growing State bureaucracy of the late 19th century and medium size commerce was the central backbone of this social group. With the War, the cleavages between an impoverished civil service sector and the "business" sector came to grow.

Corresponding levels of urbanization were low: Between 1900 and 1930, the number of city-dwellers who lived in cities or towns with more than 20,000 inhabitants grew from 10.5% to 13.9%. Lisbon stood out as the only large city in the country with 8% of the population, followed far behind by Oporto. It is here that we find the only major areas of an "urban political culture" in Portugal. From an administrative point of view, few of the cities corresponded to the average patterns of European cities as most of them were no more than "towns" or "large villages". Even considering as "urban" concentrations of more than 10,000 inhabitants, the numbers would not change significantly; the rural and village world dominated Portuguese society, accounting for more than 80% of the population in 1930.

After the significant leap in the first decades of the new century, urban growth after the 1920s was extremely slow, and maintained a modest pace throughout the period under analysis. Only in the 1960s would the rate of urban growth once again pick up steam (in 1960: 23% urban, 77% rural).

Peasant emigration had had, since the mid-19th century, a significant effect on the structure of the economy[15]. Between 1900 and 1930 close to 1 million Portuguese would emigrate, mainly to

---

[14] *Idem*, p. 198.
[15] See Miriam Halpern Pereira, *A Política Portuguesa de Emigração*, (1850-1930), (Lisboa: 1984).

Brazil and the USA. Only the war years would slow this almost constant flow. In spite of all the rhetoric and the modest yet real development of the African colonies, very few Portuguese emigrated to Angola or Mozambique during this period. This is well illustrated by the comments made by Afonso Costa, the charismatic leader of the Portuguese First Republic. Very conscious of the great difficulties a weak economy faced in exploiting the colonies, he kept repeating that, "what the colonies need is not working people but men with initiative and money, lots of money"[16]. The remittances sent home from emigrants in the "New World" thus continued to have a central position in the Portuguese economy.

We will complete this brief introduction by noting the country's low literacy rate in this period. This is decisive in the debate on the question of access to political participation after the 1910 Revolution. In 1911, illiteracy affected the majority of the Portuguese. 70% of people over 7 years of age were illiterate[17]. Illiteracy dominated the rural and provincial industrial world and increased as one moves from north to south[18]. In the areas with small holdings in the north it was lower than in the Alentejo with its mostly large holdings. Literate culture was situated mainly in the urban areas where newspaper readership levels were quite elevated.

INTERMEDIARY STRUCTURES

Political Parties

During the second half of the 19th century Portugal saw the consolidation of "oligarchic parliamentarism" (1852). For several decades but particulary between 1871 and 1890 the Regenerator Party and the Progressist Party rotated office in a reasonably stable two-party system known as *Rotativismo*. Clientelism was a key element of Portuguese politics and Government manipulation of

[16] Quoted in A. H. Oliveira Marques, *História da Primeira República. As Estruturas de Base*, (Lisboa: 1978), p. 41.
[17] See António Nóvoa, "A educação Nacional....", p. 475.
[18] See Jaime Reis, *Op. Cit.*, pp. 227-253.

local and national elections was a common practice. In this, it closely resembled other political systems of the same period, namely those of Spain, Italy and Greece[19]. Although their political programs were slightly different, the two "rotativist" parties were virtually indistinguishable.

In the late 19th century two small "ideological" parties emerged, the Socialist Party and the Republican Party. Both came from the same urban cultural setting. Nevertheless, the reformist "ouvriérisme" of the former, complemented by a "social" versus "political" strategy, would severely restrict its capacity to transcend the very small circle of the Portuguese working class.

The Republican Party rapidly became the "third party", being the central political vehicle of the urban petty bourgeoisie at the turn of the century. Republican ideology was indebted to the French Third Republic. Universal male suffrage, increasing with the secularization of education, municipal autonomy, and the separation of Church and State, were central elements of its propaganda against the oligarchy of the Constitutional Monarchy.

As the main instrument of the transition to post-oligarchic politics, the Republican Party may have played a role similar to other urban populist movements in the Balkans and Latin America in the same period. At the beginning of the century, the republican Party was directing the incorporation of the masses into the political arena in a context of very weak "horizontal" forms of political integration. Secret societies, groups of socialists and anarcho-syndicalists, anarchists students and radical republicans, remained temporarily under the Republican banner, as the "vagueness" of its program increased.

On the eve of the 1910 Revolution, the republicans were already distant from their initial urban middle and petty bourgeoisie base; they mobilized some sectors of the working classes and penetrated in the middle and lower ranks of the Armed Forces. With a national organization, strong local branches in the cities, 14 deputies in the Parliament, and control of the City Council of Lisbon, it was already possible to recognize organized factions in its struc-

[19] See Pedro Tavares de Almeida, *Op. Cit.*

tures. These ranged from moderate liberals to Jacobin nationalists. Although some attempts were made to mobilize in the Latifundio area, the rural countryside was virtually excluded from the Republican party structure. The rural world was considered hopeless in the eyes of republican intellectual and political elites.

Interest Groups

The predominance of anarcho-syndicalism over socialism in the confederations of the Portuguese labour movement was a central element of the "anti-system" role played by the Unions from the turn of the century and, above all, during the Republican period. On the other hand, and contrary to the tendency in other European labour movements in the interwar period, ideological and party cleavages in Portugal didn't produce a clear fragmentation of organized labour into several confederations.

In the late 19th century the socialists dominated the small and dispersed Portuguese unions. From then on they were challenged by the anarchists[20]. The labour Congress of 1909 and the wave of strikes of 1909 and 1910-12 marked the offensive of the anarcho-syndicalists at the confederation level. They consolidated their hegemony in the National Workers Union (1914-1919) and with the foundation of the General Confederation of Labour (CGT) in 1919[21].

The majority of "Class associations" were excluded from the political arena, but they had a modest presence in the "artisan" and "corporation" social milieu. The more active and "class oriented" were found in the Lisbon industrial belt. In the southern Latifundia area the peak in social mobilization predates the war (1910-12), when there were booming rural unions (40% of the total), strikes, and terrorist forms of social action[22]. From 1915 on, the number of rural unions declined (11% in 1920) and rural workers were ab-

[20] See Maria Filomena Mónica, *O Movimento Socialista em Portugal (1875-1934)*, (Lisboa: 1985).
[21] See João Freire, *Op. Cit.*
[22] See Pacheco Pereira, *Conflictos Sociais nos Campos em Portugal*, (Lisboa: 1982).

sent in the modest "Biennio Rosso" of 1919-21, in which the Anarcho-syndicalist CGT played a major role.

The effort of the socialists, strongly supported by the Democratic Party, led to a consolidation of their position in the more moderate areas of the labour movement. The "anti-politics" strategy of the Anarcho-syndicalists, however, "ignoring the new republican system", was an important variable in the political arena of the interwar period.

Before the Republic, examples of political mobilization of employers associations were few. Industry was very poorly represented in the political arena. Commercial and agricultural interests were organized at a local level. Particularly important were the Commercial Association of Lisbon (1860) and the Central Association of Portuguese Farmers (ACAP) (1860). The latter had been dominated from the turn of the century by the powerful interests of the Alentejo's Latifundia. In 1918, the ACAP counted 200 local associations and 50.000 members[23].

The wave of strikes of 1911-12 and the radicalism of the first years of the Republican Regime provoked the emergence of more active employers confederations and an optimistic support for Sidónio Pais's Dictatorship. Nevertheless, the unification of the interest groups associated with industry and agriculture proved difficult and unsuccessful until the post-war period.

The Employers Confederation (CP) of 1919, united 60 associations under the initiative of the "small and middle sized commercial and industrial bourgeoisie"[24]. It represented the first attempt to react to the "workers' threat" following a wave of strikes and assaults on shops in Lisbon coinciding with the "golden period" of the anarcho-syndicalist CGT. Symbols of the politicization of the employers' associations, the CP organized a small militia and created it own information service. With the end of the crisis, the CP declined very quickly, vanishing from the political arena in 1923.

[23] See António José Telo, *Decadência e Queda da I República* ..., p. 95.
[24] See Kathleen Schwartzman, *Op. Cit.*, p. 144.

The Union of Economic Interests (UIE) created in 1924, represented a political front for the employers associations. Its explicit purpose was to participate in the anti-democratic conspiracies of the post-war period. It was also the first time that an employers' association ran in the elections (1925), promoting an explicit anti-parliamentarist program. A symbol of the disaffection of important sectors of the Portuguese economic elites towards liberal institutions and the republican party system, the UIE played a central role in the final years of the liberal Republic.

3.2 THE FIRST REPUBLIC: PARLIAMENTARIANISM WITH A DOMINANT PARTY

The brief introduction given above should at least give an idea of the social fabric of 1910, when the Republicans overthrew the constitutional monarchy and began to apply parts of their political program. Even without adopting the more "extreme" theories on stages of economic and social development and consolidation of democratic systems, it seems clear that the structure of Portuguese society was far from meeting the economic, social and cultural prerequisites for "the formation of a civil political culture"[25].

The republican élites adopted a program of universal suffrage, anti-clericalism and nationalism based on the fight against dependence on Britain and on the defense of Portugal's colonial heritage. As early as 1910, legislation for rapid secularization was passed and a strong, urban, anti-clerical movement emerged. These measures, mostly inspired by those undertaken 5 years earlier by the French Third Republic, had a profound impact on the Catholic hierarchy. Suffrage, however, was not extended after all. The pretext for this shortcoming was the first monarchic revolts which broke out in Spain. Thus, the Democratic Party, inheriting part of the electoral machine of the liberal monarchy, rapidly became the ruling party.

[25] See Hermínio Martins, *The Breakdown of....*, p. 6.

Some characteristics of the Republican political system were close to Mattei Dogan's "mimic democracy". Several points must be stressed, however[26]: The "political game" was not, as during the Constitutional Monarchy, limited to the top of the social pyramid; "the landed gentry" lost direct access to the State Apparatus, or at least found new social and political mediator partners; "state and Church didn't support each other" opening new cleavages in the political arena; the State became less immune to ideological pressure than when it had been just a "tax collector for traditional functions"; political clienteles moved from semi-"traditional" forwards to more "party patronage" ones, or, to use one of many approaches, towards a "transition clientelism"; finaly, there was an important and destabilizing eruption of the urban world into the political arena. The 1911 Constitution, approved by a parliament consisting entirely of the Republican Party, established a parliamentary regime. The President of the Republic, elected by parliament, had no powers and, most specifically, could not not dissolve the Chamber. The republican elites decided against adopting universal suffrage. They left things as they had been during the constitutional monarchy, arguing that "caciquismo" in the countryside did not permit change.

Pressures for universal suffrage were very small, not to say absent, in the Republican Constitutional Assembly (1911). "Pressure from below" was also very weak, both due to the "absence" of the rural world and to the anti-participation ideology and praxis of the "active minorities" of the urban working classes[27]. Curiously,

[26] Dogan's "ideal Type" define "mimic Democracy as "a political system that imitates western competitive democracy" that is likely to appear in societies with low degrees of urbanization and industrialization", with a strong "landed gentry" and where "an immense majority of population is rural". "The State does not penetrate in society", middle classes are weak, "mass communication is very limited"; "religious feeling dominates the political culture and the State and Church support each other". "Parliament does not proceed from universal suffrage, the party in power manipulates the elections" and "the majority of citizens are not directly affected by the alternation of parties in power". See Mattei Dogan, "Romania, 1919-1938", Myron Weiner and Ergun Özbudun (Edited by), *Competitive Elections and Developing Studies*, (Durham: 1987), pp. 369-389.

[27] See Fernando Farelo Lopes, *Poder Politico e Caciquismo na Iª República* (Lisboa: 1994), p. 76.

the more conservative sectors of the Republican party that split off
very quickly after the 1910 Revolution, only occasionally debated
the problem.

The electoral laws confined proportional representation to
Lisbon (electoral fief of the Democratic Party) and to Oporto, maintaining majoritarian rule in the rest of country. Political participation, or adult male literate franchise, was small (Table I).

Table I
The Electorate and Voters (1911-1925)

Years	Electorate	Voters	%
1911	846,801	250,000*	—
1913	397,038	150,000**	—
1915	471,560	282,387	59.9
1919	500,000	300,000	60
1921	550,000	350,000	63.3
1922	550,000	380,000	69
1925	574,260	407,960	71

(*) Only 26 electoral circles voted   *Source: Lopes, 1994.*
(**) Only 28 electoral circles voted

There was a contraction of the electorate relative to that of the
latter phase of the constitutional monarchy so that the former represented just 10% of the total population and 30% of adult males.
The main differences could be found at the regional or city/coun-
tryside level, with only approximately 50-60% of the electorate
coming from the rural areas. The capital and the second city were
over-represented with 30% of the electorate.

In the Portuguese Republic the old "two party system" of the
Constitutional Monarchy was replaced by a multiparty system with
a dominant party. The Republican Party was the first semi-mass
party in the liberal party system. After the 1910 revolution, some

of the more conservative leaders left the party and created two others, the Unionist and the Evolutionist parties, which would never be more than small groups of notables.

The electoral hegemony of the Democratic Party was obvious right from the beginning as it was the inheritor of the Republican Party machinery. Its use of the State apparatus also made it "the main supplier of patronage"[28]. With an electoral system with limited suffrage, the Democratic party was able to obtain a compromise between its electorate in the urban petty bourgeoisie and some of the provincial notables, which guaranteed its dominance over the system (Table II).

Table II
Distribution of Parties in Parliament (1910-1917)
(Number of Seats)

Parties	*1911*		*1913*		*1915*	
	N°	*%*	*N°*	*%*	*N°*	*%*
Rep. P.	229	97.9	—	—	—	—
Indep.	3	1.3	12	7.7	13	8
Soc. P.	2	0.8	1	0.6	2	1.2
Dem. P.	—	—	82	52.6	106	65
Evol. P.	—	—	36	23.1	26	16
Unio. P.	—	—	25	16	15	9.2
Cathol.					1	0.6
Total	*234*	*100*	*156*	*100*	*163*	*100*

Source: Lopes, 1994.

From the turn of century on, the Democratic Party acquired a strong and reasonable stable electoral and political base and was the only national party structure in the political arena. Its radical petty bourgeois and popular urban networks were central to its sur-

[28] See Herminio Martins, "The Breakdown...", p. 8.

vival both electorally and in the streets when facing "extra-parlia-mentary" or "presidential" attempts to withdraw it from govern-ment. Until the war there was no erosion of this support. The party also complemented the "legal/electoral" functioning of the system with violent forms of attack on electoral and "extra-parliamentar-ian" opponents, namely monarchists, conservative republicans and the military.

The pattern of urban-rural political articulation was basically managed by the adoption of strong "governmentalization" of local administration. The "District Governors", were the base of the clientelistic pacts that ensured the victory of the Party in the rural areas. The quick enlistment of notables from the dissolved parties, namely from the "Regenerators", is also well documented. The Democratic party managed then to "acquire a 'double' structure and a 'double' clientele with non-competitive yet asymmetric ideo-logical orientations"[29]. Nevertheless, this uneasy coalition between urban "Jacobin" and countryside notables, while making the Demo-cratic Party win virtually all elections during the Republican pe-riod, was not "sufficient to ensure a genuine, permanent monopoly of political power (...) in the manner of dominant parties in semi-liberal politics"[30].

Both the Unionist and the Evolutionist Parties were created by center-right leaders of parliamentary factions that had left the Re-publican Party in 1912. As the main "system" parties, they were bargaining for electoral and "electoral circles" reforms, modera-tion in church-state relations, and searching for clienteles in the provinces, where they had localized "fiefs". Due to the competing rivalry between their very personalized leadership, the parties ex-ceeded all attempts by anti-democratic Party coalitions without other institutional mediators. Until the war there were no "left-wing" splits from the Democratic Party, the small Socialist Party's 2 seats being a "gift" from the Democrats.

If, up to the Sidónio Dictatorship (1918), we can still speak of the existence of a semi-loyal opposition, represented by the con-

---

[29] *Idem*, p. 6.
[30] *Ibidem*.

servative republican parties, in the 1920s all attempts at reforming the political system and at unifying the conservative forces into an electoral party failed, quickly leading to the irreversible conviction on the part of their elites that they would never achieve power by electoral and constitutional means.

ENDEMIC CABINET INSTABILITY

Electoral stability and cabinet instability characterized the entire republican period. Between 1910 and 1926, Portugal saw 45 cabinets of several types: 17 single party, 3 military and 21 coalition governments[31].

During the period between 1912 and 1917, although there was a clear dominance of single party cabinets of the Democratic Party, republican conservatives parties managed to create some independent governments. The first serious challenge to democratic hegemony came in 1915 with an attempt to bypass parliament through military intervention. The democratic cabinet ended after a military coup carried out with the complicity of the President and the conservative parties. Under military pressure the President installed General Pimenta de Castro as Prime Minister in January 1915 leading a cabinet with a strong military component. Pressures to suspend parliament, change the electoral laws and convene elections were strong. Some months later, a democratic uprising re-installed the party in power, with the support of some military units and armed civilians. Total casualties: 150 dead and 300 wounded[32]. In June 1915 the Democratic party again won the elections.

From 1915 on, preparing for participation in the War, the Democratic party led several coalition governments until the coup of Sidónio Pais in 1917. These were organized also with the complicity of the republican conservative parties. Although endemic throughout the Republican regime, cabinet turnover peaked in the immediate post-war period.

---

[31] See Kathleen Schwartzman, *Op. Cit.*
[32] See Douglas L. wheeler, *Op. Cit.*, p. 123.

Coalition governments, be they conservative initiated or "neutral" under parliament's democratic majority, proved to be no more stable. On the contrary, they experienced the greatest level of turnover and the lowest average duration: 91 days compared to the single party ones of 156 days[33].

There are nevertheless two major differences between 'pre' and 'post' war cabinet instability: in this period economic policy outweighs "political access", highlighting the growing role of socioeconomic cleavages and interest groups. A quantitative study on cabinet turnover and economic policies (i.e. pro-industry and/or pro-agriculture, urban/consumers, social pacts, etc.), clearly shows the major role played by economic interest groups in the formation and fall of cabinets. It also highlights the qualitative step taken by the "extra-parliamentary arena" in promoting cabinet instability.

As will be shown below, another new factor of the post-war period was the increasing fragmentation of the party system, with the emergence of left-wing splits from the Democratic Party, failed attempts to found a conservative electoral machine based on the pre-war Evolutionists and Unionists, as well as the appearence of the Sidonist conglomerate. It must also be stressed that the outcome of the 1926 coup was far from producing a clear-cut rupture with past Republican cabinet instability.

POLITICAL VIOLENCE

Political violence was constant in the urban world in the last years of the constitutional monarchy and in the years of the First Republic. The early twenties were the most violent. Although there were no fascist-type paramilitary formations or militias or even veterans associations such as those existing in others parts of Europe after the First World War, armed party factions, or secret societies associated with them, were to be found throughout the political spectrum.

---

[33] See Kathleen Schwartzman, *Op. Cit.*, p. 132.

Furthermore, after 1910 other poles of violence emerged associated with attempts to overthrow the republican governments and backed by sectors of the armed forces. There were two attacks by monarchists using volunteers with incipient military training who entered Portugal with the complicity of the Spanish monarchy (1911-12) as well as considerable repressive violence aimed at the waves of workers' strikes which worsened with the union movement's strategy of non-participation in the war. Nevertheless, more important and unusual was the significant presence of parallel police or militia-type structures from 1910 until after the war.

The overthrow of the constitutional monarchy in 1910 had the support of secret organizations which had a considerable number of "civilian gunners". They were often confused with the local Republican party groups, such as the *Carbonária Portuguesa* which played a decisive role in the successful overthrow of the monarchy. Between 1910 and 1913, some of these groups encouraged acts of repression and intimidation against monarchists and Catholic organizations, thus "politically accompanying" the legislation which provisional governments kept producing with lightning speed.

These groups soon became well-known, particularly the "Battalions of Volunteers" and the "Social Vigilante Groups". The ones dominated by the Democratic Party became known as the "termites". Later, similar but right-wing and mainly monarchist organizations, became known as the "scorpions".

The assassination of King Carlos and Prince Filipe in 1908 was the first of a series of attacks on and assassinations of highly-placed political leaders carried out either by individuals or secret societies. During the Republican period there were assassinations, ambushes and summary executions. Under the Sidónio dictatorship attack groups were formed by monarchists and other right-wing elements who pillaged offices, party headquarters, and newspaper offices, associated with the democrats. Such violence also marked the brief monarchist rule in Oporto, between December 1918 and February 1919, when these groups attempted to restore the monarchy and almost started a civil war. Their cooperation with Sidónio's police was marked by the so-called "death levy" in 1918 when a number of political prisoners and their police escort were murdered in Lisbon by unidentified elements hidden in neighboring buildings. At the end of 1918, came the dictator's turn to die when he was shot at Lisbon's railway station.

During the period of chronic governmental instability and following the restoration of the parliamentary regime in 1919, military and police forces used the streets to promote or overthrow governments. One such example is the National Republican Guard (GNR). This was a military police force created by the Republican regime to defend it from an army it distrusted. As far as public opinion is concerned, it was in association with the GNR that one of the period's most traumatic events, known as the "bloody night", occurred. In 1921, after a series of attacks on the GNR and its leader, a lieutenant colonel who had once been head of government, the force rebelled. Seeing he could not control them the Prime Minister resigned. On that same night, however, a group of military men, members of the GNR and some armed civilians, kidnapped the Prime Minister and other political figures and executed them. Among those murdered was Machado Santos, the military leader of the 1910 revolution. As stated above, although not specific to the anarcho-syindicalist elites, strike-related labour violence was also particularly chaotic during the first three years of the post-war period.

THE BASIC SOCIO-POLITICAL CLEAVAGES

The first political cleavage opened by the 1910 revolution was a religious one. One of the main themes of republican propaganda was secularization. In the first days following the revolution a significant anti-clerical movement swept through Lisbon. Several convents were closed. The rest followed later. Religious orders such as the Jesuits were immediately expelled from the country.

Legislation was soon passed. On November 3rd a divorce law was introduced and a month later a new marriage law was passed giving matrimony an "exclusively civil status". Strict limitations were imposed on religious ceremonies not held in churches and all religious rites associated with state institutions, such as the courts, the universities, and the armed forces, were abolished. At the beginning of 1911, about 150 priests were in prison on charges of various acts of disobedience[34]. Faced with the reaction of the hierarchy, the government forbade the reading of a pastoral letter. This resulted in the severance of Portugal's relations with the Vatican and of ties between the bishops with the State. By 1912, of all the Portuguese bishops, only one had not been dismissed from his *diocese*.

The religion/secularization cleavage soon became a focal point of Portuguese political life and lasted, in spite of later attemps at pacification, until 1926. It was in association with this cleavage that a new Catholic movement was born, closely linked to the hierarchy and showing authoritarian tendencies. The space of a Christian-Democratic style party or for a "popular" party was occupied by the Catholic Center Party whose social Catholicism rapidly became a corporatist authoritarian alternative, shown by its support for the Sidónio Dictatorship in 1917.

The second cleavage became known as the "regime question". It centered the resistance to the Republican regime by a small but relatively strong nucleus of monarchists which had very little to do with the liberalism of the parties dissolved in 1910. In 1911 and 1912 two incursions from Galicia were led by Paiva Couceiro, a caesarist ex-military officer from the military campaigns of the African occupation at the turn of the century. Returning from exile in 1914, when the government pardoned the group owing to the outbreak of war, a few of the young men who had accompanied Couceiro created *Integralismo Lusitano* (IL), a movement based on the Maurrasian principles of *Action Française*, whose influence would also make itself felt in the young Catholic party.

But the main socio-political cleavage was still that between the city/countryside or urban/rural, both at the level of interest intermediation, political access to the State and decision-making, particularly in the post war period. In the twenties, the political ex-

---

[34] See Vasco Pulido Valente, "Revoluções: A "República Velha" (ensaio de interpretação política)", *Análise Social*, vol. XXVII (115), 1992, pp. 7-63.

pression of intra-elite economic conflicts, namely between rural latifundio "traditional elite" interests and industry, and the incapacity of cabinets in dealing with them would become a central element of the regime's breakdown. This can be seen by Salazar's protection of the "traditional sector", prolonging its social and political importance by re-shaping the political arena. The New State used the political system, the intervention of interest groups and economic policy instruments to ensure this continued traditional sector domination.

THE PARTICIPATION IN THE WAR

The war had an immediate destabilizing impact on Portugal, destroying the fragile edifice built by the Republic. Portugal's possible participation in the war was unanimously agreed upon by the republicans because of the African colonies. From the turn of the century it had been known that Britain might hand some of Portugal's colonies over to Germany. For the Democratic Party, the greatest supporter of active military participation at the European front, neutrality would endanger Portugal's colonial heritage and a victory of the allies would consolidate Portugal's position in the peace negotiations.

Yet dealing with the problem of the African colonies was a long way from justifying, *per se*, active interventionism on the European front. Indeed, such action was never called for by Great Britain, even under the terms of the Anglo-Portuguese Alliance. A limited intervention in Africa, defended by the conservative Republicans, was one possible and reasonable policy, both internally and externally. Thus, it would seem natural enough that the interventionist strategy of the Democratic Party would also have internal political objectives, i.e.: to ensure control over the political system through a kind of nationalist and patriotic mobilization; to force the collaboration of the other parties by setting up an "Union Sacré"-style coalition; and to legitimize greater repressive control over political dissent and to smooth over political and social cleavages[35].

[35] Nuno S. Teixeira, *Portugal entre a Guerra e a Paz (1914-1916)*, (Lisbon: Forthcoming).

However, the expectations of the Democratic Party would founder quite quickly. The interventionist strategy caused an almost immediate division in the Armed Forces. It created a faction in favour of intervention in Africa rather than in Europe. The government did not trust the army and began to set up a special intervention force (the "Portuguese Expeditionary Corps"), appointing military officers loyal to the republic and substantially mobilizing militia officers. In October 1914, a group of officers occupied some barracks and declared themselves against participation, thus foreshadowing the events of 1915, with the temporary imposition of a military government, and in 1917, with Sidónio's coup. In spite of this the government was able to enforce Portugal's military participation. In 1916 and 1917 about two thirds of Portugal's army was abroad: 55,000 soldiers were in Flanders and 45,000 in the colonies; 35,000 of the former would either die or return home wounded[36].

The interventionist strategy of the Democratic Party took for granted the participation of the rest of the republican parties in a "union sacré" style coalition. The Evolutionist Party was willing to participate even though it abandoned it immediately afterwards, but the Unionist Party was against intervention in Europe. Both left the stage in fear of the first social and political effects of participation in the war: riots in Lisbon, raids on shops due to food shortages, the accentuation of the strike movement by unions dominated by revolutionary syndicalism which was clearly opposed to the war. As a result of these events, the government declared a "State of Siege" in Lisbon on July 12th 1917, harshly repressing a general strike in September with mass arrests of "revolutionary syndicalists".

---

[36] Nuno S. Teixeira, "A Fome e a Saudade. Os prisioneiros Portugueses na Grande Guerra", *Penélope,* 1992, pp. 91-114.

AN AUTHORITARIAN INTERLUDE:
SIDONIO'S DICTATORSHIP (1917-18)

Although Sidónio Pais used his military past to achieve a charismatic effect, the leader of the December 1917 coup d'état was a discrete member of the conservative republican élite. He was a professor at the University of Coimbra and a member of parliament for the Unionist Party. He had twice been a minister and had been ambassador in Berlin in 1916, when Germany had declared war on Portugal. The easy victory of Sidónio's coup, initially planned with the support of conservative republican notables mostly associated with the Unionist party, is explained by the rapid erosion of the Democratic Party's interventionist policy. Some of the military units that played a decisive part in the coup were getting ready to leave for the front. The ambiguous spectrum of collaborative neutrality of the coup was shown by a visit paid to Sidónio by a delegation of unions when he was still directing military operations in the center of Lisbon. The former promised Pais their support in return for the release of the unions' political prisoners.

Sidónio's dictatorship already showed some of the characteristics of the modern post-war dictatorships, especially those of a fascist nature. After some hesitations, Sidónio exiled a part of the republican élite, broke with the 1911 constitution and tried to institutionalize a plebiscitary presidentialist dictatorship. After a triumphant visit to the provinces, where he was proclaimed "the savior of Portugal" by large crowds mainly mobilized by the clergy, Sidónio Pais introduced universal suffrage, had himself elected president and took total control over the whole executive which the conservative republican parties had left in order to join the opposition. He then created a single party, the National Republican Party (NRP). No other republican party contested the elections; repression of these parties and of workers' unions would soon begin. Apart from the NRP only the monarchists and the Catholics were represented in parliament. The former supported the regime and were reinstated in a number of institutions such as the military; the latter supported Sidónio to the end, given his policy of revoking the most radical of the anti-clerical legislation and of reestablishing relations with the Vatican.

Another novelty in the new political system was the experiment in corporatist representation. Sidónio maintained the two-house system but his new senate had elements nominated by the employers' associations, trade unions, industry and the professions among others. This senate like the house of deputies, was soon scorned by Sidónio, who sent both houses on holiday and governed alone, more and more confident of his charismatic qualities.

During the war-provoked general shortages, Sidonio's political discourse was anti-plutocratic, emphasizing the struggle against party oligarchies and messianic nationalism. Sidonio was able to bring together under one umbrella the Monarchists and the Conservative Republicans. Simultaneously he efficiently used his charisma to surround himself by a group of young army officers who accompanied him at demonstrations. After he was assassinated by an ex-rural trade unionist in late 1918, a monarchist revolt broke out in the north. The republicans mobilized in the cities, and several military units declared themselves neutral, thus permitting the democrats' victory and the return to a constitutional regime.

Sidónio's regime was not able to survive the assassination of its leader and its fall marked the emergence of an army divided and politicized by its participation in the war. On the other hand, the survival of the the old "question of the regime" cleavage shattered the unity of the conservative forces and almost threw the country into civil war. The "military juntas", formed in a number of cities after the assassination of the dictator, put pressure on the government. Pronouncements of very diverse political orientations were made. A number of "military barons" associated with monarchist, "sidonist" and republican sectors made a first and lasting appearance in public opinion at this time of crisis. When Oporto proclaimed the monarchy on the initiative of the local "military junta" and when a small insurrection took place in Lisbon, the military units were divided. Many officers who had fought at the front were unhappy with the strategy of "abandonment" advocated by Sidónio with regard to participation in the war, and with the monarchist officers who had joined his regime. The Democratic Party promoted what was probably its last popular mobilization in Lisbon against the monarchist revolt as a result of which several units handed out arms to the party and others prepared to move north. The union movement's anti-Sidonism proved essential to the mobilization. At the end of January 1918, the Oporto provisional monarchist government was defeated in an armed struggle. In Lisbon, rallies and demonstrations imposed the dissolution of the parliament and of the monarchist dominated political police, and the government had to take refuge in a barracks. A few days later, the Sidonists resigned. There were several failed attempts to form a conservative party capable of fighting the elections as an alternative to the Democratic Party. In the 1919 elections, the democrats won again, obtaining 53% of the deputies, and the 1911 Constitution was re-established.

3.3 THE PORTUGUESE RADICAL RIGHT

Ideologically and politically, Portuguese fascism was profoundly influenced by *Integralismo Lusitano*. The post-war crisis saw the emergence of other movements that were not as influenced by the IL. The latter's ability to present a new reactionary ideological package, however, was decisive. This package was, despite obvious foreign influences, well legitimized within the Portuguese cultural context.

The IL's ideological vigor and its capacity to permeate the elites conditioned Fascist development and penetration in Portugal. As Herminio Martins has said, "At the time when Italian Fascist and Nazi models assumed 'world-historical' importance, those most predisposed to learn and emulate them had all been grounded in the teachings and intellectual style of IL". In fact, almost all attempts at putting together fascist parties, the last and most successful of which was NS, were shaped by the IL's pre-existance, which had already "pre-empted the ground from other influences and paradigms of the extreme right[37].

[37] See Hermínio Martins, "Portugal", Stuart Woolf (Edited by), *Op. Cit.*, p. 305.

AN IDEOLOGICAL FRAMEWORK: THE INTEGRALISTS

As the First World War was about to break out, a group of young monarchists got together and founded a journal and study-group called *Integralismo Lusitano*. They had all previously been fellow students at Coimbra, then Portugal's only university, on the eve of the October 5, 1910 republican revolution. It was the constitutional monarchy's overthrow that turned them from their literary pursuits towards political action. Some would take part in the first monarchist revolts launched from Spain. During a brief period of exile in France and Belgium they enjoyed direct contact with *Action Française*. The latter was without doubt their most important external ideological influence.

Back in Portugal following an amnesty, they founded their movement which until 1916 consisted of the publication of a doctrinaire journal. They basically began their campaign in the field of ideological struggle. Antonio Sardinha, their principal theoretician, had never himself been exiled. Indeed, he had only converted to Catholicism and Monarchism after the revolution. Others, such as the group's youngest member, Rolão Preto, were exiles who had been influenced by the culture of France's principal radical right movement.

In 1916 when the republican regime pushed Portugal into the allied war effort, IL set itself up as a political movement, launched a daily newspaper and popularized its political program. Its objectives can be summed up as the restoration of a corporatist, anti-liberal, decentralized, and traditional monarchy.

IL would leave a profound intellectual mark on 20th century Portuguese political culture. No doubt deeply influenced by the example set by *Action Française*, IL was created durable foundations for a new Portuguese reactionary nationalism. Based on numerous studies of the Portuguese national identity, it reinvented the "tradition" of an organic and corporatist society exemplified by medieval Portugal, destroyed by "imported" 19th century liberalism. To support their ideas they harked back to the forgotten theories of 19th century counter-revolutionary Portugal linked to Dom Miguel's legitimist group.

Corporatism was the central alternative to liberalism. Integral corporatism was to become the base for the restoration of the monarchy. The effort towards historical legitimation and the theoretical foundations of corporatism transcended IL's anti-liberalism, as demonstrated by the hundreds of erudite studies and explanatory notes published by its diverse leaders.

Put simply, IL constructed a coherent political and intellectual alternative endowed with its own dogma, codified into a political program. A nation organized and hierarchized according to tradition was set up in opposition to the pretense of popular sovereignty. Universal suffrage was replaced by the corporatist representation of the traditional family, the town halls, and the professions. Parliament was rejected in favor of a National Assembly of an advisory nature, representing these "live forces". In response to the Liberal State's centralization, responsible for the destruction of local life and the force behind unregulated urbanization, IL proposed an anti-cosmopolitan and ruralizing decentralization which would allow for an "eminently agricultural country the fulfilment of its historic mission." Corporatist representation was the antidote to liberal economy and the "disastrous agitation of its class struggle".

From a sociological standpoint, integralism represents a typical ideological reaction to modernization. It was for this reason that its ability to infiltrate the areas most threatened by this was successful, essentially after participation in the war destabilized the fragile Republican regime. Its political intervention was elitist, made up as it was from a rather small university network and reorganizing old provincial cells of monarchist circles.

The first integralists were quite dogmatic when it came to the question of the restoration of the monarchy, hindering good relations with other anti-liberal forces, especially with traditionalist Catholics and Conservative Republicans. Although still collaborating occasionally with other anti-democratic sectors, IL participated in the pro-monarchy attempted coups up to 1918, which was a clear cause for division among the reactionary coalitions.

Although it did suffer fascistizing changes in the post-war period, the ideology of IL's founders remained imbued with a traditionalist anti-liberalism rooted in 'historic' nationalism. and in a ruralist reaction to industrialization. Socialism and communism were for them a variant of liberalism and democracy, and were not deserving of much ideological attention. Masonry and anti-clerical and jacobin republicanism were its great enemies. The integralists' early texts proferred this anti-capitalism of ruralizing and traditional origins. It was symbolized by a modernization dominated by 'plutocrats' and industries exploiting cheap labor drawn from the countryside. Therefore their increasing progress towards power, above all during the 1918 Sidonist Dictatorship, also led them to respond to the "social question" with "organic syndicalism".

Integralismo Lusitano would never become a political league with an organizational structure comparable to the *Action Française*. Beyond subjective and ideological factors, the very nature of the republican political system could only have permitted with difficulty. Although IL spoke of the "democracy" of the republic for propaganda purposes, in reality the electoral system of restricted suffrage and caciquist hegemony of the Democratic Party led the republican conservative parties themselves to clear and incipient organization. Any ideas they had of mobilizing the rural world were unrealistic. IL's political life would go through three large phases: the first, from its foundation to the 1917-1918 Sidonist dictatorship, was characterized by almost exclusively ideological activity; the second lasted until 1922 when its activities were suspended and was marked by the attempt to create an organized political movement; and the third was more diffuse and was defined by the decentralized proliferation of its groupings until the dissolution of its Central Junta in 1932.

It was Sidónio Pais's 1917 coup that turned IL's organization into a political movement. Although a republican, Sidónio Pais invited a number of integralist sympathizers to take up ministerial posts and adopted some of their programmatic aims in his outline for corporative representation. On the other hand, in trying to organize a party to support his regime from the top down, and to which he invited the Catholics and the monarchists, he "forced" the integralists to become an autonomous organization. They would even nominate a number of deputies in 1918, on the monarchist lists, namely António Sardinha and Pequito Rebelo. In February 1917 the daily *A Monarquia* had emerged, inaugurating IL's propaganda phase. Yet its party structure, although put in practice several times, always remaine embryonic. It survived however much longer than expected given its fluidity, the number of times its activities were interrupted, and even the divisions later underwent in the 1920s.

The Central Junta was nominated, and was made up of the founders, practically unaltered until its dissolution in 1932. The party network followed the lines of the country's administrative divisions, into Provincial and Municipal Juntas. These Juntas were constituted fundamentally in the rural counties and districts of central and northern Portugal. Apart from the Alentejo which was also represented, the majority were by far concentrated in the northern and central interior where the network spread to the county level. In large urban centers there were only School Juntas, organizations of university students.

For these district and county groupings eminent local citizens were generally chosen, most of them rural proprietors and many from the minor aristocracy. A number of the legitimist party members also signed up. These were mostly "lords of the land", if not in terms of economic power at least in social power. It was they who provided the movement with economic backing and contributed to the local and national press. As university educated integralists took up positions in the county headquarters and took on a somewhat militant bent, they remained under the protection of the "land lords".

IL's organizational instructions, published in 1921, defined the movement as being "*Nationalist* on principle, *Syndicalist* (corporatist) by means, and *monarchist* in conclusion." They reaffirmed that "it is not a new party preparing to assume power; on the contrary it is a current of opinion that hopes to free the Nation from the party clienteles (...)."[38]. Its organization took after the model

---

[38] See Integralismo Lusitano, *Instruções de Organização aprovadas pela Junta Central*, (Lisboa: 1921), p. 5.

of the pre-war leagues, characterized by unyielding direction and a combination of local and provincial bodies under the direction's strict control without elective mechanisms. It was then that the Cross of Christ was adopted as the movement's emblem[39]. It would be used later by National Syndicalism.

During the post-war period a number of employees' and even workers' groups would be formed under the influence of the most radical and fascistizing sectors. However, their presence was fleeting and did not change the above mentioned description. Beginning with António Sardinha, who disappeared prematurely in 1924, their leaders never hid their mistrust of the masses and of populism. Basically, the latter were against their cultural-educational background. In the 1920s, therefore, they resisted to the fascistizing pressures of certain younger sectors.

It was also in the post-war period that IL proposed that they should set up together with *Action Française* an international congress of parallel organizations to discuss the creation of a Latin international league against "democratic tyranny" and masonry. The proposal was not well received by Maurras, who was always distrustful of any form of internationalism[40].

A number of factors contributed to IL's organizational fluidity. The first was its ideology, which defined IL as an elitist group which intervened to restore the monarchy as an almost primordial duty. Although giving positive value to Sidónio's dictatorship, they would participate in the monarchist insurrections of 1918 and 1919 immediately following his death. Some leaders were even wounded and went into exile following the battles.

A second factor had to do with its extreme dogmatism in monarchist quarrels. This sectarianism was also reflected in its relations with other conservative sectors, specifically with the social Catholics. The founding of the Catholic Center Party and its participation in parliamentary elections, which implicitly meant recognizing the republican regime, would be the cause of sharp debates and an almost complete break in relations.

[39] *Idem*, p. 3.
[40] See Hipólito Raposo, *Dois Nacionalismos*, (Lisboa: 1929), p. 143 e Eugen Weber, *Op. Cit.*, p. 541.

In the end, a rupture from within the monarchists in 1922 led to the suspension of the incipient organization of IL. IL's political activity was then suspended by decision of the Central Junta itself and freedom of action given its members. This "freedom" of action from 1922 onwards was, perhaps, one of the factors contributing to the penetration of the integralists in the diverse areas of the conservative forces. Although able to resist militia-type organizations, these conservative groups abandoned systematic monarchist restorationism and would begin to take part in radical right unitary organizations, employers associations and military conspiracies. As Manuel Braga da Cruz has remarked, "their ideological force and respective influence within conservative circles thus grew as their political organization weakened(...)"[41].

The School Juntas remained active and from October 1922 on adopted the symbolism of Italian fascism and in 1923 of the Dictatorship of Primo de Rivera. Although publicly faithful to the monarchist vision, perspectives for restoration were dimming. The official press itself revealed this tendency. In 1923 (in an issue destined to maintain title to the daily) IL's central organ affirmed in the introduction: "Mussolini and Primo de Rivera in Spain are the magnificent triumph of those truths and those methods that *Integralismo Lusitano* has been advising all good Portuguese since 1914. (...) We too have a salvation doctrine (...) And if we shall have no king, then let there be a Dictator, because he who returns Portugal to the suspended path of its eternal destinies shall be our leader!"[42].

The leaders of the Central Junta themselves began active in radical right "unitary" organizations such as the Nun'Alvares Pereira Crusade, along with the Catholics and the Sidonists. They also collaborated on politicizing employers associations, particularly in the agricultural sector. They also began to write many of the manifestos for the failed attempts at conservative military coups.

The employers associations initiated a process of progressive intervention in post-war political life. Faced with the threat of ag-

[41] See Manuel Braga da Cruz, "O Integralismo.....", p. 147.
[42] See *A Monarquia*, 26-10-1923, p. 1.

ricultural reform proposed by some sectors of the republican left, their influence grew significantly. Pequito Rebelo, founder and member of the Central Junta, played an active role in the organization of the bigger agricultural interests in the Alentejo, by creating the Alentejo Agricultural Catholic League. Later, at the time of the anti-republican shift he joined the Portuguese Central Agricultural Association.

The integralists most significant contribution to the fall of the Republic was, however, developed from within the military. The integralists were far from being the only group to influence the intervention process culminating in the 1926 coup. Nonetheless, their continued presence within the Armed Forces permited them the closest approximation to power that they experienced in their entire political life. This was so after the withdrawal of the republicans following the coup.

Practically from the time of its foundation the IL saw itself embroiled in right-wing military conspiracies. Already in 1916 it took part in an uprising opposing participation in the allied effort due to their germanophile bent. Yet it was during Sidónio's dictatorship that the IL forged closer ties with cadets at the military academy who constituted the dictator's incipient Pretorian guard. Although they could count on the growing sympathy of the younger monarchist officials, however, most looked upon them with a certain mistrust, little prone as they were to the "restorationist itch".

Sidónio's downfall and the restoration of the liberal regime threw a good number of young Sidonist military officers into the radical right's orbit. On the other hand, this monarchist revolt would be the death-knell for restorationist revolts and the integralists began to back all rightist military canditates leading the overthrow of the Republic. Much of the solidarity they eventually receive from the "May 28th lieutentants" originated with these post-war coup attempts. From this time on, the monarchist officers who were IL sympathizers took part unconditionally in the conspiracies.

Thus one finds integralists writing proclamations for and participating in a number of coup attemps as "civilian links". This was specifically the case of the coup of April 18, 1925, the attempt which immediately preceded May 28. Given a political education much superior to the low levels found in the armed forces, they went about giving a more precise ideological content to the notion of "order on the streets". On the other hand, given their widespread collaboration in the coup attempt, they were able to consolidate contacts with the more radical "lieutenants" and with Gomes da Costa, the unstable general who finally led the uprising.

Although the integralists did play an important role in the first phase of the Military Dictatorship, the new political situation created new divisions within their already somewhat diluted sphere of influence. The fascist option was adopted by a large part of the youth sector and among the military sympathizers. Central Junta hardliners remained faithful to the monarchy, supporting all projects looking to install a new and radically anti-liberal corporative order. They eyed Salazar's rise and the formally hybrid political institutions created by him with distrust. A good part of the network withdrew into various fascistizing organizations which had sprung up in the interim and which culminated with National Syndicalism (1932). A number of the so-called second integralist generation immediately took on membership in the Salazarist order. Such was the case of Marcello Caetano, Salazar's successor in the late 1960s.

FASCISM AND THE POST-WAR RADICAL RIGHT

The most striking characteristics of the rise of fascism in postwar Portuguese society are, on the one hand, the precociousness with which the example of fascism's first external paradigm (Italian fascism) was followed and, on the other, the feebleness and fragmentation of its expression as a national party.

Portugal's first political experience with fascist learnings occured during the brief Dictatorship of Sidonio Pais. During the post-war period *Sidonismo* acted as a reference for Portuguese fascism and for young officers, intellectuals and Republican rightist students above all, the latter groups created numerous parties which increasingly cited the example of Mussolini's party. Althought it is not worth mentioning all these groups, the most important of them will be pointed out and their social base characterized. Many of these groups can not even be defined strictly as fascist. The concept of radical right is more appropriate, even if fascism is now understood to include Mussolini's party and the hodgepodge of ideological elements that it brought together. Some of these groups had their origins in *Sidonismo*, uniting intellectuals, students, and young officers from Republican and secular backgrounds. In order to get a better idea of rising military participation in these groups, we can take as an example the 1921 Sidonio Pais Center; 19 out of 33 of its leaders were officers, mostly from the army. Many of these intellectuals, such as Antonio Ferro, were active participants in the Portuguese futurist movement. Later on Ferro moderated his fascist ideas and served the Salazar regime as its propaganda chief. Less influenced by IL, these men were active propagandists of the Italian fascist word.

1923 saw the first publications carrying the subtitle "Portuguese fascism". The first fascist party, *Nacionalismo Lusitano* was also founded. NL was not just involved in merely ideological activity; it was a militia-type movement oriented towards the masses. A few months beforehand, Rolão Preto, director of IL's "social" sector, had rehearsed the creation of a "syndicalist" section. He founded a newspaper called *Revolução* (1922-1923). From the paper's name, its political program and to its principal director, the paper differed little from the NS founded in 1932. The selfsame Rolão Preto was also invited to lead the *Nacionalistas-Lusitanos*. However, attempts to found these fascist parties were condemned to failure and they rapidly disappeared from the scene following the military's first serious coup attempt against the liberal regime in April 1925.

Rolão Preto and IL's "Organic syndicalism"

Rolão Preto was the youngest of *Integralismo Lusitano*'s founders. As an emigrant monarchist student he had been the first

secretary of *Alma Portuguesa*, a magazine published in Belgium
in 1913 by young monarchist exiles some of whom had taken part
in the anti-republican incursions in 1911 and 1912. Born in the
Beira Baixa region in 1896, Rolão Preto was only 17 years old
when he was the managing editor of this first integralist organ,
one of the many publications founded by emigrant students in
France and Belgium under the direct influence of *Action
Française*.[43].

Although they were from completely different generations and
political worlds, Preto would always recognize the following two
names as having inspired him: Sorel and Valois. The former was
his great master. As he would reaffirm many years later, "he was
the one who did perhaps everything"[44]. Without denying Maurras's
formative impact on IL the latter had diminished somewhat in the
post-war period. In the 1920s it was Valois, the pro-fascist dissident, who continued to be the main reference. Rolão Preto's political and intellectual journey from Integralism to Fascism did not
make him an IL dissident, yet his trajectory was comparable in
some way to that of the founder of *Le Faisceau*.

Having returned to Portugal on the eve of Sidonio Pais's coup
d'etat and at the time that IL was debating its transformation from
ideological pressure group into political movement, Preto rapidly
consolidated his responsibility for the "social" area of the movement. As opposed to other IL founders, beginning with António
Sardinha himself, Preto separated himself from them right from
the start, placing emphasis on political action over the mere cultural and ideological activities which had characterized the
movement's short life up to that point.

Although sharing the same intellectual ideas as IL's founders,
longer exile and the adventure of the war led its youngest member
to forge closer ties with French intellectual pre-fascism and, in a

[43] See Eugen Weber, *Op. Cit.*, pp. 525-547.
[44] See enterview with João Medina, 27 de Junho de 1975, in *Salazar e os
fascistas. Salazarismo e Nacional-Sindicalismo. A história de um conflito (1932-
1935)* (Lisboa: 1977) and, J. R. Jennings, *Georges Sorel. The character and
development of his thought*, (London: 1985).

rare if not unique case for IL's founders, with Italian pre-fascism. The influence of Italian neo-nationalism, of Corradini and the *Idea Nazionale*, and of D'Annunzio's gesturing also decisively marked this integralist leader.

The traditionalist mark would never disappear from Preto's action and discourse, despite the "revolutionary" language of the fascism adopted in the 1930s. Nevertheless he was able to introduce certain ideas which, had they been taken up by the movement as a whole, would have led it directly to fascism in the 1920s.

Rolão Preto's political activity between 1918 and 1934, when National Syndicalism was declared illegal, was dominated by the attempt to steal the Portuguese working class away from socialism, anarcho-syndicalism, and later, communism. He hoped to "nationalize" the working classe via "organic syndicalism". In 1918 he tried to reconcile "syndicalism with the monarchy"; the 1930s found him brandishing the same "integral corporatism" now led not by the King but by a charismatic fascist-type leader.

The "Organic Syndicalist" program derived from the "integral corporatism" model which was supposed to replace the classic representative mechanisms of liberalism. In spite of suffering numerous setbacks, it suffered few changes from the time it was elaborated by Rolão Preto and other integralists immediately following the war - accompanying the launching of IL's "syndical" sector.

The new utopia proposed by IL to the petty bourgeoisie and most particularly to the working class was that of an "organic society" which would "make the nation great". Some Integralist anti-capitalist elements were used to justify the antidote: to the interests of capitalism's growing "denationalization", whose centers knew no frontiers and threatened to destroy national realities; of a savage industrialization which created a miserable proletariat manipulated by socialist and revolutionary ideologies; of a political class corrupted by international capital. The antidote was expressed through a protective "social" discourse for the working classes, advocating limits on exploitation and giving value to workers' symbolic place in "national production".

IL's corporatist project as developed by Preto foresaw a vast network of workers' and employers' syndical institutions based on region and productive sector to be overseen by 'Syndical Chambers' which would regulate salaries, arbitrate work conflicts and represent each sector in the system's upper bodies. It would be not only tedious but also practically impossible given the number of variations, to refer in detail to all the organigrams of the project which would henceforth constitute the programmatic platform of the first integralist Unions. Initially vague and very schematic, it was referred to constantly in the 1920s, adopted in the 1930s and then well developed, becoming National Syndicalism's central platform. It was, however, used as a propaganda and agitation banner from war's end on, allowing IL a new language in which elitist aristocratism would metamorphosize into "anticapitalism", and permitting the radicalization of the anti-plutocratic themes strictly associated with republican liberalism.

Joining the board of the integralist daily in 1920 upon its director's arrest, Preto multiplied his journalistic activities, writing editorials and signing articles commenting on international events almost all of which focused on the "social question". His *de facto* directorship of the newapaper allowed him to publish instructions for education of the syndical sector set up that year on an almost daily basis. Until the suspension of IL's political activity in 1922, Rolão Preto dedicated himself to setting up these first integralist unions. They found greater echo among the petty bourgeoisie employed in the service sector than among the working class.

Along with most of the rest of the Portuguese radical right, and most likely with the Catholic Center's quiet approval, Rolão Preto enthusiastically welcomed the march on Rome. However, even before taking power he noticed the new synthesis which fascism represented, uniting the ideological principles of his Italian nationalists comrades with the primacy of "revolutionary" political action. The Italians that Preto recognized as fellow travellers from 1914 onwards were Corradini's nationalists or the Italian "integralists". It was only from 1921 that Preto began to refer to the adventures of the "fasci di combattimento", founded two years earlier. Until then his references were focused on the nationalists and on D'Annunzio's campaigns[45].

Rolão Preto began to support fascism when that movement got over its initial ideological confusion and became an electoral and political force in 1921[46]. From the start, the great admiration that he expressed was for the methods of political action and the preeminence given to action. As for ideology, fascism was on his opinion only confirming the principles that he and the nationalists already believed in. In July 1922 he wrote that "our organic syndicalism is, in essence, the base for the present-day syndicalist thought of Mussolini's friends."[47].

Keeping a close eye on fascism's advance in the summer of 1922, Preto immediately styled himself as its defender in a debate in the pages of the newspaper *A Época* between himself and a journalist and Catholic priest. There was one point, however, on which both Rolão Preto and the Catholic journalist were agreed, albeit for different reasons: the impossibility of "organizing at present in our country a movement with the characteristics of Mussolini's party"[48]. In spite of proclaiming that "the day will come in which we, Portuguese nationalism, shall also march on Rome", Preto still held reservations as to the possibilities for the success of such political action in Portugal[49].

Although he made Italian fascism the most quoted example of the overthrow of the liberal order, Preto did not give in to the mimicry of imported ideas from 1922 onwards. In his view, integralism disposed of an ideology and organizational base for a Portuguese fascism, and certain specificities of the Portuguese political situation were not favorable to its implantation.

---

[45] See Rolão Preto, "Alma Nova" e "Fiume - Cosa fatta capo ha", *A Monarquia,* 26-9-1919 and 12-11-1919. See on D'Annunzio, Michael A. Ledeen, *The First Duce. D'Annunzio at Fiume,* (Baltimore and London: 1977).

[46] See Emilio Gentile, *Storia del partito fascista, 1919-1922. Movimento e milizia,* (Bari: 1989).

[47] See Rolão Preto, "Crónica Social", *Nação Portuguesa,* 2ª série, nº 1, Julho de 1922, p. 34.

[48] See *Idem,* 13-11-1922.

[49] See Rolão Preto, "Crónica Social", *Nação Portuguesa,* 2ª série, nº 6, Dezembro de 1922.

As for political action, Rolão Preto would arrive at the conclusion that his unknown Catholic Center opponent reminded him of during the polemic: "Fascism's actions on the occasion of Bolshevik excesses and tumults was a military action. Fascists did what a regular Army that knows its duty would have done"[50].

In 1921, as the integralists unions were being formed, Preto created the organization's Central Economic Council which was to coordinate that sector. Early in the following year the newspaper *Revolução* was founded. It was a "monarcho-syndicalist paper" destined to serve as the mouthpiece of the syndical sector[51]. Beginning with the title and ending with its program, this first fascistizing experience launched the bases for the upcoming National Syndicalism.

The paper was founded by younger IL members and was directed principally towards the working classes and the petty bourgeoisie. Rolão Preto developed his concept of a "social Monarchy" in it. Guides for the creation of integralist Unions were published and he tried to periodically respond to the anarcho-syndicalist CGT's daily *A Batalha*. IL's program was popularized in the *Cartilha do Operário*. A new language speaking of "comrades", "revolution", and "bourgeoisie", attempted to show the class "perturbed by internationalism" the path towards a reconciliation with a "nationalism" that was also "anti-powers' that-be".

In March 1922 a "manifesto of the Integralist Unions" was prepared, but its actual potential was relatively weak. In Lisbon there were Unions of Civil Construction, of Commercial Employees, of Banking Employees, and another, still being organized, of Metallurgic workers. A number of others spread throughout the country were of tenous existence, such as the Covilhã Commercial Workers' Union. With the exception of Civil Construction, which was in any case headed by a contractor, the integralist organization was unable, following its philosophy of creating mixed workers/employers Union, to establish itself outside the service sector.

---

[50] See *Época*, 13-11-1922.
[51] Nº 1, 5-2-1922.

This movement was abruptly interrupted by what IL saw as the "treason" of the Paris Pact signed by the representatives of King Dom Manuel and the heirs of the legitimate candidate which recognized the rights of the former to the throne. The integralist Central Junta announced the movement's auto-dissolution and IL, despite once again taking up doctrinaire activity at the end of the year, never put itself back together again in organizational terms. It was doubtful that the most important IL leader, namely António Sardinha, had ever wanted to go beyond the elitist action that had characterized the movement up to that point. For Rolão Preto, however, the first opportunity to 'fascistize' the IL had disappeared.

The suspension of IL's activities could have permitted, and in fact did permit, the integralists' taking part in the activities of groups directly inspired by fascism and whose bases originated with the Sidonist republicans that had sprung up in the interim. Nevertheless, Preto would remain faithful to IL, either for ideological reasons, or due to doubts as to the chances for success for such a movement. This in spite of his being a reference for the IL youth and of having been invited to take on the leadership of various projects looking to constitute fascist movements.

In 1923 Preto refused to take on the leadership of *Nacionalismo Lusitano*, the movement led by João de Castro Osório and directly inspired by Italian fascism. Suspecting that IL would remain dogmatic on the question of the monarchy's restoration, "alarmed that they are ready to accept a nationalist dictatorship"; and being republicans, Castro Osório had attempted a number of times to convince Preto to defend his project before the integralist leadership a number of times. Soon after he invited him to assume the leadership of his movement.

In trying to bring back to life the integralist union organization, João de Castro hoped to create a "National Labor Confederation" "which we have to set up to oppose the CGT", "the anarcho-syndicalist central union". The integralist leadership, however, would not furnish the *Nacionalistas Lusitanos* with the material and political support that they had asked for. Preto supported them from a distance, not believing in the venture subsidized by various employers' sectors which would rapidly disappear.

With the armed forces' progressive participation in political life, Preto, along with the integralist leadership, would turn to the formation of groupings within the Armed Forces, taking part in a number of the post-war conservative conspiracies. It would be impossible to account for all of them here; some were never more then mere sideline manouevers whilst others made it to the streets. The abandonment of the temptation to constitute a real political organization reduced sectarianism and the priority given to the monarchy's restoration, allowing IL to strengthen its political and ideological influence. The integralists began to unite with other sectors of the radical right within the Army, particularly the Sidonists, and took part in the reorganization of various employers' associations, namely in agriculture. They also found places in political organizations such as the Nuno Alvares Crusade, which after a number of hesitations, turned into an ideological and political forum for the defense of fascism, although with an elitist intervention, in the mid-1920s.

In late 1923, the slogan "Let's go!" (*Vamos a isto!*), which accompanied Preto's political activities meant more for military than for civilian organizations. Nonetheless, some of these considered themselves as civil support organizations for military coups[52]. Outpacing other leaders, he went beyond the "regime question" and began the search for military leaders disposed towards leading the conservative alliance. In 1925 he was with Filomeno da Camâra during the April 18th coup, and on the 28th of May, 1926, he accompanied Gomes da Costa to Lisbon[53]. Only in 1926, immediately following the coup which had overthrown republican Parliamentarianism, did Rolão Preto associate himself with the constitution of a fascist movement, already aligned with the "28th of May lieutentants".

---

[52] See Rolão Preto, "Vamos a isto! Os triunfos do Fascismo e de Primo de Rivera aproximam a hora resgatadora do Luzismo", *A Monarquia*, 26-10-1923, p. 1.
[53] See José Plácido Machado Barbosa, *Para além da Revolução... a Revolução. Entrevistas com Rolão Preto*, (Porto: 1940), p. 108.

The failure of IL's constitution as a political organization, the abandonment of the objective of restoring the monarchy, and the dispersal of its members, along with the premature death of its leader and principal ideologue, allowed Preto and the reduced fascist faction a peaceful coexistence within the integralist "family". It was a family that had lost some of the dearest ideological dogmas of its founding generation as it flourished, gaining many new sympathizers - students and young military officers influenced by the example of fascism.

"Lusitanian Nationalism"

Founded in 1923, *Nacionalismo Lusitano* represented the first attempt to create a fascist movement outside the integralist orbit and within the parliamentary Republic. The subtitle of its mouthpiece, *A Ditadura*, read as follows: "periodical of Portuguese fascism". Its life, however, proved to be short. Founded in 1923, it had for the most part ceased activity by the time of the military coup on the 18th of April, 1925 - the immediate predecessor to the overthrow of the parliamentary Republic.

Unlike *Revolução*'s "syndicalist" experimentation, the initiative for the creation of *Nacionalismo Lusitano* came from intellectuals who were somewhat distanced from IL and who had marked republican leanings. The "fascistizing" process they underwent had much more to do with Sidónio Pais's Dictatorship. Moreover, despite having been created upon the collapse of IL as a political movement, NL's founder, João de Castro Osório, looked towards IL leaders for support from the beginning. He even invited Rolão Preto to take part in the venture.

Castro Osório was the son of a well-known republican, Ana de Castro Osório. He had recently obtained his law degree and had launched himself into the literary world with a few ultra-nationalistic theatre pieces. He was the author of the political program of the movement co-founded with Raul de Carvalho. The latter had come over from the neo-Sidonist organizations and been a member of Sidónio's political police. His connections with employers associations and banks made some of NL's financial support possible.

In July 1922, João de Castro took part in an unsuccessful military coup attempt promoted by the Sidonists and the integralists, and as a result spent a short period in prison[54]. He founded the movement following his release. In June 1923 he founded *Portugal*, an organ of *Acção Nacionalista*, including Sidonists and rightist radicals with integralist roots.

Acção Nacionalista's manifesto called for the organization of a new syndicalism against "the mercenaries who live on the sweat of the workers"[55]. It was, indeed, the neo-syndicalists' guiding idea that the principal organ of the Portuguese union movement, *A Batalha*, warn against the dangers posed by such organizations. In 1923 the fascist theme began to occupy an important place in the Portuguese labor press, be it anarcho-syndicalist or from the upstart Portuguese Communist Party. Yet the articles, which were almost always translations, basically referred to the rise of fascism in other European countries. *A Batalha* on the other hand, denounced the creation of the NL right from the start.

The movement's first manifestos, outlining its program to deal with the political situation in1923, were encouraging for the employers' associations, calling for "national dictatorship; re-establishment of the death penalty, [for the] abolition of the GNR", as well as announcing that "a fascist militia shall be created in all cities, composed of volunteers with no remuneration whatsoever", in response to the "crimes of the syndicalists and communists"[56].

The fascist model was adopted for the ritualization of militancy. When becoming members of the organization, initiates swore an oath that synthesized the program: "as a Portuguese I desire the nation to be strong and national and to free itself from secret societies, from political clienteles, from speculators, all responsible for the present crisis; that it should enjoy the direct representation of

---

[54] See Visconde de Porto da Cruz, *Paixão e Morte de Sidónio*, (Funchal: 1928), pp. 80-82.
[55] See *A Batalha*, 5-7-1923, p. 1.
[56] See *O Imparcial*, 26-7-1923, p. 1.

the social forces of the Nation, transforming the present system of national representation of social, municipal, and organized professional forces; that family, corporation, town hall, and church shall all be free and privileged; that the Army should be strengthened and dignified for the defense of the nation; that property should be defended in its rights and obliged to fulfill its duties with the nation and most especially with the workers. The declaration committed members to "take the side of any Portuguese government against foreign and Bolshevik agression", to "obey the leader of *Nacionalismo Lusitano* in the fullfillment of all acts of voluntary national service", to "carry out all propaganda so that the Portuguese organize themselves around the principles of *Nacionalismo Lusitano* against the political oligarchies and plutocracies that are tyrannizing and annihilating the Nation."[57]

The parties on the republican left and from the union movement demanded that the Ministry of the Interior immediately abolish NL. *A Força* accused them of banding together an "irresponsible armed youth", and defined the initial core group of the "Loreto fascist host" as "integralist monarchists, fugitive republicans of various stripes, namely from the Sidonist group, young officers full of ambition, and union runaways from the professional unions, anarchists without ideals"[58].

This portrait was not far from the truth; actual activity was, however, rare. Towards the end of 1923 NL put pressure on Ginestal Machado's government to dissolve parliament, heavily criticizing the former when his Cabinet fell due to the parliament. From then on hopes turned to Cunha Leal: "Dictatorship is salvation. The living forces of the country demand it. The Army wants it. The people think so as well (...) so why wait? For a man? But that man has a name (...) and that man is Cunha Leal."[59]

Until the aborted military coup attempt on April 18th, 1925, it is easy to verify the inside manoeuverings of the movement in the military conspiracies and its dependency on certain factions among

[57] See *A Ditadura*, 4-1-1924, p. 2.
[58] See *A Força*, 4-11-1923, p. 2.
[59] See *A Ditadura*, 19-4-1923, p. 1.

employers and in the market. Financial support was evident through the advertisements that at times took up to 60% of the paper's space. The main subsidy came from the Industrial Alliance Society, but a number of banks such as the Portuguese Industrial Bank and the Portuguese Popular Bank also contributed generously.

The last coup attempt that counted on NL's participation was the one on April 18th. On that day *A Ditadura*'s proclamation was directed at the "soldiers and farmers" ("you who were crucified by the volleys of the enemy in Flanders"), calling for popular participation in the coup. Raul de Carvalho was arrested but did not come to trial[60]. From then on its organizational structure dissolved.

Of all the fascistizing groupings founded in the early 1920s in Portugal, NL is perhaps the one which most resembles the classic paradigm, notably in its organizational model, in the framework of its elite and in its political program. It was composed of a youthful elite on the periphery of the cultural and political system; it adopted a virulent and paramilitary style with nationalist slogans appealing to veterans, to the young, and to the working class; it adopted a confusing and contradictory political program, looked upon with suspicion by the traditional conservative movements, particularly by the monarchists and the Catholics. Its mobilization, however, was scarcely worth mentioning and it played no role in the overthrow of the parliamentary republic. NL members and press contributors later took up membership in other fascistizing organizations, specifically in the May 28th League and in National Syndicalism, but its leadership left no significant mark.

The "Nuno Alvares Pereira National Crusade"

As opposed to the NL, the Nuno Alvares Pereira National Crusade, an organization with a more significant position on the eve of the 1926 coup d'etat, had a much greater political and cultural importance to advance it, particularly in the last years of the par-

---

[60] See *Idem,* 19-4-1925, p. 1.

liamentary Republic. A small nationalist league founded at the height of Sidonism, the Crusade had a heterogeneous base. Founded in July 1918, the Crusade was only sporadically active until 1926, both in terms of political action and strictly in terms of organizational continuity. The very makeup of its leadership changed each time it re-launched itself. It was its founder, Lieutenant João Afonso de Miranda, who invited elements from all the conservative parties (republicans, Catholics, and monarchists) as well as various members of the military to be part of the leadership. All these elements were brought together by slogans such as the "defense of the fatherland" and "the creation of a patriotic mentality"[61]. In spite of the fact that in the strictest sense of the word it could not be considered a fascist party, be it due to its social or its organizational base, it did develop a pro-authoritarian propaganda campaign in the last years of the liberal regime for which fascism was an important reference.

After auspicious beginnings under Sidónio's regime, the Crusade practically disappeared in the years which followed, only to reappear in 1921 with a "manifesto to the country". In it, yesterday's vague nationalism became a more clearly defined critique of liberalism, calling for the reform of the State: "Order on the streets. Order in spirit. Order at home, at last. Without order, the State cannot live", proclaimed the Crusade upon re-initiating its activities yet again[62]. Its program then took on a more authoritarian bent. It continued to consider itself a respectable organization destined to "intensely lift up the energies of the Portuguese people, waking them up and grounding them in the love for the land and the cult of their heros". However, it added to this a definite political program which aimed to "reconstitute the traditional family"; "nationalize the scientific spirit"; "promote the moral unity of the nation and consequently to join in the search for a solution to the problem of public order"; and "equitably solve all conflicts between capital and labor"[63].

[61] See João Afonso de Miranda, "Para a história da Cruzada Nacional", *Cruzada Nacional Nun'Alvares*, nº 1, Novembro de 1922, p. 40.
[62] See Cruzada Nacional D. Nun'Alvares Pereira, *À Nação*, 20-9-1921.
[63] See *Idem*.

Right from the outset, this program for the restoration of order was accompanied by a discourse for historic/patriotic legitimation. As referred to in the 1921 manifesto, the Crusade aimed merely to "reintegrate the Fatherland into the cult of its violated tradition, that is, into the cult of its civic and domestic virtues; into the cult of private and public honor; into the cult of its heros and great men, into the cult of order, of law, of benevolence, of tolerance"[64]. Considered by the recently founded *Seara Nova* to be revealing "of what our country's conservative mentality consists of and what matters to it", this manifesto marked the revitalization of the Crusade. Throughout the following year it was able to count on district-level leaderships in most of continental Portugal[65].

During the first years of a somewhat irregular existence the Crusade's political activity can be summed up as the organization of a few conferences and proclamations, the point of reference being a vague nationalist discourse indispensable for uniting divergent sectors, from the conservative opposition to the Democratic Party, all under one roof. Among its members there were leaders of conservative republican parties such as António José de Almeida, as well as monarchists, republican ministers, senators, various deputies, and even an ex- President of the Republic - Teixeira Gomes. In 1922, the Catholic members of the Crusade were, Oliveira Salazar, Cerejeira and José Maria Braga da Cruz, among others[66]. Such a pluralistic devotion to the Master of Avis was attacked by the IL from the start. More specifically, it was attacked by António Sardinha at the time of the Crusade's foundation[67].

It was a fragile convergence, and any attempt to transform the Crusade into a league based on disciplined political action was condemned to failure. Nonetheless, the simple fact that it had brought together such diverse personalities from political figures to intellectual traditionalists, and conservatives, demonstrated the progressive "negative" unification of a part of the conservative

[64] See *Idem.*
[65] See *Seara Nova*, n°1, 15-10-1921, p. 21.
[66] See *Cruzada Nacional Nun'Alvares*, n° 1, Novembro 1922, pp. 5-2.
[67] See *A Monarquia*, 30-7-1918, p. 1.

establishment against the parliamentary Republic. The very names mentioned above were distinguished members of political parties or pressure groups with which they were more firmly bound in ideological and political terms than they were with the Crusade. For many of these individuals lending their name was the limit of their activities within the League.

Until 1926 when its ideological turn towards fascism became obvious and its propaganda campaign developed hand in hand with the May 28th conspiracy, the Crusade continued to appear and disappear from the political scene periodically[68]. Nevertheless, each time it reappeared, its leadership organs showed a significant and progressive isolation from parliamentarianism. Raul Proença, a close observer of the Crusade, was surprised by the respectable names which signed the "monstrosities" written in the Crusade's proclamations, noting "that there are republicans (...) greater enemies of the future than the most reactionary integralists."[69].

1922 saw industrialists such as António Centeno, integralists such as Pequito Rebelo, general Gomes da Costa, and conservative republicans such as Egas Moniz associated with the Crusade. Two years later even João de Castro, the founder of *Nacionalismo Lusitano*, became a member. Between 1922 and 1924 the Crusade enlarged its internal structure, creating local and district sections. It even founded a "ladies central commission"[70].

In January 1926, the Nun'Alvares Crusade re-structured its leadership yet again, this time emphasizing the interventionist and fascistic component. Filomeno da Camara, an April 18th conspirator and future extreme right coup planner during the Military Dictatorship, assumed the organization's Presidency. Also elevated to the leadership at the time were Martinho Nobre de Melo, an ex-minister of Sidónio and the Crusade's main ideologue in the movement's last phase. There were also other well-known names from the extreme right of the political spectrum[71].

[68] See José Machado Pais, *Op. Cit.*, 1983, p. 219.
[69] See *Seara Nova*, n°1, 15-10-1921, p. 21.
[70] See *Cruzada Nacional*, 8-2-1924, p. 61.
[71] See *A Reconquista* n° 1, 15-1-1926.

In organizational terms, the Crusade now adopted a more militant model. Its new mouthpiece, *A Reconquista*, also called itself the "organ of the Labor and Academic League of the Supreme Commander". Among the latter, it had no echo at all. Nonetheless, the academic propaganda commission began effective agitation at the Universities. On the 9th of January, 1926, the Crusade organized a rally at the Geographical Society which according to the press was attended by "thousands". Its discourse was already more radical and the contents of its political program clearer. In April 1926, calling on Gomes da Costa, it was stated that "We would like the Chief of State to really be a *chief* and not a parties' rubber-stamp man"; "we want a (...) representation of the permanent and real interests of the nation and not the transitory and egoist interests of the party clienteles"; "we want the elimination of direct or immediate interventionism of the State" in the economy; "we do not want obligatory organic syndicalism but one with social and political privileges"; "theoretically, we want liberty and privileges for the Catholic religion, in a Concordat regime"[72].

In the first months of 1926, the Crusade considered itself to be something like a driving force of "a great national movement with the purpose of putting an end to the sterile inter-party struggle for the technical organization of the public government (...)"[73]. It would be too hasty were one to consider the Crusade as the main inspiration for the victorious May 28th, 1926, coup. Nonetheless, its last leadership did unify a small but powerful pressure group which attempted to dominate the Military Dictatorship; the interventionist incidents associated with General Gomes da Costa went on to prove this.

Revealing of the political vigor acquired by the Crusade early in 1926 was the growth of membership which came from the integralist and Sidonist organizations, even though the former had not merged into the Crusade. Another element worthy of note which the Crusade cultivated from the outset, was the military. Among

[72] See *A Reconquista* n° 5, 1-4-1926, pp. 67-69.
[73] See manifesto "Às Academias do País" da Comissão Académica de Propaganda in *A Reconquista* n° 6, 15-5-1926, p. 96.

its founding members was one of the May 28th lieutenants, Mário Pessoa. The student presence was also heavy in the academic section. Worthy of note is Castro Fernandes, a founder of National Syndicalism in the 1930s. Thus, the names more closely associated with republican conservatism gave way to a younger and more virulent extreme right.

References to fascism and to the Primo de Rivera Dictatorship remained basically confined to the Geographical Society, and did not go out onto the streets. In 1926 the only players called onto the streets by all the conservative sectors were the military. The Crusade, like others before and after it, was merely preparing to get on the conspiratorial bandwagon which had been on the move from 1925.

3.4 THE FINAL CRISIS AND BREAKDOWN OF THE REPUBLIC

Portugal's participation in the First World War did not cause any serious damage to the productive or social structure comparable to that suffered by contenders in Central Europe. Neither did it favor the conditions for the emergence of groups able to form the first basis for fascist movements through the enlargement of the original nuclei of intellectuals founding them. Portugal suffered her war "humiliations", the decimation of her battalions at the front, right in the middle of the Sidónio Dictatorship. It was under the same regime that she ended her military participation in the war. The republicans managed to mobilize many veterans and turn them against the Sidónio Pais Dictatorship; they had been "betrayed" by the monarchists that had supported the military regiments that had refused to leave for France. There was, however, no "veterans" phenomenon as the latter were either rapidly absorbed into rural society or emigrated. The "vitoria mancata" was also moderate as Portugal managed to safeguard her colonial heritage and had no territorial claims in Europe.

THE PARLIAMENTARY AND ELECTORAL ARENA

The Sidonist Dictatorship and its outcome, the near state of civil war that followed the regime's end, allowed for the first pact among political parties for the revision of the 1911 Constitution to give more stability to the political system. The conservatives were strongly pro-presidentialist and the Democratics allowed the President the power to dissolve parliament after a clear definition of the restricted powers of cabinets between dissolution and elections (1919). The management of this power would prove to be difficult, opening an important direct channel to the President from extra-parliamentary pressures.

There were important changes in the party system in the post War crisis: the "historic" leaders of the pre-1917 period went. Afonso Costa, the strongman of the democratic party, did not return from exile and António José de Almeida and Brito Camacho left the Evolutionist and Unionist Parties; the Democratic Party suffered splits on the left and on the right; small but highly ideological parties appeared both in the parliamentary (Catholics, "Democratic Left", etc.) and extra-parliamentary arenas (Communist Party -1921, Sidonists -1919, etc.). The main characteristics of the pre-war period prevailed, however. Universal suffrage was not implemented and the formal political system remained basically unchanged.

An increasing fragmentation of the party system characterized the Post War period (Table III). In 1919, the conservatives (Unionist, Evolutionist and Centrist Parties) were able to unite under the aegis of the the new Liberal Party, an embryonic electoral machine opposed to the dominant Party. For the first time in the electoral history of the Republic the Democratic party was defeated, and its monopoly seemed to be in jeopardy (1921). The liberal cabinets, however, would fall due to an insurrection of the National Republican Guard, explicitly aiming to dissolve the 1921 parliament. From 1921 on, conservative representation would split again into several parties ("Governamentais", Nationalists, "Populares"), and authoritarian ideological pressures increased.

Table III
Distribution of Parties in Parliament (1919-1926)
(Number of Seats)

Parties	1919-21		1921		1922-25		1925-26	
	N^o	%	N^o	%	N^o	%	N^o	%
Democratic P.	86	52.8	54	33.1	71	44.6	83	50.9
Evolution. P.	38	23.3	—	—	—	—	—	—
Unionist P.	17	10.4	—	—	—	—	—	—
Independents	13	8	5	3.1	5	3.1	19	11.7
"Reconstituintes"	—	—	12	7.4	17	10.7	—	—
Socialist P.	8	4.9	—	—	—	—	2	1.2
Catholic P.	1	0.6	3	1.8	5	3.1	4	2.4
Liberal P.	—	—	79	48.5	33	20.8	—	—
Monarchists	—	—	4	2.5	13	8.2	7	4.3
"Dissidentes"	—	—	3	1.8	—	—	—	—
Regionalists	—	—	2	1.2	2	1.3	—	—
"Populares"	—	—	1	0.6	—	—	—	—
"Governamentais"	—	—	—	—	13	8.2	—	—
Nationalist P.	—	—	—	—	—	—	36	22.1
Democratic Left	—	—	—	—	—	—	6	3.7
U. I. E.	—	—	—	—	—	—	6	3.7
Total	*163*	*100*	*163*	*100*	*159*	*100*	*163*	*100*

Source: Lopes 1994 and Marques 1975.

Despite some splits (the "Reconstituintes", on the right in 1920 and latter the the "Democratic left" in 1925), the Democratic Party survived as the system's dominant party. But its "asymmetric" clientelistic machine caused it to suffer severe losses among urban social voters, while the manipulation and violence surrounding electoral acts increased dramatically. The "indefinition" of its policies when in government was also reinforced by the emergence of two main tendencies within the party structure, a moderate and another more left-wing, which broke off in the 1925 elections.

Having survived the post war economic and social crisis, the 1925 elections put the Democratic Party in government again, by now, however, the main arenas for political battle were already outside parliament. One new element should be stressed nevertheless: the emergence of the direct representation of a federation of employers associations (UIE), with a clear anti-democratic platform using elections and parliament to express itself.

THE EXTRA-PARLIAMENTARY ARENA

1919-1922 were perceived by the State, the employers in urban industry, commerce and services, as the years of the "red threat". The golden period of the anarcho-syndicalist CGT, with the first communist split from its ranks, was marked by a wave of strikes, affecting a range of sectors such as the state civil service and commerce. As the union movements declined in strength terrorism emerged; clandestine organizations such as the "Red Legion" were popularized by the conservative media. The Democratic Party gave new impetus to the Socialist Party, opening its electoral machine and seats in parliament (with average number of 2, the Socialists got 8 seats in 1919), all attempts at "political integration", however, failed[74].

As already stressed above, the employers' associations most affected by these almost exclusively urban movements improved their federations and increased their intervention in politics dramatically. Nonetheless, by the end of 1922 the "red threat" was over and labor confrontations were on the decline. Recent studies on the politicization of employers' associations and the authoritarian takeover of power, best illustrated by the UIE's activities from 1924 on, prove convincingly that "intrabourgeois" economic conflict far outweighed the bourgeois-worker conflict"[75].

The most important factor inifying the new extreme right in the twenties was the "postponement" of the republic/monarchy cleavage. In this external influences such as Italian fascism and the Primo de Rivera's Dictatorship, as well as a new generation of young Sorelian integralists played an important role. The results of this change were already apparent in organizations like the Nuno

---

[74] It should be mentioned that the Communist Party, born from a split from Anarcho-Syndicalism and very "working class" based in terms of its first elites, played a very insignificant role in the final crisis of the Republic.

[75] See Kathleen Schwartzman, *Op. Cit.*, p. 184

Alvares Crusade, whose reorganization in the 1920s included Sidonists, Catholics, integralists and fascists as members. The role of groups such as the integralists was more important in terms of conspiracy and propaganda for the dictatorial option than the Catholic Center, which was connected to the church hierarchy, and thus more cautious. The integralists had significant support within the armed forces and played an important role as an anti-democratic radicalizing element among some of the conspiratorial groups. But the presence of both in organizations such as the Nuno Alvares Crusade, and its influence within the army shows how an important sector of the civilian radical right lent support to the coup supplying the military with a political program which transcended "order in the streets and in the government."

From the outset the conservative republican parties and small groups of notables connected to interest groups had become accustomed to using extra-parliamentary means of gaining power. After the war, there had been some coalition governments and even some conservative ones, but always in connection with crisis situations. The radicalization of the small conservative republican parties was a key factor in the fall of the Republic; it led them to appeal to the military when the Democratic Party was again victorious, after the elections of 1925. From this spectrum of parties some charismatic figures emerged, joining the appeal of the small, elitist extreme right for military intervention as well as and above all for the constitution of organized groups inside the armed forces. Cunha Leal, a leader of the Nationalist Party was one of these leaders. From 1923 at least, Leal had been advocating military intervention and negotiating a *post-factum* political position with military factions.

ARMY INTERVENTION

Military intervention in Republican politics precedes the post war period and the persistence of organized factions in its ranks does so as well. The main difference between the post-war interventions and the 1926 coup, is, perhaps, the multiplication of "corporatist" tensions between the army as an institution and the government and their increasing "unity" when interventing in the political arena[76].

Tracing the roots of the 1926 coup by examining previous conspiracies and essentially personalized military role-players is a "evenementielle" trap. In fact, as one American historian put it, Portugal had been living "in the kingdom of the Pronunciamento" from 1918 onwards[77].

The pre-civil war situation of December 1918-February 1919 was particularly devastating for the Army, bringing with it the creation of "Military Juntas" all over the country, as well as the reopening of the "regime question" upon the proclamation of the Monarchy in Oporto. The Sidonist regime was also able to attract an increasing number of young cadets and military officers that were associated with a segment of a civilian radical right involved in various conspiracies throughout the early twenties. But there were various poles of civil-military tension that had arisen during the Republic's last years that must be considered.

The Democratic Party was confronted with a new Army after the war. The army had acquired a troop core twice its 1911 size, with new prestigious leaders from the battle front as well as a new militarist ideological dimension. The main problem, however were the close to 2,000 supposedly temporary militia officers. When elsewhere in Europe officer corps were being reduced through demobilization, in Portugal the government incorporated militia officers into the regular corps. This "political" incorporation produced 4,500 regular army officers in 1919, as opposed to 2,600 in 1915[78]. Whether a strategy of "integration' due to the fear of demobilization, or an instrument of "political patronage", the result was the emergence of a "corporatist" tension with the civilian government. This was particularly so during the hyper-inflationary period, when the purchasing power of a captain was eroded down to 60% of its 1914 value.

[76] See Maria Carrilho, *Op. Cit.*, and José Medeiros Ferreira, *Op. Cit.*
[77] See Douglas L. Wheeler, *Op. Cit.*, p. 193.
[78] *Idem*, p. 181.

Suspicion of the Army led to the staff and heavy armament reinforcement of the GNR, especially during 1919-1921 (5,000 in 1911; 11,000 in 1922). The GNR "was strengthened as an urban defender of the State" against both the working classes and the army, and "became one more element of the bureaucracy associated with the Democrats' control of the government"[79]. A second "corporatist" tension was thus created. A Democratic Prime Minister would later be obliged to weaken the GNR, to discourage insurrections coming from within the force but also to "calm down" the army.

On April 18, 1925, some military officers carried out the first open coup attempt, in name of the Armed Forces themselves. The resistance of some units and of the GNR aborted the insurrection. A few months later a military court sent those involved back to the barracks. The appeal for a military interregnum from parliamentary politics was at its height. If there is a difference between this coup and the one of 1926, it is probably in the increase of political support in the form of an "anti-system coalition".

The military coup of May 28th 1926 which ended the parliamentary republic represented more than a praetorian military intervention in political life. Republican liberalism was overthrown by an army divided and politicized due to Portugal's participation in World War I, which received calls for a coup from organized factions within its ranks ranging from conservative republicans to social Catholics to the integralist extreme right and its respective Fascist appendices, the latter particularly influencing the young officers. Let us not forget that these officers constituted the base of the first modern dictatorship established in Portugal, the brief dictatorship of Sidónio Pais, which already showed some of the traits of Fascism, with its anti-plutocratic populism.

Although the work of conspiratorial groups, the ins and outs of the coup were common knowledge both to the public and the parties. The splits among the different factions of the conspirators were more important than the resistance of the government. General Gomes da Costa, contacted by one of the groups of conspirators,

---

[79] *Ibidem*, p. 185.

became the coup's leader. He began his descent from Braga in the
north of Portugal to Lisbon, simultaneously negotiating his new
powers with the conservative republican component headed by
Admiral Cabeçadas. The journey took several days and the Lisbon
press kept everyone up to date on the negotiations. There was hardly
any serious military resistance to the coup and no civilian mobilization. The legacy of the Liberal parliamentary Republic, the outcome of its legitimacy crisis was, however, an unstable Military
Dictatorship for years to come.

SOME FINAL REMARKS

Following the analysis of Portuguese fascism's post-war characteristics, we need to assess its role in the overthrow of liberalism, and the precise nature of the May 28th 1926 coup.

One of the merits of more recent research on the fall of the parliamentary republic in 1926 has been finding proof of the extreme
ideological and political diversity of the political players commited
to its overthrow upto the coup of May 28th 1926. On the other
hand, it is also worth emphasizing the severe political instability, a
constant feature of the early years of the ensuing military dictatorship which initiated a period marked by a tumultuous struggle for
hegemony.

The most appropriate analytical perspective from which to examine the fall of the republican regime is the angle of civil-military relations in a crisis of legitimacy. Appealing to the military
was a constant in post-war politics period. By definition the republican political system did not have Linz's "loyal opposition",
as it was obvious to the political actors that the possibility of achiev-
ing power through elections was virtually nil.

Given the heterogeneity of the elements which moved back-
stage of the military intervention, the movement leading up to May
1926 fits somewhere between the two patterns for the fall of democratic regimes indicated by Juan Linz. It was a military coup which
co-opted part of the political elite of the liberal regime (which,
like many in the military, aimed for the establishment of a reformed

constitutional order), included the "disloyal opposition" and excluded the dominant party from power[80]. The outcome was a Military Dictatorship which rapidly got rid of part of the republican component in later coups, but was unable to institutionalize itself. The lesser partners in this coalition, the fascists, found room for manoeuvre within the new regime which brought them close to the new authorities briefly.

The small but pugnacious workers movement of anarcho-syndicalist hegemony frightened the ruling classes given the republican regime's notorious inability to promote its inclusion. However, the role of the Portuguese "bienio rosso" in the authoritarian wave which overthrew Portuguese liberalism should not be exaggerated. Some economic and social cleavages were superimposed onto this wave among the factors contributing to the fall of the Republic. To quote Organski's model, cleavages between city and country or traditional and modern élites were typical of a "dual society" like that the Portuguese in the twenties, and are of more use when analyzing the fall of Portuguese liberalism than the cleavage between the industrial bourgeoisie and the working class.

Some researchers have tried to "solve" the problem of the absence of a Fascist movement in Portugal by drawing attention to its contribution, albeit fragmented and weak, to the movement which led to the overthrow of liberalism. This rather voluntarist exercise was hasty and showed little sensitivity to scale. Attempts were made to prove that Portugal, after all, had everything that the classics pointed out as the "origins" of Fascism (modernism and futurism, nationalism, traumas from the first world war, a workers' offensive, anti-communism, young military officers politicized by the extreme right, the "avant la lettre" Fascism of Sidónio Pais, the "massification of politics", liberalism's legitimacy crisis and even Fascists...). One should note, however, the scale of the above and explain why fascists were not the protagonists either in the overthrow of liberalism or in the authoritarian order which followed[81].

---

[80] See Juan J. Linz and Alfred Stepan, (Edited by), *Op. Cit.,* p. 82
[81] See António Costa Pinto, "O fascismo e a crise da 1ª Republica: os

If we assume that the processes of overthrow of democracy associated to fascism were characterized by "the takeover of power by a well-organized disloyal opposition with a mass base in society, committed to the creation of new political and social order, and unwilling to share its power with members of the political class of the past regime, except as minor partners in a transition phase"[82], the main factor to emphasize in the Portuguese case is the absence of a Fascist movement contribuing to the overthrow of liberalism and to the building of the authoritarian order. The very coalition of political forces which supported its overthrow was characterized from the start by a predominance of conservative and elitist radical right-wing pressure groups. Fascism, now seen as a movement, was the eternal loser in 1925/26, during the Military Dictatorship and in the thirties when Salazar was already in power.

More then anything else the crisis of Portuguese liberalism goes back to the problem of the complex relationship between Fascism and the different political families which made up the conservatists during the first half of the 20th century. It seems clear today that the rise of Fascism was only possible in coalition with ideologies, factions and the electorate which up to then had been represented by different conservative parties. Mixing them together, however, does not help us to understand their novelty and singularity. As Blinkhorn said "It cannot seriously be denied that as movements, parties and political ideologies, conservatism and fascism occupied very different positions within the early and mid-twentieth century European right, converging at some points and conflicting at others."[83]

Even though doubtful "structural" causalities are not examined here, it does seem clear that the second rate role played by the fascists was particularly evident in those countries whose economic development, social structure, and political system were closer to that of Portugal in the 1920s, i.e., on the Eastern and Southern European periphery.

nacionalistas lusitanos (1923-25)", *Penélope* n° 3, Junho de 1989, pp. 43-62.

[82] Juan J. Linz, *Op. Cit.*, p. 82.

[83] See Martin Blinkhorn (edited by), *Fascists and Conservatives*, (London: 1990), p. 13.

The crisis suffered by the Portuguese Republic in the post-war period was a typical example of the difficulties that fascism found in societies with only an incipient "massification of politics" and in which political competitors had to a certain extent, "filled" the available political space[84]. Another important factor was the presence of ideological and political right-wing competitors, closely linked to the two cleavages above mentioned.

The secularization cleavage was perhaps the most important of those created by the First Republic. Even in cultural terms, Portugal was a clear example of how there is little space for the emergence of a "fascist intelligentsia" when "the hostile response to modern society and the concomittant rejection of liberalism and democratization remain embedded in traditional religious forms, and reactionary or conservative politics is linked to the defense of the position of the church (...)"[85]. The Church and the Catholic Center thus constituted a powerful obstacle to the "fascistization" of the university and intellectual elites, occupying a key political space in the anti-democratic reaction. Another important cleavage was that of the regime. Monarchist restorationism continued to inhibit, both ideologically, via integralism and politically, by destroying the populist mobilization of Sidonism. It was also the "question of the regime" that broke the understanding between integralists and social catholics, both defenders of an authoritarian corporatism as an alternative to liberalism.

The employers' associations, which, in the early 1920s, offered some support for the tentative fascist movements then created, organized an electoral movement and negotiated directly with the military and conservative pressure groups. The prospect of military intervention also robbed the militia of potential followers. The militia was made redundant from 1925 on, when disorder prevailed, not among the working class streets but within parliament and government.

---

[84] See Juan J. Linz, "Political Space and Fascism as a Late-Comer", Stein Ugelvik Larsen et alli (Edited by), *Op. Cit.*, pp. 153-189.
[85] *Idem*, p. 164.

Following the mobilization of the popular urban and middle classes, progressively distanced from the Democratic Party, there exist no traces whatsoever of populist mobilization in the conservative countryside by the anti-republican reaction. In the north, the Republic had not shaken up the traditional structures of domination, and had established clientelistic pacts with local notables. In the south of the latifundia, rural unions had almost disappeared after their significant rise between 1910 and 1912. They were not a constituent part of Portugal's "bienio rosso" in the 1920s. The social conflict inherent in the development of Italian rural fascism did not happen in Portugal.

Although occasionally contradicted by the relative success of some movements in Eastern Europe the pre-"massification" nature of conservative political and social representation in Portugal in the twenties, and the existence of clientelistic relationships in the political system, were certainly decisive elements in the type of transition to authoritarianism which took place in Portugal.

Chapter IV

FASCISM AND SALAZARISM
- Problems of interpretation

As soon as the Republican regime was overthrown, the Military Dictatorship immediately found negative solutions for some of the problems most worrisome for the conservative bloc. The Democratic Party was ousted from power and its leaders exiled, the working class lost its right to strike and the unions' room for legal maneuvering was considerably restricted. Revolutionary action against the dictatorship was carried out almost exclusively by the republicans, with the exception of a failed general strike in 1934, when Salazar established the corporatist system. The Catholic Church blessed the 1926 coup and immediately offered up its secular members for possible ministerial positions, albeit cautiously in view of the presence of many republican officers and civilians.

Salazarism grew out of the Military Dictatorship established in 1926. The Dictatorship imposed by the military was permeated by a succession of conspiracies, palace coups and even revolutionary attempts, which clearly expressed the fight for leadership within the vast conservative coalition on which it was based. The difficulties in consolidating an authoritarian regime came one after the other, given the political diversity of the conservative bloc and its ability to penetrate the armed forces. Curiously, it was under the Military Dictatorship that the Fascists enjoyed some influence; given their presence in the young officer class, they attempted to create some autonomous organizations and played a role in driving out the republican military component. It was this "limited and self-devouring pluralism", mediated by the military, that Salazar gradually came to dominate.

The National Union (UN) was legally established in 1930. It was an "anti-party" which aggregated the civilian forces that supported the new regime. In 1933 a new Constitution declared Portugal a "Unitarian and Corporatist Republic", creating a compromise between liberal and corporatist principles of representation. The former were eliminated through subsequent legislation and the latter limited and relegated to the background. The result was a Dictatorship of the Prime Minister and a National Assembly dominated by the UN through non-competitive elections. To avoid any loss of power, even to a House dominated exclusively by the government party, the executive was made almost completely autonomous. General Carmona remained as President to guarantee military interests. The censorship services eliminated any suggestion of political conflict and devoted their attention both to the opposition and, initially also, to the Fascist minority of Rolão Preto that insisted on challenging the new regime. The political police were reorganized and used with remarkable rationality. All this was done "from above" without any particular Fascist demagogy and the process depended more on Generals and Colonels than on Lieutenants, and more on the Ministry of the Interior than on "the mob". By 1934, after a few hitches, liberalism had been eliminated and the old republican institutions replaced.

The more rebellious fascist leaders were exiled but most of them "got jobs" in minor positions, especially with the onset of the Spanish Civil War, which frightened the regime. The great republican figures were forgotten in exile after the brief optimism caused by the Spanish popular front. One by one the anarcho-syndicalist leaders went to prison or died in Spain leaving the leadership of the clandestine opposition to the small and young communist party.

The regime institutionalized by Salazar was admired by many on the fringes of the European radical right, above all by those of Maurrazian and traditional Catholic origins, given the very similar cultural origin of the "New State". This identity transcended a mere "order" program but did not include the "totalitarian", "pagan" aspects that were bringing Nazi Germany and Fascist Italy closer and closer. *It is within the ideological spectrum of the radical right as well as in anti-liberal social Catholicism that the cultural and political origins of Salazar's regime are to be found* .

4.1 FROM MILITARY DICTATORSHIP TO SALAZARISM

THE MILITARY, CONSERVATIVE REPUBLICANS AND THE RADICAL RIGHT

"Dictatorship without a dictator" was how one contemporary observer put it, for the regime established on the 28th of May, 1926 was unaccompanied by any alternative to republican liberalism. The dictatorial regime resulted from a tentative compromise, brokered by the military, and went through several diverse (and contradictory) phases until the consolidation of authoritarianism in the 1930s, by then under the direction of Salazar.

It is not easy to "read" the dizzying sequence of political events during the early years of the Military Dictatorship with the help of the numerous typologies normally used by students of the inter-war right. This is partially due, as has been previously mentioned, to the nature of the republican political system and to the subsequent incipient nature of right-wing political representation under the overthrown regime. On the other hand the military nature of the new regime brought to a climax not only the corporative tensions inherent to the military institution, which had already survived many conflicts, but also determined the formation of true political factions within the armed forces.

Yet in spite of these limitations, it is possible to define a tripartite typology of the political/ideological spectrum of the Portuguese right, which may have some analytical use for the study of its political attitudes during the early years of the Military Dictatorship[1]:

[1] See António Costa Pinto, "The Radical Right and the Military Dictatorship in Portugal: the 28 May League (1928-33), *Luso-Brazilian Review,* Vol. 23 (Summer 1986), pp. 1-15.

The former, a kind of "conservative liberalism", had representatives in the conservative republican parties. These tried to enlist the support of the military while backing the Military Dictatorship as a temporary regime which would allow them to reform the republican constitution of 1911 towards a more presidentialist system with limited parliamentarism and a remodeled party system. A strong conservative party would be created with the support of the state, capable of standing up to the Democratic party once constitutional law had been re-established.

The latter, "authoritarian conservatist" strain, was markedly antiliberal. It proposed the establishment of an authoritarian regime which would eliminate the old system of Republican parties and introduce a one-party system. The new party would be created by the state machinery, building mechanisms for corporatist representation. These would be based on Catholic corporatist ideology and on the theory of governments of "technocratic competence". This current was supported by Catholics, monarchists and authoritarian republicans.

Finally, the radical right, which proposed a complete break with the liberal system, aimed at the construction of a nationalist, corporatist, integralist state based on a charismatic and totalitarian leadership. The building of the new regime would begin with the creation of a mass party, and the Military Dictatorship would lead the nationalist reform of the state. The ideological basis of this right was the radical conservatism of *Integralismo Lusitano*, which merged with other ideological currents after the war.

However, the new situation created by the military provoked a noticeable alteration to the political spectrum, and many of the attitudes taken by political figures, especially in the military, can only with difficulty be understood in light of the above-mentioned typology. Erratic courses multiplied and it would be far too time consuming to go over them in detail. Yet the stances taken by some party formations in the Dictatorship's early years can perhaps be better studied if we do take them into consideration.

Noteworthy among the diverse political movements that immediately placed themselves in the camp supporting the Dictatorship and which constituted an important counterweight to the radical right, was the Catholic Center, which was closely dependent on the Church hierarchy itself, as well as a number of conservative republican parties. Some of these, notably Cunha Leal's Liberal Republican Union and the Nationalist Party, saw their plans to manipulate the new powers frustrated during the Dictatorship's first years. Nevertheless they constituted a support of the regime alongside the conservative military elite facing the offensives by the radical right.

Both the Church and the Catholic Center placed themselves in the camp supporting the Military Dictatorship. Until 1928, the date of the inauguration of Salazar's leadership, the Center was a powerful pressure group, which only faded when the recently nominated minister of Finance neutralized it after consolidating his power in the early 1930s. As will be shown below, his positions were decisive in the blockade of the radical right during the first years of the new regime.

The significant role played by the conservative republicans should also not be underestimated. A number of party formations maintained an important influence over the Army, especially with certain generals who were included in the government and who would later even oppose Salazar, such as Domingos de Oliveira, Vicente de Freitas, and others. Their importance was written into the compromise final text of the1933 constitution that the regime was based on.

Even though many republicans immediately went into opposition (mostly those connected to the democratic party), the small conservative parties did supply the dictatorship with a number of ministers and they always enjoyed major influence. Once they lost direct influence, their ability to influence a large number of officers continued to be significant, and even President Carmona remained always sensitive to the sector.

Between 1926 and 1930, the Military Dictatorship failed to achieve institutionalization and on several occasions was the target of attempted coups d'état, both by the pro-democratic opposition (the most serious occurred on February 7, 1927) and by the far right. The conservative republicans, the Catholics, and the far right were now in the limelight and they tried to convert young officers who constituted a somewhat parallel power in the barracks, fortified by the nomination of many among them to local administrative posts. At the governmental level, however, a more cohesive group of conservative generals organized around General Carmona progressively consolidated its authoritative order. It was in this atmosphere that Salazar, following a major economic crisis, was named finance minister and negotiated ample powers over the other ministers.

The unifying pole of a fascistizing current within the Military Dictatorship was established under the very brief consulship of General Gomes da Costa in 1926. Rolão Preto, along with young officers and other exponents of the radical right, immediately set up a militia organization to support the new regime, emerging into the political spotlight behind the figure of the old general.

In June 1926, Martinho Nobre de Melo, an ex-Sidonist minister with an integralist background and a leader of the Nuno Alvares Crusade, presented the new dictatorship with a genuine political program, which proposed that the nationalist "militias" become para-military organizations of a fascist type[2]. In July of that year, General Gomes da Costa dismissed a series of ministers and assumed a number of ministerial portfolios. Martinho Nobre de Melo and the integralist João de Almeida entered the government. Two days later, however, the generals sent Gomes da Costa into exile in Azores, dismissed the ministers, and banned the organization.

This first attempt to 'fascistize' the nascent Military Dictatorship died at birth, due to the coup carried out by generals Carmona and Sinel de Cordes, which sent the old general into exile and neutralized the ministerial remodeling he had undertaken under the group's pressure. In the years that followed, however, the far right,

[2] See António José Telo, *Op. Cit.*, Vol. 2, (Lisboa: 1984), p. 220.

closely linked to the May 28th "lieutenants", participated in a number of coup attempts until the founding of the more stable May 28th League two years later. Following the overthrow of Gomes da Costa, the most radical sector of the "integralist family" staked its bets on the creation of a fascist party able to dominate the Military Dictatorship and Rolão Preto returned to "national syndicalist" propaganda.

A second attempt was launched soon after the failed February 1927 pro-democratic revolution, by the Lusitanian Militia[3]. It was undertaken by the same group and was immediately opposed by the conservative republicans and the Catholic Center. The integralists, as well as some of the "May 28th lieutenants", supported the initiative. On the other hand, Cunha Leal's Liberal Republican Union denounced the group from the start, in the name of significant numbers of its supporters[4]. As for the Catholic Center, it called attention to the dangers of a "paganized nationalism" that went about perverting and poisoning the "new generation", and reaffirmed the idea that only the Church could prevent such "excesses"[5].

Following a period of contradictory attitudes towards the Militias, the Dictatorship dealt them a final blow in an official note which emphasized that "everything that has been said about the government's interference in the organization of any militia body is premature"[6]. A subsequent initiative to form a party supporting the Dictatorship, by the Catholic Center, shed light on the enormous contradictions plaguing the governments of the Military Dictatorship.

In late 1927, when the conservative republican sector again attempted to launch a group "to support the Dictatorship", the answer of the far-right was to create the May 28th League. This organization, once neutralized, became the platform which launched the National Syndicalist movement.

[3] See Arlindo Caldeira, "O partido de Salazar...", pp. 944-949.
[4] See *A Situação*, 19-3-1927.
[5] See *Novidades*, 17-2-1927.
[6] See *A Voz*, 3-3-1927.

Fascism arose in Portugal towards the end of the 1920s, attempting to cut across the right-wing political spectrum. It was supported by numerous young officers with influence in the barracks and local administration; unlike the government party it had locally based support groups; it also inherited the small militias hurriedly set up by military "barons"; and began to mobilize sectors of the petty bourgeoisie, in the context of an unstable Dictatorship already dominated by the Catholic "dictator of finance". Thus, Rolão Preto saw the moment for the unification of the sector into a fascist party.

As an organized movement, NS was not in and of itself the beginning but the end of fascism in Portugal, a latecoming unifier which aimed to be an alternative to the regime, and in the context of the Military Dictatorship, to the consolidation of Salazar's authoritarian order.

PRETO'S NATIONAL SYNDICALIST MOVEMENT

The first steps towards the organization of National Syndicalism were undertaken in the summer of 1932[7]. Its foundation was legitimized as an "economic and social" force destined to be not only the embryo of the new corporatist system but also simultaneously the vanguard force for the construction of a "Nationalist State". Its political program was based on the "12 principles of production" drawn up by Rolão Preto in the 1920s, concentrating "all economic, social, and political theory, away from the bourgeois molds of monarchies and constitutional republics, away from the unnatural criminal insanity of Marxism, yet within human truth at a revolutionary and traditional pace (...)"[8].

The first regulations did not give any particular pre-eminence to a personalized leadership - the organization was to be led by a six member "pre-corporatist" directorate. It was only in 1933, fol-

---

[7] On the National Syndicalist Movement see António Costa Pinto, *Os Camisas Azuís. Ideologia, elites e movimentos fascistas em Portugal, 1914-1945* (Lisboa: 1994).

[8] See António Pedro, "Nacional Sindicalismo. O que pretende e o que é a nossa organização", *Revolução*, 10-10-1932, p. 1.

lowing the growing anti-Salazarist radicalization, that Rolão Preto signed statutes which brought the NS closer to the fascist model. NS represented the fascistization of a significant part of the IL, which had succeeded in mobilizing and directing a considerable segment of the Portuguese radical right. The NS counted on a solid organizational base, including various working head-offices, a network of close to eighteen regional and local newspapers, and several thousand members. But unlike previous organizations, this one unambiguously modeled itself along fascist lines organizationally, ideologically, and in terms of political action.

Mobilization Themes

By the end of the 1920s the Military Dictatorship had already literally robbed native fascism of some of its mobilizing themes. But for NS's founders everything was, and dangerously so, still to be decided. Some of fascism's "antis" had already been removed from the political scene, namely democracy and the radical republicans, enabling the NS to reinforce the drive towards the corporatist reorganization of the State, the creation of a militia to educate the new regime elites and to conquer the "masses".

To the remaining political forces and pressure groups supporting the Dictatorship, National Syndicalism presented itself as the vanguard of the "National Revolution". Its leaders proclaimed themselves supporters of a true reform of the State which would eliminate the last vestiges of liberalism and block the return of the Republic's old "caciques". In exchange, they were ready to offer the Dictatorship mass support and to dispute the communist and anarcho-syndicalist hegemony of the union movement in order to transform it into a disciplined support for the new regime.

Another aspect of the NS's propaganda was the predominance of a simultaneously corporatist and charismatic principle over an electoral principle. The latter, supported by sectors of the Dictatorship, was seen to be the product of "a spirit of compromise and transigence [which] could not in any way interest the Integral State"[9]. The fascist press reacted to any conciliatory sounding

---

[9] See Rolão Preto, "Comunicado de Guerra", *Revolução*, 23-2-1932.

speeches given by the Dictatorship's leaders which favored Conservative Republicans. It was the "social question", however, which lay at the heart of NS. The NS was seen as "the rational and foreseeable interpretation of all the revindications of those repressed by the old liberal-democratic society, and the triumph of the sacred instincts of the national community over individualism and the base procession of its instincts"[10].

The fascist "anti-conservative" dynamic was above all reflected in the aims of mass mobilization, of the creation of militias and nationalist unions, as well as in the anti-plutocratic and populist discourse, the creation of a "bottom up" dynamic of State reform. Its organization stigmatized the government party as representing precisely the Dictatorship's dominant elite, unified in an "eclectic [party] of the genre of Primo de Rivera's Patriotic Union, electoral and conservative"[11].

In early 1932 National Syndicalism's public demonstrations introduced Portugal to fascist choreography, characterized by paramilitary parades, combat songs and the charismatic ritualization of Rolão Preto's leadership. NS's street presence peaked during the Lisbon and Oporto rallies and the commemoration of the military coup, on May 28th, 1933, in Braga. This growing public support for National Syndicalism, led the anti-fascist opposition to initiate various actions against the movement and confrontations become widespread from mid-1933 onwards.

The "Labor Temptation"

National Syndicalism made extreme right's most successful attempt to penetrate the Portuguese labor and union movement. In March 1934, already in open conflict with Salazar, Rolão Preto pointed with pride to the appearance of a new workers "elite" associated with NS, "a beautiful elite of propagandists" which had "arisen after just a few months of nationalist and corporatist doctrination"[12].

[10]   See Rolão Preto, "República? Monarquia?", *Revolução*, 8-11-1932, p. 1.
[11]   See Rolão Preto, "El Movimiento Nacional Sindicalista", *Acción Española*, nº 34, 16 Octubre 1933, p. 203.
[12]   See Rolão Preto, "Novas Elites. Propagandistas operários", *União Nacional*, Leiria, 11-3-1934, p. 1.

In a country where industry was barely concentrated and where small and medium-sized factories carried the most weight, it was mainly in the north, along the Oporto/Braga axis, that NS made its presence felt. The very geography of legal and clandestine left wing denunciations coincides with the largest NS mobilizations and with the violent confrontations between the fascists and the communist and anarcho-syndicalist opposition throughout 1933 and 1934. In the rural world National Syndicalism did not leave a significant mark. Its mobilization of the agricultural proletariat was almost non-existent in the latifundium South, carrying out some agitation in Évora. In the North, some monarchist notables organized rallies and enrolled new members. In the countryside NS discourse was primarily directed at property holders. They supported the claims of the "live forces" of farming that "median farming" that was the "base of the national economy"[13].

Rural rallies were sporadic and provoked a great deal of suspicion amongst District Governors. The NS press placed a certain emphasis on propaganda activities focusing on the rural world in districts such as Castelo Branco, Guarda, Aveiro, and Leiria; these, however, were soon prohibited. NS activity in rural zones was perceived by the governments' representatives as agitation respectful of traditional social hierarchies[14].

Organization and Social Base

NS's organization was built around a charismatic figure who united elements of pre-existing groups clearly dominated by IL. Given this characteristic, NS's formation process illustrates the *penetration* model in the formation of party organizations; based on a single individual and "political entrepreneurs" associated with him, the movement was established, creating its own local groups (or reorganizing them on the basis of a new loyalty)[15].

[13] See Rolão Preto, "Acuda-se às classes médias!", *União Nacional*, Leiria, 10-12-1933, p. 1.
[14] See Relatório do Governador Civil de Leiria ao Ministro do Interior, 19-7-1933, Maço 463, Arquivo Geral do Ministério do Interior/Arquivo Nacional da Torre do Tombo (AGMI/ANTT), Lisbon.
[15] See K. Eliassem and L. Svaasand, "The formation of mass political organi-

Towards the end of 1933, various NS leaders, notably Rolão Preto, announced that the party had 50,000 members[16]. Some months later, in a confidential letter addressed to CAUR's general secretary, the head of NS foreign relations revealed that the movement had "a total of 30,000 comrades", a somewhat more modest number[17]. The disappearance of the organization's membership files and archives does not permit a thorough study of the profile of fascist adherents. One has to make do with the membership lists occasionally publicized by the National Secretariat, which identify up to 3800 members. This approximately 15% on whom data exists permits a closer, albeit limited, glimpse of the social and political profile of both members and leaders, as well as allowing for comparison with the one party with which it shared power in 1933 - Salazar's National Union (Table IV)[18].

Socially, other than the classic student and employee categories, NS had two characteristics that are worthy of note, namely its influence among young army officers as well as the considerable number from the popular social groups, workers in particular.

The military members of the organization had a very important place within NS but for the most part they did not formalize their membership. NS's Military Secretariat was composed solely of members, but they gained an impressive network of sympathizers, as proven by the number of army officers present at public demonstrations. The great majority of members were recently promoted lieutenants and captains.

The social ties and political solidarity between these officers and the movement's founders date from the early days, after the 1926 coup. In the period leading up to the foundation of the 28

zations: an analytical framework", *Scandinavian Political Studies*, 10 (1975), p. 90; Angelo Panebianco, *Modelli di partito. Organizzazione e potere nei partiti politici*, (Bologna: 1982), pp. 104-110.

[16] See Peter Merkl, "comparing fascist movements" in, Stein U. Larsen et alli (edited by), *Op. Cit.*, p. 756.

[17] See Carta de José Campos e Sousa a Augusto Pescosolido de 26/5/1934, "Movimento Nazional-Sindacalista Dissidente in Portogallo", Miniculpop, Busta 404, A.C.S., Roma.

[18] See António Costa Pinto, "As elites políticas e a ...", pp. 575-613.

Table IV
Social and Professional Distribution of NS Members

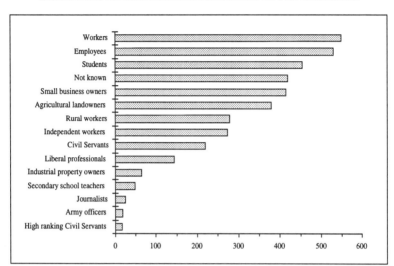

Source: Costa Pinto, 1992.

May League in 1928 these ties were consolidated through different groups, schemes, and publications. The IL's post World War I ideological influence among the military, whether in the 1918 "Sidonio's cadets", or the 1926 "lieutenants", should also be remembered.

For a number of years the fascists were able to exploit and exalt "lieutenantism", organizing themselves into a political party claiming to be a faithful depository of the spirit of the "May 28 revolution". They were apologists of militarist values and the radical replacement of the conservative political elite by the civilian and military youth which had participated in the 1926 coup. It was a military group that resisted the stabilization that would inevitably lead to the re-establishment of the hierarchy.

The significance of working class membership is somewhat relative. A reasonable number of workers does not necessarily imply fascist success among popular social groups or the creation of a alternative fascist elite within the union movement. This influence developed under a dictatorial regime that had already imposed severe limitation on unionism's margin of maneuver. However, presenting itself as an embryo of the corporatist system allowed it some success with mobilization. It also permitted the training of various officials (more in the service sector that among the working class) who eventually joined the "National Unions" of Salazarist corporatism.

NS and Salazar

From May 1933 onwards, Rolão Preto was faced with attacks against NS by various sectors of the Dictatorship and he accused the conservative republicans of maneuvering the UN against National Syndicalism. He cited internal service orders in order to prove that he had never been hostile to the government party and denied any conflict whatsoever with Salazar. This was, however, a tactical expedient, given that he was simultaneously counting on Salazar's eventual removal from power under military pressure.

The organization's internal correspondence reveals a clear distancing from Salazar and a bet on his replacement by a military supporter of National Syndicalism. However, many members, particularly those in the countryside, were sincere Salazarists and they were surprised by disagreements with the leader of the Dictatorship. Although very careful when making direct attacks on Salazar, the National Syndicalists were intransigent when it came to State's fascistization, the rapid implementation of a corporatist order, the refusal to integrate the government party, as well as ceding to the principles of Republican Liberalism.

At the Lisbon and Oporto rallies Rolão Preto became open in his demands for power. Addressing Salazar at Lisbon's Edward VII Park he stated: "your excellency, listen to the national soul that is vibrating; listen to the youthful vote for: Alea jacta est". In an Oporto demonstration of sympathizers, he harangued against the "social conservatives" and the infiltration of "oppositionism", advising that: "we announce the revolt and are ready to march one day, to save the Terreiro do Paço (...). The hour that we march on

Lisbon (when I give the necessary word) I cannot see what could possibly move Dr. Oliveira Salazar against us!"[19].

From 1932 onwards, having gained power in spite of the opposition of the chiefs of the movement, Salazar maintained a prudent distance from the National Syndicalists and lost no opportunities to differentiate himself from them both in terms of doctrine and policies. In the interviews granted to António Ferro which, apart from his speeches are the most important source of information on his political thought, Salazar distanced himself from the European fascisms and their national counterparts. Salazar separated himself from totalitarian fascism which "tends towards a pagan caesarism, and brings about a "New State" which knows no limits of the moral or juridical order". In his view, were such a movement to gain legitimacy "the Nation would not endure it... we are a poor, sick country (...) we go slowly, step by step"[20]. In various parts of the interview the leader of the *Estado Novo* ideologically rejected nationalism and integral corporatism; politically he denounced party violence, militia actions, and the charismatic leadership of the fascist dictators.

On the 28th of May, 1933, while Portuguese fascists marched in Braga in commemoration of the 1926 coup, Salazar denounced the "always feverish, excited, and discontent (...) who will continue shouting, faced with the impossible: more! More!"[21] The still delicate political situation however did not permit him to suppress National Syndicalism immediately as the UN lacked capacity for intervention and the instruments for repression and political control were not yet under its direct control. Furthermore Salazar's somewhat risky dependence on the President of the Republic and on the military, a group which clearly placed Carmona under pressure, did not permit him much room to maneuver.

In September 1933, the government backed a schism within National Syndicalism, offering official recognition in exchange for the removal of Rolão Preto and his followers from the leadership.

---

[19] See *Comércio do Porto*, 9-5-1933, p. 6.
[20] See António Ferro, *Salazar. O homem e a sua obra*, (Lisboa: 1933), p. 148.
[21] Oliveira Salazar, *Op. Cit.*, p. 225.

The schismatics, however, emerged as losers at the Congress. In their resistance to government and the attacks of government's backed schismatics, Rolão Preto's group relied essentially on the army, exploiting its differences with Salazar, as well as pressuring Carmona to remove him. The NS military faction had in any case taken part in anti-Salazarist maneuvering from late 1933 onwards.

During the summer of 1934, after a long meeting with the head of the political police, Salazar decided to abolish NS. On the 4th of July Rolão Preto was taken to Lisbon as a prisoner. Monsaraz, the General Secretary, would be arrested a few days later. On July 11th the Council of Ministers decided to expel the two supreme National Syndicalist leaders from the country for a period of six months, subject to prolongation. There had been a number of spontaneous demonstrations by members who had taken to the streets with their "hurrahs for Rolão Preto"; a good number of protest telegrams, blocked at origin, received no response from the organization. Announcing the radicalization of some local groups, one of these protests from the Oporto leaders ended as follows: "the UN does not pass as more than a swindle imposed by Your Excellency upon those who helped you (...), we advise you and at the same time remind you of the recent death of the Austrian chancellor (...), we shall not disarm but wait for the moment"[22].

On the 10th of September, 1935, with Rolão Preto actively participating, the NS along with other opposition sectors, May 28th deserters, as well as exiles from Spain, attempted to overthrow Salazar. Contrary to previous conspiracies in which NS members had been simply an element of military maneuvering, this time the leadership itself outlined and negotiated the political program[23]. NS's participation dominated the coup attempt and its announced defeat marked the end of organized fascism in Portugal.

A few days later, in an extensive and highly ideological note, Salazar already felt sufficiently confident to offer an account of his differences with this restless group of civilians and officers. The themes, already current in previous speeches, were now crys-

[22] See Arquivo Oliveira Salazar (AOS) /CO/PC-3F, ANTT.
[23] See Vasco da Gama Fernandes, *Depoimento Inacabado. Memórias*, (Lisboa: 1975), p. 55.

tallized into three questions: the conflict "between force and violence"; between "politics and administration"; and of the "constitutionalization of the national Revolution". In the first point, he stressed his hatred of "violence within the Government (...) without moral limitations and with no precise definition of its legal state." The second point reaffirmed that "politics had killed the administration of this country". As for the "constitutionalization" of the new regime, he looked upon it as the guarantee "that the fundamental principles of the system [would] bear fruit" against those who "would see the Dictatorship continue in wavering and uncertainty"[24].

***

The fascist alternative was quickly crushed with the "constitutional pacts" between the military elites and Salazar who was able to group the conservatives within the National Union, as well as dominate the poles of fascist resistance, administratively and through repression. The tension between the fascists and other authoritarian pressure groups that dominated the Portuguese Dictatorship were the manifestation of a conflict that featured in most processes of transition to authoritarianism with weak fascist movements[25]. Its more rapid resolution in favor of the new authoritarian government in Portugal, with the consequent elimination of the fascists, may be explained by the factors briefly listed below.

From the first decade of the century, there had been competitive ideologies and political movements in Portugal. They easily collaborated with the Dictatorship's military leaders, without threatening their functions, values and positions within the new regime. As Juan J. Linz has pointed out, within the framework of a transition whereby the military takes on a central role, they tended to turn more to the bureaucratic elites and the conservative parties, rather than the fascists[26]. This was so in spite of the fact that some

[24] See Oliveira Salazar, *Op. Cit.,* Vol. II, (Coimbra: 1945), p. 69-78.
[25] See Roger Griffin, *Op. Cit.*, pp. 116-145.
[26] See Juan J. Linz, *Fascism, Breakdown...*, *Cit.*, p. 71.

of the younger members were fascist sympathizers. Such was the case of the Portuguese Military Dictatorship.

It was in the government that one sector of the civilian elite made up mostly of university law professors and headed by the young finance minister Oliveira Salazar negotiated, at times under great tension, the "constitutionalization" of the Dictatorship and the progressive distancing of the military. Throughout this process the fascists were a "negligible factor". The existence of an authoritarian right supported by powerful institutions such as the Church, the principal hierarchy of the Armed Forces, and some of the agricultural and industrial interest groups, blocked off space and working room from the fascist radical and mobilizing pole.

There seems to be no doubt that it was the transformation of the military coup d'état into a prolonged civil war that allowed neighboring Spanish fascists, whose numbers and sociological significance matched that of their Portuguese counterparts, to leave an important mark on the dynamic of Francoism. In Portugal, a successful military intervention resulted in a preventive Dictatorship, and there were a number of crises of institutionalisation that gave the fascists a capacity for maneuver. Nonetheless, both at the internal and external level no factor empowered the role of the fascists in Portugal.

The external factor is not insignificant. In a number of eastern and northern European countries and in Vichy France it was the outbreak of the Second World War that forced many right-wing dictatorships from going ahead with the destruction or quick abolition of native fascism. With the probable exception of Romania, the process was already underway by the time "German Europe" was born. Even the fascist movements that lived on countries where democracy survived were negligible phenomena on the eve of the German occupation. Such was the case of Belgium, Norway, or Denmark.

In Portugal, just as in Brazil, a situation less different than is supposed, no single international variable conditioned the spontaneous decision of the government elites to eliminate a contentious native fascism. Many of these Dictatorships used the fascists "for certain functions such as propaganda, control of the mass media

(...)", etc[27]. In Portugal, the "integration" process of the fascists into Salazar's new regime was weak, and suffered the bureaucratic cautiousness imposed by the *Estado Novo*'s elite. They were channeled into secondary regime institutions. The recalcitrants tried their luck in the 1935 coup attempt, and developed a "leftist and social fascism" that carried a few of them into the post-1945 opposition to Salazar. The majority reconverted to the regime, especially when the Spanish Civil War introduced a certain fascist choreography.

4.2 THE POLITICAL SYSTEM OF SALAZARISM

In 1935, a delegate of the CAUR, Baldi-Papini, visited Portugal and sent a long report back to Rome expressing his views on Salazar's regime and quoting from conversations with Portuguese political leaders[28]. Placing the process of the overthrow of the liberal order and Salazar's rise to power in a historical context, Papini stressed the differences with Italian fascism. In Portugal, "a policing operation by the Army was enough, while in Italy there was a civil revolution with all its bloodshed, its March and its collective spirit of regeneration. Thus, no Duce, no elite, no doctrine, no revolutionary faith born and cemented in the battlefield had filled the soul of the people from the very start"[29].

Referring to Salazar, he emphasized that "the leader and founder of the "New State" took no part in the movement and eventually created a "personal regime without a personality". After analyzing its institutions and recognizing the mark and inspiration of Fascism here and there, he concluded: "in short, while Fascism is a system of thought rather than a system of government, the "New State" is merely a system of government to which an idealized content is imparted"[30].

---

[27] *Idem.*

[28] CAUR, *Relazione sulla Missione Compinta dall' Avv. U. Baldi Papini in Portogallo*, Agosto 1935, Miniculpop, Busta 404, ACS, Roma. On this organization of Italian fascism see M. A. Ledeen, *Universal Fascism* (New York: 1972).

[29] *Idem.*

[30] *Idem.*

A "CONSTITUTIONALIZED DICTATORSHIP"

The institutions of the *Estado Novo*'s political system were essentially defined by the 1933 constitution. It was a constitution that represented an early compromise with conservative republicans and was thus weak in its liberal principles and strong in its corporatist and authoritarian dimension. Rights and liberties were formally maintained, but were actually eliminated by government regulations. Freedom of association was maintained, but parties effectively eliminated through regulation. The UN never had formal status as a single party, although from 1934 on it was one.

The UN president would be Salazar, who would nominate the National Union deputies to parliament. The constitution maintained the classic separation of powers, and gave relatively few powers to the chamber of deputies and none to the corporatist chamber, making the government autonomous from any control. Theoretically the members of the corporatist chamber ought to have been designated by the corporations, but in reality Salazar would nominate most of them. The constitution maintained a president of the Republic elected by direct suffrage and a president of the council of ministers, and Salazar was only answerable to the first. During the early years this would be the only constitutional threat to Salazar. The president of the Republic was always a general, a legacy of the Military Dictatorship that would eventually cause some problems to the dictator, especially after 1945. In sum, the definition of a "constitutionalized dictatorship", to use a phrase of the time, reflected the real nature of the regime.

Reduced to mere "advisory councils", both the Chamber of Deputies and the Corporatist Chamber represented, as did the single party, the regime's "limited pluralism". The contradictions between those favoring a restoration of the monarchy and republicans, between integral and moderate corporatists, cut across the chambers. In the 1950s different lobbies arose among defenders of agricultural and industrial interests.

The *Estado Novo* inherited the repressive apparatus set up by the Military Dictatorship and strengthened it. Censorship, established in 1926, was reorganized and later controlled by the propaganda services. The same occurred with the political police, which was transformed into the true backbone of the system. The growing autonomy of the political police was progressively decreed until it ended up answerable only to Prime Minister Salazar. Aside from repressing the clandestine opposition, controlling access to public administration was of central importance. Mechanisms to control judiciary power were increased. Political crimes, for example, were placed under the jurisdiction of special military courts, and special judges were nominated. Furthermore, the political police were given ample powers to determine prison sentences.

In 1936, with the basic outlines of the legal system consolidated, Salazar authorized the founding of a militia, the Portuguese Legion, and also set up youth and women's organizations dependent on the ministry of education. A fascistic choreography thus emerged more clearly.

One important problem remained, namely, relations with the military. Throughout the regime's long life this was the institution that Salazar was most sensitive about and the one he most feared. Nonetheless it is clear that the subordination of the military hierarchy to the regime was a fact on the eve of the Second World War. The process was slow, and numerous tensions arose, but the movement to co-opt and control the military elite was the central element in the consolidation of Salazarism.

Salazar's 1938 speech at an officers' demonstration symbolically marked the victory of "a civilian police dictatorship" over the old Military Dictatorship implanted in 1926[31]. In political-administrative terms, the two most important steps of this control process went from the arrival of Salazar in the War Ministry in mid-1936, after several previous attempts disallowed by Carmona, to the reform of the Armed Forces in 1937.

After taking charge of the War portfolio in 1936, Salazar had a final, albeit tentative word on all high-level promotions and transfers. In spite of the "temporary" nature of his position, Salazar was Minister of War until the end of the Second World War. It was as

---

[31] See Maria Carrilho, *Op. Cit.*, p. 423, and José Medeiros Ferreira, *Op. Cit.*, pp. 175-202.

Minister of War that he presented his reform bill for the Armed
Forces in 1937. It constituted the most significant piece of legislation for ensuring government control over the Armed Forces. This
reform provoked the most important quantitative and qualitative
reduction in the Armed Forces to occur since the First World War.
In the years that followed the officers corps would decline by 30%.
Already significantly affected by resignations and transfers into
the reserves of those implicated in the dozens of attempted coups
and revolutions after 1926, it reached "the lowest levels registered
since 1905"[32]. Apart from this control "from above", a number of
legislative measures strengthened ideological and police control
over the Armed Forces. These measures heralded the political hegemony of the Dictator's aide for the Armed Forces, Captain Santos
Costa. He was promoted Sub-secretary of State and his domain
went unchallenged until the late 1950s.

Salazarism was no affront to international order. Its nationalism was based on the legacy of the past and on its colonial patrimony. Its system of alliances was based on the Anglo-Portuguese
Alliance which was never questioned and which ensured the English government's discrete support of the dictatorship. The geography and progress of the Second World War determined Portugal's
non-involvement. Salazarism focused on maintaining neutrality and
continuing the old system of alliances.

As far as the political system is concerned, little or nothing
changed with the profound alteration of the international order after 1945. The only concession was the opening for the emergence
of a legal opposition - a month at a time every four years - for
which no constitutional reform was necessary. In 1958, following
the "scare" provoked by the presidential candidacy of a dissident
general, Humberto Delgado, the President was indirectly and "or-
ganically" elected by the National Assembly and the representatives of the Municipal Chambers.

---

[32] *Idem*, p. 422.

SALAZAR: A "STRONG" DICTATOR

Many studies of modern dictatorships ignore the leader. In the case of the "New State" it would be a mistake to do so. Salazar had a world view and ran the whole institutional design of the regime. Once he became the unchallenged leader little legislation, be it the most important or the most trivial, was passed without his approval[33].

Salazar played no part in the 1926 coup d'état. Nor was he listed as a candidate for dictator during the last years of the parliamentary regime. He was born to a poor rural family in a village in central Portugal, in Vimieiro near Santa Comba Dão. Oliveira Salazar received a traditional Catholic education and completed most of his intellectual and political education before the 1st World War. He attended a seminary but abandoned the ecclesiastical path on the eve of the fall of the Monarchy in order to study law at the University of Coimbra. A reserved and brilliant student, he led the best known Catholic student organization at Coimbra, the CADC. His friendship with the future cardinal patriarch, Cerejeira, dates from this time. He pursued a university career as a professor of economic law and his only political activity under the liberal Republic occurred within the strict limits of the social Catholic movement. He was one of the leaders, but not the only one, of the Catholic Center and was elected deputy by the party in the early 1920s.

It was because of his expertise in finance and his membership in the Catholic Center that his name was suggested a number of times for Finance Minister immediately after the 1926 coup. As it was of course in that capacity that he joined the Military Dictatorship in 1928. His rise within the government was initially due to the ample powers he negotiated on his arrival at the finance ministry. Only later did he turn his attention to the political institutions.

The image that Salazar cultivated was that of a reserved puritanical and provincial Dictator, an image which held sway until his death and one which he never attempted to change. As a young

---

[33] We are still waiting for a good biography of Salazar, meanwhile see the one written by one of his Ministers, Franco Nogueira, *Salazar*, 6 vols., (Coimbra: 1977-85).

Catholic militant he left Portugal only once to take part in a Catholic congress in Belgium. After taking power, he made a single trip to Spain to meet with Franco. He ruled over a "colonial empire" but never visited a single colony during the 36 years of his consulship. He never went to Brazil, the "brother country", either. He flew once and didn't like it. Yet it would be a mistake to assume that his provincialism implies a lack of political culture. Salazar was an "academic" dictator who closely followed international politics and the ideas of the times.

Salazar always evinced some ideological traits connected with his cultural background: he was a traditional anti-liberal Catholic integralist in a context of secularization and accelerated modernization. For him the latter were symbolic of the First Republic. He was ultra-conservative in the most literal sense of the term. He steadfastly defended his rejection of democracy and its ideological heritage, favoring an "organicist" vision of society based on traditional and Catholic foundations. As national leader he was aware of the inevitability of modernization but was always acutely aware of the threat it represented.

In their systematic and cartesian simplicity, his speeches provide a good indication of his political thought[34]. He always spoke to the elite. When the District Governors mobilized the peasants, Salazar maintained, come hell or high water, his principles. Everything else derived from or was added to this. He was a professor of finance and had clear ideas about the management of a State's balance sheet. Portugal's dictator rejected the Fascist model of charismatic leadership both out of ideological training and political choice; not for pragmatic reasons and even less out of suitability to any characteristic nature of Portuguese society, the social structure of which was not unlike many of those which underwent a populism closer to Fascism. As a "strong" dictator he rarely decentralized decisions and relied above all upon a docile administration.

---

[34] For the 1930s, see Oliveira Salazar, *Discursos*, Vol. I, (Lisboa: 1935).

THE NATIONAL UNION AND AUTHORITARIAN SINGLE PARTIES

The National Union was a variant of a particular type of party which Juan Linz has labeled "unified parties", due to their origins. Sartori considered the same type of parties "single authoritarian parties" generally representing a "coalescence, from the top, of various elements to create a new political entity", which forced other forces to either integrate or be excluded.[35] In some cases these parties fulfilled a number of the functions assumed by the single parties of totalitarian and fascist regimes. Their origins, ideology, organization, and relationship with both the state and society, however, were different:

- The key determining factor is that these parties were created in an authoritarian situation, where political pluralism was already absent or severely handicapped. The impetus for their formation came from the government with the decisive aid of the state apparatus. In general their establishment entailed varying degrees of compromise on the part of other parties or pressure groups leading or participating in the winning coalition.

- They fulfilled legitimizing functions which were particularly important for "elections" and other constitutional "pretenses". After institutionalization these functions became less important. Generally, they did not have a monopoly on representation and coexisted with other "organic" political institutions over which they had no control. They were not the exclusive channel to power. They were not mediating agents between institutions such as the Armed Forces and the Government. Interest groups and religious institutions among others also had their own channels. Their capacity was also limited as far as the creation of a new political elite is concerned. Their aim was to "prevent dissidence, rather to organize consensus"[36]. Though they had been created by regimes gen-

---

[35] See Juan J. Linz, *Authoritarian and Totalitarian....*, p. 266, and Giovanni Sartori, *Op. Cit.*; Marco Tarchi, *Partito Unico e Dinamica Autoritaria* (Napoli: 1981), p. 99.
[36] *Idem,* p. 114.

erally not, or only occasionally, mobilizing they themselves were not mobilizing.

- Given the above, party organization was weak, dependent on the Government or the administration. Leaders were usually Government appointed. The basic organizational structure did not penetrate society. They lacked cells or organs for training or agitation and they did not control mass (or paramilitary) organizations. Membership fluctuated and hardly ever reflected ideological concerns. Not infrequently, they had little social prestige. Under mobilizing single party regimes apoliticism maybe an obstacle to access to the ministerial elite; in these cases, however, it could be an advantage.

- These parties had a vaguer and less codified ideology than the fascist parties given the more heterogeneous nature of the coalition overthrowing the previous regime and the important role played by institutions like the Armed Forces, the Church or even traditional political parties. Ideology was less codified because it was "produced" after the installation of the dictatorship rather than developing in a pre-dictatorial, competitive environment. Thus, the values expressed are vaguer and more negative.

In Portugal and Spain, parties of this type had antecedents and were modeled on those which thrived under Sidónio Pais (National Republican Party) and Primo de Rivera (Patriotic Union)[37.] Similar and more or less successful projects were also promoted in the 1930s by authoritarian regimes, particularly in Spain, Austria, Hungary (National Union Party), and Poland (Camp of National Union)[38].

---

[37] See Shlomo Ben-Ami, *Fascism from above: The Dictatorship of Primo de Rivera in Spain, 1923-1930,* (Oxford: 1983) and José Luis Gomez Navarro, *El Régimen de Primo de Rivera,* (Madrid: 1991).
[38] See   Stuart Woolf (Edited by), *Op. cit.,* (London: 1981), pp. 117-150 and 171-189; Edward D. Wynot, *Polish Politics in Transition. The Camp of National Unity and the Struggle for Power, 1935-39,* (Athens: 1974).

A single party that approaches this model in terms of origins is Franco's. In 1937, Franco forced various previously independent parties that were part of the coalition that ultimately won the civil war to unify under the banner of a single political party. The end result was an organization strictly controlled by Franco but with distinct factions acknowledged by the party leadership.[39] The identity and preponderance of the groups was reflected within the party or through the ministerial elite. Nonetheless the Francoist single party was quite similar to the Italian fascist model, at least initially. This was never the case in Portugal where the National Union merged with the State apparatus such that it depended on it from the first to the last day of its life. Its very existence was at risk during certain phases of the regime. This was particularly true when, paradoxically, its survival seemed to be most important — namely during the "fascist era".

Regardless of ones view of Party/State relations in single-party regimes, Portugal will always be at one extreme of the spectrum when compared to its European counterparts during the period between the two world wars. Some party system typologies, such as Giovanni Sartori's, have gone as far as excluding the *Estado Novo* from the family of "single parties" since the National Union does not appear to fulfill the role that its counterparts played[40].

The Organizational Structure

Salazar created the UN in 1930 just as he was emerging as the dictatorship's main political leader as Finance Minister. The launching of this organization, however, was accompanied by statements that were vague, regarding its role and membership. Salazar's Government-led organization welcome all of the Dictatorship's sympathizers, whether republican, monarchist or Catholic. For the first two years, the National Union was completely dependent on the Ministry of the Interior[41]. The Ministry's dispatches directed the

---

[39] See Ricardo Chueca, *El fascismo en los comienzos del régimen de Franco. Un estudio sobre la FET-JONS*, (Madrid: 1983), p. 166.
[40] See Giovanni Sartori, *Op. Cit.*, pp. 235-236.
[41] See Circular do Ministro do Interior aos presidentes das comissões distritais da UN, 29-12-1931, Maço 452-Caixa 5, AGMI/ANTT.

government's party while the District Governors were influential in the establishment of the local committees. During the initial phase, the Minister of the Interior could replace local leaders who would normally depend on the District Governor[42.]

This dependency marked the life of the party. Contrary to what one might expect, its lethargy was especially notorious during the 1930s. Once its leaders had been appointed, its statutes established and its candidates to the National Assembly chosen, the UN practically disappeared. In 1938, the dictator himself recognized that the UN's activity had "progressively diminished almost to a vanishing point."[43.] Thus, it was only immediately before 1945 that the UN acquired visibility once again, when opposition mounted and disaster at the polls threatened.

The frailty of the UN's internal structure was also clear in the absence of departments that most other authoritarian single parties possess, notably propaganda, ideological training, and cultural intervention. It also lacked socio-professional organizations which in neighboring Spain, for instance, could be found in the FET[44.]

Salazar's *Estado Novo* later created state departments for propaganda, the Portuguese Youth, or the "Doppo Lavoro", but these were not linked to the party. Only occasionally did the state turn to the party network, and then only to carry out specific well-defined tasks. Finally, if the Constitution of 1933 represented a formal commitment to liberal principles of representation, the National Union clearly represented an organizational commitment to conservative republicanism at the local level.

One of the CAUR delegates who came to Portugal on political missions in 1934 and 1935 considered Salazar's single party and the absence of any youth involvement "una delle debollezze più tragiche"[45]. In his introduction to his chapter on the Salazarist party, delegate Baldi-Papini described the UN as a "skeletal" body, a kind

[42] See AOS/CO/PC-4, ANTT.

[43] Cit. in Manuel Braga da Cruz, *O Partido...* , p. 140.

[44] See Ricardo Chueca, *Op. Cit.* pp. 169-398 and Sheelagh Ellwood, *Prieta las Filas. História de Falange Española, 1933-1983,* (Barcelona: 1984), pp.113-154.

[45] See CAUR, *Op. Cit.*

of "council of wise men", "far from the masses". Its organization lacked militancy and no obligations united its members. "No discipline unites them, they have no duty. They know nothing of the military character of Italian Fascism or German National Socialism"[46].

Although the regime adopted some of the institutions of fascism later on, the founding characteristics of the party endured throughout Salazar's regime.

The National Leaders

The first leaders appointed to the National Union's central committee created more of a "college of cardinals" than a typical party elite. They represented the Military Dictatorship's different "sensibilities". Their average age was 50, far above that of the *Estado Novo*'s 1st National Assembly deputies and, for that matter, generally higher than within the regime's other institutions.[47.]

Salazar had called upon individuals with monarchist, conservative and republican backgrounds with a common trait — they all had links to the state by virtue of previous ministerial public office, or military positions. The Central Committee came into being in 1932 by which time almost all regional and local structures had been set up. Salazar assumed the presidency and Albino dos Reis, ex-member of a conservative republican party, was appointed vice-president. More conservative republicans, an ex-Integralist, and a Catholic Center leader, were invited to preside the first Central Committee. All others were either ministers or ex-ministers of the Dictatorship with a few military officers completing the cast.

One ought not believe that this diversity meant that Salazar felt the need, as Franco eventually did, to "integrate" or control certain sectors in order to later make them part of the governing elite. Francoism allowed one or diverse sectors to lead the party and in proportional representation at the government and administrative levels. Under Salazarism, however, no such thing occurred.[48.] Be-

[46] *Idem.*

[47] See Philippe C. Schmitter, "The social origins, ...", p. 443.

[48] See C. Viver Pi-Sunyer, *El Personal Político de Franco (1936-1945). Contribución empírica a uma teoria del régimen franquista*, (Barcelona: 1978),

coming a UN leader was the equivalent of "retirement" or marking time at a less than prestigious government post. There was no real National Union-to-Government movement.

Political Origins of Local Leaders

At the end of 1930, the Minister of the Interior instructed the District Governors to investigate the political affiliations of the National Union's district and county leaders prior to May 28, 1926. Despite subsequent changes, a basic picture emerged of what became the single party of the Salazarist regime, after the elimination of its rivals.

In accordance with a chart provided by the Ministry, the District Governors divided the leaders into four broad categories: republicans, monarchists, Catholics and independents, with the first category being subcategorized whenever possible by party affiliation[49]. The identification of the political origins of the 806 county leaders from eight districts of continental Portugal provides an insight into the trends that affected the selections made by the Government in 1931 (Table V):

Table V
Political Origins of the National Union's Local Committees

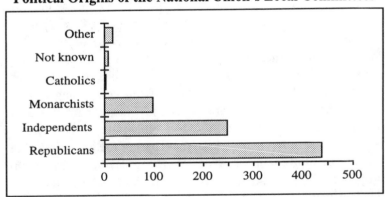

Source: Costa Pinto, 1992.

pp. 145-231 and Miguel Jerez Mir, *Elites Politicas y Centros de Extraccion en Espanha, 1938-1957*, (Madrid: 1982), pp. 49-178.

[49] See Maço 451-caixa 4, AGMI/ANTT.

The survey confirmed what many had already sensed. There was a markedly larger percentage of republicans. The large percentage of independents, however, raises questions. A more detailed examination might well significantly lower their 30% share of the total in favor of the republican parties, as it is likely that their number included former republicans who had temporarily distanced themselves, before the fall of the parliamentary republic.

The District Governors did not include in the category of monarchists the integralists. They identified only seven which, even if a flawed count is taken into account, indicates their resistance to the National Union. This is not unexpected given that a number of Integralists whose names appeared on the Government rolls either resigned or were excluded in the years that followed.

The figures in the chart above can only be revised by case studies. Nonetheless, the number of "independent republican" leaders (without party affiliation), must clearly have been much higher, with the largest number obviously in the conservative republican parties.

Foremost among them were the Nationalist Party and Cunha Leal's Liberal Republican Union, backers of the 1926 *coup d'état* and former Democratic Party opponents. Many of the militants in these parties contributed entire county committees to the National Union, even thought their leaders disagreed with Salazar.

In the early phase at least, the National Union's efforts were more clientelistic rather than properly ideological. There appears to have been an attempt to adopt a good part of the conservative republican parties' networks. Not surprisingly, political discourse was considerably more moderate than that characteristic of the regime during the second half of the 1930s.

Membership and Social-professional Background

Between 1930 and 1933, adherence to the UN can be described as "open"[50.] The UN's statutes themselves failed to contain a section on the "rights and duties" of its "associates", who were simply required to be "adults capable of fully exercising their political

[50]   See Maurice Duverger, *Les Partis Politiques*, (Paris: 1957), p. 93.

rights." It was only later, when the local committees were inundated with "requests", asking for "favors", that the UN instructions began to successively stress more control and care over membership.

Other than being occasionally drafted for a trip to Lisbon for a demonstration, members had no "rights and duties" whatsoever. In effect they did not participate in the organization which explains why the government was never minimally concerned with cries of "infiltration". Most of these were not "political infiltrations" but simple patronage, in any case.

Salazar's party do not pursue a popular, mass basis. The dictator once publicly stated that "we need neither fawn on the working class to get their backing nor provoke their ire only to have them later shot for their excesses."[51.] The single party was never behind any of the instruments of "consensus" directed at the popular social groups (Table VI).

Table VI
Socio-economic Distribution of UN Membership

Upper classes	42,4
Middle classes	25,6
Low classes	27,4
Not known	4,6

Source: Cruz, 1988, p. 235-237.

The social-professional composition of the single party consisted primarily of upper class (42.4%) and middle class (25%) elements, with a good number of proprietors and upper level technical and administrative officials.[52].

---

[51] Oliveira Salazar, *Op. Cit.*, p. 178.
[52] See Manuel Braga da Cruz, *O Partido...*, pp. 235-237.

The Single Party and Political Elite

The presence of the single party in Portugal was not an important factor in the formation of Salazarism's political élite as its functions in this field were limited. It did, however, strengthen Salazar's authority and limit the organization of blocs and pressure groups as well as allow for a certain "technocratic" pluralism of choice.

The first parliamentary elections held in 1934 had clear legitimizing intentions. These elections were synonymous with the non-mobilizing character of the regime. Held regularly, they were always acts which never intended to simulate 99% participation. Civil servants were mobilized and despite the already restricted number of registered voters, electoral rolls were manipulated. The "New State" was never a "dual State". Salazar governed over and through the administrative apparatus, relegating the truly "political" institution to a second place. This characteristic of the Portuguese regime differentiates it from the typical tension between party and state in Fascism[53].

To wit: the UN played a significant role in the control of central and local administration; in the unification of the diverse political factions that supported the regime; and in the supply of political officials - especially, once again, in the provinces.

Despite the continuing lack of studies on the Salazarist political elite, the few which exist make it clear that the party was not seen as necessary to gain access to the most important positions posts. According to one study, out of the 608 parliamentary deputies of the *Estado Novo*, only 45% were members of the UN[54]. The figure is even lower for members of the Corporatist Chamber, never higher than 15%[55]. For the ministerial elite the number was obviously higher although still quite low - only 29% of the ministers were members of the single party[56].

---

[53] Cf. Emilio Gentile, "Le Rôle du Parti dans le Laboratoire Totalitaire Italien" and Philippe Burrin, "Politique et Société: Les structures du pouvoir dans L'Italie Fasciste et L'Allemagne Nazie", *Annales ESC*, mai-juin 1988, n° 3, pp. 556-591 and 615-637.

[54] See Manuel Braga da Cruz, *O Partido...*, p. 176.

[55] *Idem*, pp. 176-177.

[56] *Idem*, p. 176.

In neighboring Spain one can identify the regime's different phases according to the changing composition of its political elite. A similar exercise is not possible for Salazarism. The Party, the Armed Forces, the Catholics and Monarchists, although significant pressure groups, did not condition the selection process of the elite as they did in Spain. Or at least such cycles of influence and decadence have not been identified. A closer analysis of Salazar's ministerial elite proves this.

According to one of the few studies on Salazar's ministers, most ministers came from the ranks of the armed forces or public administration, but the majority were from the "technocracy" (Table VII)[57].

Table VII
Occcupational Recruitment of Ministers, by Period

Period	Military	Politicians	Technicians
1932-36	6	2	11
1936-47	5	7	4
1947-58	5	5	9
1958-68	8	3	22

Source: Lewis, 1968, p. 640.

When ministers holding positions within the single party or the militias are considered as "politicians" then the fact is there are notably few of them. It is worth noting that of the 17 considered, 14 were university, mainly law professors, the institution that by far provided the *Estado Novo* with the most ministers. The proportion of university professors was even higher in the "technicians" category.

Ministers also had little room in which to maneuver. Salazar put a stop to ministers' council meetings early on, dealing privately with each one and controlling practically all proposed legislation.

---

[57] See Paul H. Lewis, "Salazar's Ministerial Elite...", p. 640.

Under Salazarism, Ministers were practically reduced to a class of Director Generals of their Ministries.

Beyond the political-administrative "technocracy", only the military maintained a steadfastly constant presence. This was especially the case in the early phase, given the military nature of the Dictatorship established in 1926. Yet it is clear that the military were a strong presence within the regime's elite, both within the single party and the militia organizations, as well as the repressive apparatus. The military presence within the political police, though small, remained strong until the end of the Second World War, and continued to be stable in areas such as the censorship service. The Presidency of the Republic, lest we forget, was also always the domain of the military.

THE CORPORATIST APPARATUS

The *Estado Novo* was essentially legitimized by corporatism. It was written into the Constitution and played a central role in determining institutional structures, ideology, relations with the "organized interests" as well as the State's economic policy under Salazarism.

Corporatism was one of the key elements of Italian Fascism, as well as covering a wide ideological spectrum of the authoritarian right from the beginning of the century. Italy however was far from having a monopoly on. As far as authoritarian regimes are concerned, corporatism was not specific to Fascism and it is doubtful whether it can even be considered as part of German Nazism[58]. It did, however, constitute a central element for the legitimation of most of the post-war authoritarianisms, such as those of Austria, Spain, Vichy and Portugal.

Salazarism did not give a monopoly on representation to the corporatist sector, against the will of the radical right. The electoral principle was maintained and the Corporatist Chamber retained merely consultative powers in a National Assembly which

---

[58] See Peter J. Williamson, *Corporatism in Perspective. An introductory guide to corporatist theory*, (London: 1989).

was anyway practically powerless. The corporatist structure itself was never completed, despite the original plans. Its effect on economic policy or its capacity to act as a buffer against social conflict, are worthy of detailed study. Though there were no actual Corporations to represent the "organic elements of the nation" in the Corporatist Chamber, there were also no intermediate organizations. The distance between the bases and the members of the Chamber was maintained by the State. The Procurators were chosen by the "Corporatist Council". This Council, however, consisted of Salazar himself as well as the ministers and secretaries of state of the sectors involved.

The cornerstone of the corporatist structure was the *Estatuto do Trabalho Nacional* (ETN) (1933) as well as the "industrial conditioning" law. Although tempered by the *Estado Novo*'s strong Catholic learnings, as a declaration of corporatist principles the ETN owed a great deal to Italy's "Carta del Lavoro". Approved in September 1933, the Statute was publicized by a political discourse which sought a clear synthesis of the Italian model with the ideals of "social Catholicism".

The founder of the Portuguese corporatist system was a friend of Salazar's, Pedro Teotónio Pereira, a former integralist who brought a group of young officials together in his department both from the radical right and from social Catholic origins. The new social engineering was quickly, albeit bureaucratically, established, given reluctance to include the Rolão Preto fascists who had meanwhile been suppressed.

With the ETN approved and the appropriate control mechanisms created, labor became the first sector affected. The government gave the unions two months to either accept the new system or be disbanded. Substantially weakened after the 1926 coup, the unions accepted the new legislation, although only by a slight majority[59]. But the most important among them were simply dissolved when they rejected the legislation. In January 1934 there was a revolt against the so-called "fascistization" of the Unions; these were then

---

[59] See Fátima Patriarca, *Processo de implantação ....*

recreated from the top down by officials from the corporatist apparatus.

From the start the new Unions were subjected to total control by so-called National Institute of Labor and Welfare (INTP). Their statutes and leaders were submitted for State approval. If they diverged from the ETN's path, they were summarily dissolved. Even the use of members's dues came under official scrutiny. Finally, "national" representation was avoided, thus maintaining the unions in a submissive state.

The *Casas do Povo* encompassed the rural world. The regime recognized no social differences in rural society which was overseen by the large landholders, set up as "associate protectors". And as opposed to the world of labor, the old rural unions were simply abolished, particularly in the latifunda dominated south.

In order to ensure that the working classes were provided for culturally, the National Foundation for Joy at Work was created, which worked in coordination with the Secretariat for National Propaganda (SPN) to organize the activities of the *Doppo Lavoro* — an obviously Italian-inspired body[60].

The corporatist system's role becomes clearer if seen within the context of the state's intervention in the economy from 1930 onwards. In effect, a fourth category of institutions existed which were considered pre-corporatist according to the 1936 laws, and which ensured smooth relations between the state and the emerging corporatist institutions: these were the Organizations of Economic Coordination. According to the political discourse, these were meant to disappear gradually over time as the corporatist edifice neared completion. In practice they became central features, gaining total control over the *Gremios* ("Guilds"), especially in agriculture and the weaker industrial areas, as well as in the agrofood export sector. Wheat, milling, wine and related business, olive oil, wool and wool products, as well as canned products including fish, all depended on the state commissions for all decisions regarding production quotas, prices and salaries.

---

[60] See Victoria de Grazia, *Mass organization of leisure in fascist italy* (Cambridge: 1981).

The integration of employers' associations into the new corporatist system was asymmetrical from the start, especially when compared to labor. Decrees affecting the *Gremios*, looking to the forced organization of employers and the liberal profession were more moderate and prudent. The old employers' associations remained tentatively active in a "transitory" manner and in many cases they lasted as long as the regime itself. Formally, the *Gremios'* organizations were either voluntary or mandatory, with the state taking the initiative under the broad definition of the "national economic interest". Indeed economic intervention strategies determined the organization required, rather than a search for any coherence in the corporatist structure. The economy's more modern sectors had greater autonomy, but agriculture and the large associated trade sectors (wine, olive oil, cereals, etc.), along with the milling and industry, among others, would rapidly be forced to unite in the *Gremios*, within the framework of the corporatist system.

Corporatist labor Relations

Unlike the Vargas and Peron dictatorships, the "New State" did not attempt to promote intense working class mobilization, opting instead for the establishment of a passive and paternalistic consensus. There was little stimulation of National Unions be these Conservative Catholic or of the more fascistic variety, both of which existed under the Dictatorship. Populist mobilization was, for the most part, absent.

Asymmetry between labor and capital increased during the *Estado Novo*, and social demagoguery was more traditional and paternalistic than fascist. The employers' resistance to "class collaboration" was evident throughout the 1930s, the 'golden years' of corporatism. A number of case studies on the corporatist system in the 1930s have pointed to the extremely slow pace of negotiations stemming from the enormous resistance of employers' associations, which were by then much stronger than the state-dependent union movement whose bargaining power was so restricted.

The only study on this issue indicates the following key tendencies: control over the adult male labor market, restrictions on women's entry into the market, preferential access to family members in certain professional sectors; minimum or non-existent salary increases although there were greater discounts for Social Welfare on both sides; and finally, dominant state legislation governing social benefits for the working classes as well as labor protection.

Employers' resistance was demonstrated by the successive postponement of negotiations with the unions as well as by the reaction to the regime's labor laws. There were successive examples of this ranging from work schedules to the minimum wage. Employers reacted badly to "forced collaboration" and in many cases they ignored the laws. Whenever "the free will of all parties" was permitted it was actually the "free will of the employers" which invariably won the day. Given the unions' weakness, the corporatist apparatus was able to undertake further radical action that eventually clashed directly with employers. The state's tendency to fix salaries by government decree increased, and became particularly strong during the war years. The State found that it was forced to "compensate" for the imbalances caused by the increasingly statist nature of the syndicalist system. Indeed, the INTP's corporatist officials were finally the ones who struggled to maintain pressure on employers at many labor conventions[61]. On the other hand, the *Acção Catolica*'s organizations which participated in the National Unions were also active, often entering into conflict with employers and even with the State.

A number of researchers have pointed out that "concerns with social justice [under the *Estado Novo*] were somewhat autonomous and constituted a certain value per se"[62]; the violently accusatory tone of contemporary reports written by corporatist officials demonstrated the tensions that emerged between the State and employers. There is no doubt that this problem existed among certain sectors of the regime and particularly among young INTP officials. When compared to the Liberal Republican period, however, the more reliable redistribution indicators show a negative balance for

---

[61] See Fátima Patriarca, *Processo de implantação....*
[62] *Idem.*

the *Estado Novo*. This is amply demonstrated by the fact that the only study on State Health and Welfare expenditures during the 1930-45 period shows that the "guarantee of the functioning or the health and welfare system (...) was partially abandoned by the *Estado Novo*, and would only seem to reappear" after the Second World War[63].

It is obvious that employers gained much more from Salazarism. There was peace and social order, wages were kept low, market protection was ensured, particularly with the colonies, and financial stability was guaranteed. All this was ensured through the State's intervention by means of the Organizations of Economic Coordination as well as the "industrial conditioning" law[64]. The most sensitive areas, notably agriculture and exports, were governed by "mandatory cartelization", while the entry of new companies was conditioned.

One important dimension of the corporatist system was the influence of its extremely powerful rural lobby, particularly in the southern latifundia region. Rural policies produced a significant legacy transcending the question of the absence of agricultural reforms. The wheat producers' protectionist lobby was able to convince the government to promote the "wheat campaign" between 1929 and 1936. It was an enormous program designed to support grain production. It was detrimental for the industrial sector which was obliged to buy at prices well above those on the international market. This is but one example of a political system whose ruralist stamp persisted until the end of the 1950s. In the 1930s only the sectors which were less dependent on agriculture escaped more extensive intervention.

"Industrial conditioning" had profound consequences for the structure of Portuguese industry. Government authorization became an integral part of the process of creating new companies. These were even dependent on the State for approval of any changes in 'installed capacity'. This resulted from the protection of the inter-

[63] See Nuno Valério, *As Finanças Publicas Portuguesas no Período entre as Duas Guerras Mundiais*, Ph. D. Thesis, Lisbon University, 1982.

[64] See Fernando Rosas, *Op. Cit.* and José Maria Brandão de Brito, *Op. Cit.*

ests represented by the *Gremios* which conditioned the market entrance of new competitors, thus reducing innovation and the flexibility of the economy. The corporatist model established the infrastructure for the development of Portuguese capitalism in the 1950s. The debate on the impact of its "modernizing" legacy is, however, a far from peaceful one: the system was based on protectionism, import substitution, the development of infrastructure and on the containment of labor. Simply speaking, it favored traditional agriculture and prolonged its social importance without modernizing technology; it "froze" the weaker and dispersed traditional industrial sectors in time, guaranteeing protected markets in the colonies; it offered protected employment to skilled workers at miserable wages, maintaining a good number of the active population occupied with subsistence farming. By the 1950s this part of the population again began to emigrate.

MILITIA AND YOUTH ORGANIZATIONS

Students of the *Estado Novo* have stressed the impact of the electoral victory of the Popular Front and the breaking out of the Civil War in Spain. The possibility of a "red" victory was obviously seen as a threat and the regime's reaction to this challenge was to develop a new political discourse and symbology and to set up two militia organizations. This has been interpreted by many as the "fascistization" of the Salazar regime.

Until the eve of the Spanish Civil War Salazar refused either to create a militia type organization or to permit the top down fascistization of the single party. During the Military Dictatorship a number of attempts to create such bodies failed. In 1934 Salazar crushed Preto's National Syndicalism and refused to take up the offer made by loyal dissidents. In the same year the first youth organization which was backed by the philo-fascist propaganda chief António Ferro, the School Action Vanguard (AEV), was disbanded[65]. In 1936, however, the regime created a para-military

---

[65] See António Costa Pinto and Nuno Afonso Ribeiro, *A Acção Escolar Vanguarda (1933-1936)*, (Lisboa: 1980).

youth organization and permitted the appearance of a militia organization directly inspired by the fascist model.

The Portuguese Legion (LP) was founded in September 1936 in the wake of an anti-communist rally organized by the "National Unions". It resulted from the genuine "pressure" of certain sectors which had recently joined to the regime. Salazar authorized its formation and decreed its strict submission to the government. As was his custom, he moderated its declaration of principles and made the military responsible for it, avoiding the selection of officers who had been prominent in the radical right and within National Syndicalism.

The same sort of "pressure" led to the foundation of the Portuguese Youth (MP). In this case, however, these pressures were stamped out. Various projects aiming to unite youth sectors in a para-military organization to replace the moribund AEV were drawn up by the Education Ministry. Between May and September of 1936 immediately after the MP was founded, there was a tendency towards indiscriminately accepting members including those who were not in the schools. This dynamic was associated to the victory of the Popular Front in Spain. The MP's voluntary character permitted youngsters from the "lower middle classes", business and service employees as well as workers to sign up. During these first months, the MP's social base "approximated that of the National Syndicalist Movement"[66]. This movement was rapidly interrupted, with the transfer of the non-student volunteers to the LP. From then on, the MP embraced only schoolgoing youth. Participation was compulsory and the MP became dependent on a strengthened Ministry of Education. The MP was also rapidly "Christianized", coexisting with other, essentially Catholic, youth organizations due to a campaign of criticism promoted by the Church hierarchy.

The Dictator's authorization of the creation of a more voluntary and politicized militia such as the LP can only be seen in the context of the radicalization provoked by the Spanish Civil War.

[66] See Simon Kuin, *Mocidade Portuguesa: "Mobilization" of Youth during the Portuguese Estado Novo Regime (1936-1974)*, (Florence: 1991) (Mimeo.).

It is interesting to note, however, that this was one of the demands of a splinter group within NS which had led it to abandon Rolão Preto and join Salazarism in 1933. In 1935 a group of corporatist unionists and Preto dissidents had made a similar but failed attempt. The driving force behind the LP was this same group[67]. It is not by chance that the inaugural rally was convoked by the corporatist apparatus, and supported by a number of NS dissidents. Salazar chose Costa Leite (Lumbrales) as the first president of the central committee, a professor from the University of Coimbra who had led the anti-Preto breakaway faction in 1933 with the support of Salazar.

The LP has left a much greater mark on the collective memory of the *Estado Novo* than its scant weight within the regime warrants. Together with the MP, its 30,000 members, "uniformed, disciplined, and instructed", dominated the regime's choreography between 1937 and 1939[68]. With the end of the Civil War in Spain and the discreet return of the Portuguese volunteers who had fought on Franco's side, the LP's presence and even its choreography declined significantly. It was reduced to carrying out actions of provocation and information during the brief post-war electoral campaigns. The LP was right from the start headed by military officers. Even in times of peace it was headed by the Ministry of War. Of its five leading members, two had to be from the military and one a commander. Its district commissions were also entrusted to army officers.

Relations between the LP and the other institutions of the regime were not peaceful. This was particularly the case of relations with the National Union and the MP. Salazar separated the MP from the Legion and all proposals to place it under the control of the latter were rejected. As for the single party, which was always suspicious of militia organizations, it continued to dominate local administration and constituted the principal "channel" of communication between the State and the country as a whole. There was no formal link between these two organizations.

[67] See Luís Nuno Rodrigues, "A Legião Portuguesa...", pp. 21-25.
[68] See Relatório confidencial a Salazar do Presidente da Junta Central da Legião Portuguesa, 27-4-1939, AOS CO-PC, ANTT.

After an initial shakeup, both the Church and the Army had their prerogatives assured by the two institutions. The first kept its organizations and "Christianized" the MP within the context of a school apparatus whose reform it largely led. The second dominated the structure of the Legion and sent an appreciable number of reserve officers into the organization, armed with a salary complement. There were some differences, however, between the two organizations that are worthy of note. Whereas the MP was quickly depoliticized and Christianized, the LP was more of a militia. It was more politicized and it had the discourse, organizational structure and social composition typical of a fascist militia.

Comparison of the two organizations with those of the other European authoritarian and fascist regimes will not be undertaken here. But it worth pointing out that they were much more modest and much more strictly dependent on the State apparatus. Their fleeting presence on the political scene, and their choreographic nature in particular meant that they were never as developed as their counterparts, even if one takes into account the Vichy example, whose ideological and political precepts were close to Salazarism. With the Spanish Civil War over, the LP feared that it would be relegated to a secondary role, and put pressure on Salazar in order that it would not be dissolved. It was claimed that "there is still much to do in our patriotic reinvigoration, and the Legion thus believes that its mission should not be terminated"[69]. Salazar did not dissolve it but it went into irreversible decline nonetheless.

***

When referring to the rise of single-party systems, Giovanni Sartori emphasizes that "the more modernized and/or developed the society, the more anti-partyism gives way to uni-partyism — at least in the sense that the latter solution is revealed to be much less fragile and much more efficient than the former"[70]. The above seems to be the case of authoritarian and fascist regime experi-

---

[69] *Idem*, p. 10.
[70] See Giovanni Sartori, *Op. Cit.*, p. 61.

ences between the world wars. Indeed, in the liberal and democratic countries in which there were parties with a popular base and eliciting widespread political participation, the ensuing single regime party was generally more important and a better mobilizer, independently of the degree of its dependency upon the state.

The single parties in Spain or Italy, although dependent and controlled, exerted many functions within the political system which are absent in Portugal. This difference is undoubtedly due to the prior existence in both countries of fascist parties and strong right-wing movements. In both Spain and Italy the new single party manifested several tendencies. In Italy it was the fascist party that assimilated other groups, such as the Nationalists[71]. In Spain there was greater parity in the movement given the relative weakness of the Falange. In Portugal, the right-wing parties responsible for the overthrow of the liberal order had never been more than ideological pressure groups or clusters of "notables". They drew their strength from two central institutions: the Army and the Church. Some of the reasons for the relative weakness of Salazarism's single party have already been considered. Comparison, however, permits the addition of various other elements. The emergence of National Syndicalism reflected the intention of creating a mass fascist party. Ironic as it may seem, its rapid growth seems to confirm, albeit in a limited way, the factors governing the political modernization of Portuguese society, particularly of the urban centers.

From this perspective, the UN appears to be one of the single parties closest to the "anti-party" ideal proclaimed in official discourse. Apart from its functions as a legitimizer of the new regime and its "exclusion" of activist candidates, it was important as an instrument for the "political channeling" of local notables rather than the masses.[72] One may even venture to say that, if in Italian fascism the government controlled and directed party mobiliza-

---

[71] See Emilio Gentile, "La natura e la storia del partito nazionale fascista nelle interpretazione dei contemporanei e degli storici", *Stória Contemporanea*, n°3, Giugno 1985, pp. 521-607.

[72] See Giovanni Sartori, *Op. Cit.*, p. 63.

tion, the National Union in Portugal was a state agency responsible both for the "integration" of local elites and broad political "demobilization".

Institutions like the MP and LP were based on the Fascist example, but they were channels of nothing which was essential. Almost all the other dictatorships of the period showed similar characteristics and inspirations but basically the Portuguese "New State" did not share the mobilization tensions of its Fascist counterparts. The regime isolated the small urban universe, distrusted even mass mobilization and relied on four important forces: the police, bureaucracy, local notables and the church.

The regime skillfully mingled the administration and party, which included notables, relied on the traditional élites and on the political police to maintain the social order. The cooperation of the church was sufficient to maintain the provinces in a state of unchanging peace. In the south, dominated by large estates where the agricultural proletariat was active, the police was more alert. In the rural areas in the rest of the country, however, this was unnecessary.

4. 3 STATE, POLITICS, AND SOCIETY

NATIONALISM, CATHOLICISM AND EMPIRE

Salazarism did not represent a clear break with the fundamentals of modern Portuguese nationalism of the turn of the century. As one Portuguese historian has said, "The 'New State' amply, coherently and totally defined discourse on national tradition faithful to the positivist theoretical model, even though serving political objectives that were contrary to the republican movement that preceded it in power and in use."[73]

---

[73] See Fernando Marques da Costa, "Imaginário histórico, imaginário político", in *Nação e Defesa*, 46, April-June, 1988, p.11.

What Salazarism did do with notable tenacity, was to consolidate and "massify" within the cultural fabric the late 19th century idea of "national regeneration"[74]: The colonial dimension and "imperial" pretensions of Portugal as the heart of Portuguese identity and national independence; a historicist nationalism that peaked during the discoveries, i.e., a Portugal small in Europe but large in global terms[75]. Two important dimensions were later added: the reconciliation between traditionalist Catholicism and corporatism, henceforth both considered as emanating a "national tradition" which had been threatened and almost destroyed at the turn of the century by the secularizing adventures of "imported" liberalism[76]. Catholicism reemerged tightly woven into the "nation's" historic formation through its ritual and through official discourse, thus reinforcing the idea of Portugal's medieval genesis in the process of the "Christian reconquest". A true "re-christianization" was undertaken from the early 1930s onwards. Beyond the immediate function of "eliminating class conflicts", corporatism became the official ideology. With an "organic" Medieval Portugal as a paradigm, the image which the "New State" hoped to foster was that of "a society without conflicts", be these political, social, local or cultural.

With the "New State", the movement to "reinvent the past" took a qualitative leap forward, as demonstrated by the cultural strategy of the Propaganda apparatus, or the museological policy of restoring national monuments. Any memory of Arab culture and of cultural diversity in general, already weak even in the south of the country, was the target of disdain or covered by silence. The north, the "Christian cradle of nationhood" was valued above all. It was symbolically represented by Guimarães, a small Northern city

---

[74] On this topic see, Ronald W. Sousa, *The Rediscoverers. Major Writers in The Portuguese Literature of National Regeneration*, (University Park and London: 1981), and Roger Griffin, *Op. Cit.*

[75] See Valentim Alexandre, "Ideologia, economia, e política. A questão colonial na implantação do Estado Novo", *Análise Social*, 123-124, 1993, pp. 1117-1136.

[76] António Costa Pinto and Nuno G. Monteiro, "Probleme der nationalen...", pp. 15-26.

which had been the first seat of the medieval kingdom. The preservation strategy for national monuments consisted of the notably efficient reconstruction of all symbols of the "Christian reconquest", particularly of castles as well as military fortresses in general. Whenever possible, any memories of the North African presence were eliminated. National heroes from the time of the nation's foundation or its maritime conquests became the objects of well-programmed graphic, cinematographic, and monumental development. The regime used all these mass means as best it could.

An eminently "organicist" conception dominated the image that the regime tried to project of itself and of the country. As far as propaganda was concerned, it could be said that the project of the Integralist radical right, blessed by social Catholicism, was applied. It was indeed in the cultural field that the similarities to regimes like that of Vichy were most obvious.

The myth of the "empire" was also central to the ideology of the "New State" and the effort to create a colonial mentality through the school apparatus and propaganda reached its height during this period. A series of colonial exhibitions were organized in the 1930s and propaganda on the "colonial world" reached its zenith with the 1940 "Portuguese World Exposition". The survival of the colonies was at the heart of the nationalism of the *Estado Novo*, and it was the key variable in the Dictatorship's foreign policy which was clearly fearful of any Nazi German or Fascist Italian expansion outside Europe. After the Second World War and in anticipation of the resistance to decolonization, Salazar changed the "imperial" rigidity of the 1930s, favoring a more "pluri-racial and pluricontinental" model. As the international scene turned progressively hostile, colonialism gradually became "the regime's fifth essence" and "replaced corporatism" as the ideological heart of the *Estado Novo*[77].

---

[77] See Boaventura Sousa Santos, quoted in Manuel Braga da Cruz, *O Partido...*, p. 45.

The Propaganda Apparatus

In 1933 the regime created the SPN headed by António Ferro. In the cultural field, Ferro had nothing to do with Salazar and was a cosmopolitan journalist connected to futurist and modernist circles and an admirer of Fascism since the 1920s[78]. He enjoyed the dictator's confidence and, depending on him directly, Ferro created a machine which greatly exceeded the needs of Salazar's image management. Although he had little to do with the Leader's provincial integrism, or perhaps precisely because of this, António Ferro gave the regime a "cultural project" which skillfully combined "modern" aesthetic resources with a true "re-invention of tradition". It was the SPN that coordinated and fed the regime's press, ran the censorship services, organized the mass demonstrations sporadically 'transported' to the capital and that encouraged the leisure activities designed for the popular classes in close association with the corporatist apparatus. It also organized numerous activities for the élites and promoted cultural relations with foreign countries. The SPN was skillful in recruiting intellectuals and artists who, without Ferro's "modernistic" intervention, would hardly have been attracted by the profile of the Head of Government.

The cultural combination of modern and traditional was openly dominated by the latter. Like other authoritarian regimes, Salazarism's cultural project sought the "systematic restoration of traditional values."[79]. Particular attention was given to a whole "ethnographic/folkloric" movement which included the revitalization of local folk groups, the restoration of the symbols of the "Christian reconquest" as well as the social deployment of these images. The title "most Portuguese" became the object of official competitions such as the "most Portuguese village in Portugal", destined to "increase in the Portuguese the cult of tradition", developing

[78] See Artur Portela, *Salazarismo e Artes Plásticas*, (Lisboa: 1982), and Jorge do O, "Salazarismo e cultura", Joel Serrão and A. H. Oliveira Marques (Dir. de), *Op. Cit.*, pp. 391-454.
[79] See Christian Faure, *Le projet Culturel de Vichy. Folklore et Révolution Nationale, 1940-1944*, (Lyon: 1989), p. 7.

one of the basic elements of the traditionalist nationalism of the "New State": the village as microcosm of a traditional society, without conflicts, "harmonic", god-fearing, and immune to urban and dissipating vices[80]. The SPN can also take credit for the great majority of the statuary on nationalist intervention in 20th century Portugal as well as the introduction of popular cinema exploring historical themes.

In 1940 the "New State" organized a huge commemorative fair: the "Portuguese World Exposition". It celebrated two of the nation's most mythic dates: the 1140 "founding of the nation" and the reconquest of independence in 1640 following 60 years of Spanish occupation. Taking place in Lisbon at a time when the rest of Europe was involved in a war, it perhaps represented the "ideal type" of Salazarist nationalism at its apogee: an old nation with a glorious maritime past and possessing an empire that extended from the Minho in the North of Portugal to Timor, part of an island shared with Holland until decolonization[81].

Selective censorship also clearly indicated the "organicist" ideal type. In a society where conflict had theoretically been abolished, nothing was published that might testify to its existence. Indeed the regime did not ban or systematically dissolve the publications which supported the opposition. These publications survived throughout the thirties, isolated or reduced to an intellectual readership who were allowed to engage in debates about the social significance of art or the German-Soviet pact as long as they stayed strictly within the limits of Lisbon's cafés and stayed well away from the working class. As for the rural and provincial bastions, Salazar did not have to worry about them as he trusted traditional structures. As Salazar once said "politically speaking, only what the public knows to exist exists (...)"[82]. Needless to say, the censors were ruthless when it came to compulsory "social peace".

[80] See Joaquim Pais de Brito, "O Estado Novo e a aldeia mais portuguesa de Portugal", AA.VV., *O Fascismo em Portugal...*, p. 508.

[81] See Jorge Ramos do O, "Modernidade e Tradição -Algumas reflexões em torno da Exposição do Mundo Português", AA.VV., *O Estado Novo. Das Origens...*, pp. 177-185.

[82] See Oliveira Salazar, *Discursos...*, p. 259.

The School System: "God, Fatherland, Family"

The *Estado Novo* paid obsessive ideological attention to education. This was not synonymous with a will to modernize, particularly in the 1930s. This once came later in the 1950s. The debate on the advantages of illiteracy became famous, and in 1933 even Salazar said that "the constitution of vast elites is more important than teaching the people to read". What was at stake was the primarily ideological reorganization of what had been the pride of the liberal republican elites: The secular state-run school, particularly at the primary level.

The "ideal type" Salazarist ideology - "God, Fatherland, Family, Work" - affected professors who were ideologically controlled, led to the authorization of single textbooks and to a special decoration of classrooms. More than any imperialist and combative mystique, it was the value of resignation and obedience that characterized new primary school teaching, as well as the values of an "organic" society that had no knowledge of conflict or "politics" clearly reserved for a paternalistic elite headed by Salazar. Christianization was another official obsession which affected everything from the contents and the decoration of classrooms to school rituals.

From the 1930s onward the educational system rigidly codified the "official" version of Portuguese history which was be revised and its relative pluralism eliminated to fulfill the slogan "everything for the nation, nothing against it". As early as 1932 the Minister of Education drew up a new policy that greatly strengthened "the family as a social cell", "faith, as (...) an element of national unity and solidarity", "authority" and "respect for the hierarchy" as "principles of the social life"[83]. The heroes of the past were purged of all vices, and their saintliness eventually confirmed by scientific investigation. The sole objective of the "Maritime Discoveries", for example, was noted to be the "spreading of the faith and of the empire", and the positivist view of the discoveries as a "mercantile adventure" was eliminated[84].

[83] Quoted in Arlindo Caldeira, "Heróis e Vilãos na Mitologia Salazarista", *Penélope*, n° 15, (Forhcoming).

[84] See Maria Filomena Mónica, *Op. Cit.*, p. 303.

The youth organizations of the Regime were set up within the framework of the nationalist and Catholic reform of the education system. Rather than promoting the modernization of the school system, the *Estado Novo* controlled what it inherited. Spending on schools remained stagnant from 1930 to 1960, although the ideological control of professors and students progressively increased. Once the early confusion had been overcome, the MP became a para-scholastic instrument for training under the aegis of the Education Ministry. The former focused on the training of youth in high schools to which, until the leap forward in the 1950s, only the urban middle classes had access.

The education ministry founded an official women's and women's youth organization when the separation of the sexes in high schools began. Education was an area in which an increasing number of women professionals were involved (in 1940 76% of primary school teachers and 33% of those in high schools were women)[85].

It was under Salazarism's first National Assembly in 1934 that three women deputies entered the building of the Portuguese Parliament for the first time. Their number was always small, but their arrival was praised even by what remained of the Portuguese feminist press of the 1920s. Salazar announced the fact as "a novelty" in an interview with a Lisbon daily paper during his preparations to choose the regime's first deputies: "in both the one and the other Chamber there will be a number of women, which doesn't mean that the State or they themselves have been converted to feminism".

The first three deputies, although conservative, Catholic, and unmarried, were not members of the single party or the small fascist movements, but of the school apparatus. One of them, Maria Guardiola, the principal of one of the capital's high schools, played a central role in the creation of Salazarism's women's organizations. Their speeches in the National Assembly had mostly to do

[85] See Anne Cova and António Costa Pinto, "Femmes et Salazarisme", Christine Fauré (Sous la dir. de), *Encyclopédie politique et historique des femmes*, (Paris: Forthcoming).

with teaching, namely proposing the introduction of courses dealing in child welfare, the reform of the school system, guided by the "principles of doctrine and Christian morality traditional in the country".

In 1936, following a study trip to fascist Italy by a group of women, among them Maria Guardiola, the *Estado Novo* set up the Mothers' Work for National Education (*Obra das Mães para a Educação Nacional* — OMEN) as a dependency of the Ministry of Education and, a year later, the Portuguese Female Youth (MPF). OMEN's leaders mostly coincided with those of the official female youth organization[86]. The national commissioner of the latter, Maria Guardiola, remained at the top position for 30 years, stepping down only in 1968.

OMEN was dependent on the Education Ministry, and as such it had at its center a core of women loyal to Salazar and his regime. Its patrons were figures from Lisbon's social elite, and at times the aristocracy. Delegations were founded in the main cities, but its activity was mainly within the area of ideology. Once the Portuguese Female Youth had been created, OMEN formally continued as an organization with autonomous functions, but in reality it never grew. Besides overseeing the new group, it continued to organize the annual "mothers week", among other duties, along with the official youth organization.

With no organic connections to its male counterpart, the MPF had as the main theme of its statutes the education of young women "in the love of God, Fatherland, and family" as well as the training of "Christian and Portuguese women"[87]. Nationalist training, evidently more important in the men's sector, was in the case of women almost entirely replaced by the cult of the medieval queens of Portugal, especially Queen Leonor, the founder of aid organizations, as well as by the cult of the Virgin Mary. "Home economics", hygiene and nursing, as well as "maternal science - the most useful science for family and Country", were the basis of education[88].

[86] See Vitória De Grazia, *How Fascism Ruled Women. Italy, 1922-1945*, (Berkeley: 1991).
[87] *Mocidade Portuguesa Feminina* (Lisboa: Sd), p. 6.
[88] *Idem*.

CHURCH, STATE AND SOCIETY

It would be difficult to fully comprehend the political system and the ideological foundations of the "New State" without taking into account the determining influence of traditionalist Catholicism present in all of the regime's major texts and institutions, from the Constitution, the declaration of the principles of corporatism, the weakness of the party and the paramilitary organizations to propaganda. Many of the definitions of the type "clerico/..." analyzed above represent attempts to take this essential dimension into account. It is a dimension comparable with similar phenomena under Franco, Dolfuss and even Vichy. All of these received important support from the Catholic Church and, like the Portuguese case, were also set up after republican secularization programs.

The Portuguese Catholic Church did not only contribute towards the ideological mould of the regime. Apart from all the Catholic symbolism that the regime used with the explicit approval of the Church hierarchy, there was an actual "christianization" policy in all institutions and especially in the school system.

When some organizations directly inspired by Fascism were created, (MP and LP) they were immediately taken over by the religious services, omnipresent in both institutions. In the case of the youth organization, a sensitive matter indeed in Church-State relations under the Fascist regimes, care was taken to neither dissolve nor integrate the Catholic organizations which maintained their autonomy, as well as to ensure their influence over official organization.

The close association between the Church and the State in Salazarism transcended a mere convergence of interests; it is possible to speak of an ideological and political nucleus common to the Church and the regime, including corporatism, anti-liberalism and anti-communism.

Catholic Church and Fascism

The Portuguese Catholic Church hierarchy and the Catholic Center Party, key elements of the political periphery of the Dictatorship since the Consulate of Gomes da Costa, acted as in important brake on fascist and radical right-wing groups and tendencies that had emerged since 1926. Their progressive rise was slow and cautious, particularly during the period of the regime's institutionalization. One of the reasons for this prudence was doubtless the strong influence of the conservative republicans, even among the high level officers who headed the Dictatorship, though the presence of the Catholic Center at the ministerial level was immediate and decisive.

Despite this support, both the Constitution and the regime's fundamental texts maintained the formal separation of Church and State, and the *Estado Novo* did not transform itself into a "confessional state" as under neighboring Francoism. The history books record the episode between Salazar and Cardinal Cerejeira, a close friend from Salazar's youth and the head of the Catholic Church during the *Estado Novo*. The latter wrote him reminding him that he was prime minister as "an emissary of the friends of God". Salazar answered in a speech that he was there "by the legal nomination of the President of the Republic"[89]. On the other hand, when Salazar founded his single party, he immediately called for the dissolution of his own party, the Catholic Center, provoking some tension.

During the phase of institutionalization of the regime, the Church starting fighting the fascist parties. Their attitude towards National Syndicalism was one of radical denunciation. Whenever possible, they expressed their fear at the possibility that those in Power (particularly certain members of the Military) might in some way support the fascists. From the autumn of 1932 onwards, the attacks increased. NS's political and ideological attitudes were considered anti-Catholic, reminiscent of the old quarrels between the Catholic Church and *Action Française*, and Italian fascism. The more "officious" Catholic press condemned "pagan and agnostic nationalism disdainful of eternal destinies as a heresy which adored the deified State".

Thus emerged the most systematic refutation of NS's ideas and political practice from the perspective of Social Catholicism. This

---

[89] See Franco Nogueira, *Op. Cit.*, Vol. II, pp. 9 -11.

criticism of NS anticipated some of the Church hierarchy's resistance, when the Salazar regime founded a number of organizations susceptible to threatening what the Church considered to be its own territory some years later. At a time the hierarchy looked to the central task of a "new crusade for the Christian reconquest of Portugal", the Church reacted against any fascist attempt to take up this space.

Although the "Catholicization" of the *Estado Novo*'s institutions was a founding element of Salazarism, the Church feared the possible totalitarian bent of some state organizations after 1936, as well as the possibility of the "forced integration" of its youth organizations within official, Catholicized bodies. This fear, however, turned out to be groundless. On the contrary, the regime "offered" the church the symbolic and ideological structuring of large sectors of society, particularly those closer to traditional rural society, and opened up social space for the Church's own organizations. When Salazar institutionalized the *Estado Novo* and his Catholic Center Party was disbanded, he gave the Church hierarchy the task of "rechristianizing" the country after decades of Republican and Liberal secularization. The Catholic Center was restricted to the social arena and barred from the political arena.

Catholic Church and Society

The Portuguese Catholic Action (ACP) was founded in 1933 by the episcopate and acted as a guarantee of collaborative autonomy with Salazarism and its institutions for many years, particularly the corporatist ones[90]. Strictly dependent on the hierarchy and present in a number of governmental organizations, the Catholic bodies represented a powerful instrument of conservative socialization with only occasional centers of dissidence, particularly after 1945. The large number of clerics in the leadership of the movement's groups reduced tensions between the regime and the sectors closest to the corporatist system, although these did nonetheless occasionally crop up.

---

[90] See Maria Inácia Rezola, "Breve panorama da situação da Igreja e da religião católica em Portugal (1930-1960)", Joel Serrão and A. H. Oliveira Marques (Dir. de), *Op. Cit.*, pp. 222-255.

In Portugal, therefore, apart from the Catholicization of the official organizations, the Church successfully resisted all attempts at integration. It maintained and developed Catholic Action. Catholic Scouts were never abolished and developed alongside the MP. The Catholic Action organizations linked to the corporatist system maintained their autonomy. A significant private and Catholic education sector emerged. Without great difficulty the Church won over republican conservative resistance and fascistizing tendencies.

Discourse and action by the *Estado Novo*, and by the Church hierarchy reached their zenith in the late 1930s. In 1940 the concordat that crowned the commitment between the Church and the regime was issued, setting the rules for the close collaboration which was de facto already common practice. The last of the republican legislation to be abolished with the concordat was divorce, which was prohibited in the case of religious marriages. Soon after, a revision of the constitution included the phrase that the Catholic religion was "the religion of the Portuguese nation"[91].

The *Estado Novo* thus gave the Church, as stated by Salazar, "the possibility to reconstruct (...) and recuperate (...) their leading position in the formation of the Portuguese soul", and the Church, in the words of Pope Pius XII, labeled Portugal a model, where "the Lord has provided the Portuguese nation with an exemplary head of government"[92].

When the ideological vitality of the regime began to diminish, especially after 1945, the Church gradually became the New State's ideological haven and the vitality of the Catholic organizations increased. Early in the 1940s, the Catholic Action organizations already had almost 70,000 members, most of them in youth organizations. In 1956 their number surpassed 100,000[93]. At the popular level, the Fátima phenomenon, "managed" by the hierarchy and the regime, symbolized the two ideological pillars of the *Estado Novo*'s survival after 1945 — Catholicism and anti-communism. Only the crisis and the war which affected the third pillar, colo-

---

[91] See Manuel Braga da Cruz, "As relações entre o Estado e a Igreja...", p. 211.
[92] *Idem.*
[93] See Maria Inácia Rezola, "Breve panorama...", p. 238.

nialism, created a number of cracks in the armor in the period of decadence.

Traditionalist Catholicism and the Church, the ideology and the institution, were, on the one hand, one of the dictatorship's most powerful elements and yet, on the other hand, limited the regime's fascistization, in effect becoming the main driving force behind the "limited pluralism" of the *Estado Novo*.

4.4 SALAZARISM, FASCISM, AUTHORITARIANISM

Many students of Fascism using the binomial authoritarianism/ totalitarianism tend to emphasize the fact that regimes like Salazar' were non-mobilizing. If this is understood merely as synonymous with an absence of extensive mobilization and of totalitarian tendencies, this is certainly true. Even during the "Fascist Era", the "New State" was deeply conservative and relied more on traditional bodies like the Church and the provincial élites than on mass organizations. It did, however, ensure social control by creating a whole cultural and socializing apparatus to which it intended to link its ideology.

Salazar once said to Henry Massis that his aim was to "make Portugal live by habit"[94]. Apart from the conscious demagogy of the statement, this "maitre-mot" which so delighted his French supporter perfectly sums up the traditionalism of Salazarism. A functionalistic interpretation might argue that Salazar's dictatorship did not undergo the totalitarian tension of Fascism because it did not need it, given the nature of Portuguese society at the time. This interpretation, however, does not wash since this tension existed in societies either as industrialized as or less industrialized than the Portuguese. Salazarism was, rather, voluntarily non-totalitarian and allowed most of the population to "live habitually" as long as they did not "get mixed up in politics", an activity reserved for the ruling minority.

---

[94] Quoted by João Medina, *Salazar em França,* (Lisboa: 1977), p. 50.

It is, nonetheless, a mistake to confuse Salazar's regime with a "pragmatic" dictatorship, at least in the period under study (1933-45). Salazarism officially instituted an "organic" vision of society and persevered in using all the ideological and social instruments of control, administrative, corporative, educational, propagandistic as well as the elite, the state and Church, to make that vision a reality. On the other hand, it reinforced the presence of the state in the economy, limited the autonomy of the economic élites and disciplined them with an iron hand.

SALAZARISM AND THE EUROPEAN AUTHORITARIAN WAVE

From the perspective of cultural origins and ideology as expressed in official discourse, the Dictatorships closest to Salazarism were obviously those where Maurrasianism and Catholicism dominated -the cases of a dominant sector in Francoism, Vichy, or the Dolfuss regime. When comparing transitions to fascism and its essential agents, the fall of liberalism and the military dictatorship which ensued was an integral part of the authoritarian cycle of the 1920s. This is especially the case in those transitions which were caused by military interventions supported by right wing parties. Examples of the latter include Hungary in 1919, Poland, Greece as well as Lithuania in 1926.

Nonetheless, of all the European Dictatorships which emerged in the 1920s, Salazar's *Estado Novo* was the most institutionalized and the one that lasted the longest. The second element, is less important as far as this study is concerned. Had severe international constraints not existed at the time, many of the dictatorships in the countries on Europe's southern and eastern periphery would probably have survived with features quite similar to the Salazar Dictatorship. Regimes such as Pilsudski's in Poland, or Smetona's in Lithuania, and later Dolfuss's Austria and Horthy's Hungary emerged as integral parts of the same post-war authoritarian wave and had features rather close to those that presided over the institutionalization of Portuguese authoritarianism. Conditioning factors that were more external than internal were responsible for the "freezing" of the institutionalization of those regimes, leaving the rising process of "political engineering" unfinished.

All these dictatorships were established on the heels of traditional coups d'état; they represented a compromise between civilian and military conservatives; they set up single party or hegemonic party political systems; the fascist parties were either minor partners in the coalitions that took power or were absent. In varying degrees, the elites and political movements that inspired the Dictatorships were influenced by fascism, but the principles, the agents of institutionalization and the type of dictatorship they founded largely transcended the specificity of fascism. These authoritarian regimes, "as defined in the Linzian taxonomy, became the typical response to the pressures of mass politics and modernization in most of Southern and Southeastern Europe during the interwar period."[95]. Some of their features effectively became the dominant model for 20th century rightist dictatorships.

FASCISM: MOVEMENT AND REGIME

There are numerous generic definitions of Fascism, but few of "Fascist regimes". The definitions limit themselves to the characteristics associated to the movements as well as the classification of associated regimes with political systems in which the values, methods, and political action of the Fascists penetrated the Dictatorships[96].

It is clear that the fascistization of the dictatorial regimes was linked to the movement, its ability to influence the State and institutions as well as to mediate its relationship with society. The specificity of the fascist phenomenon lies precisely in this movement-State-society tension as well as in the "degree of fascistization". It was stronger in National Socialist Germany than in Fascist Italy, but was also strongly felt in other dictatorial regimes. Thus

---

[95] See Stanley G. Payne, "Authoritarianism in the Smaller States of Southern Europe", H. E. Chehabi and Alfred Stepan (edited by), *Politics, Society and Democracy. Comparative Studies (essays in honor of Juan J. Linz)*, (Boulder: Forthcoming).

[96] See Stanley G. Payne, *Historia del Fascismo* (Madrid: Forthcoming).

Francoism's first phase (1939-45), Romania under the short legionary regime, or Hungary under the Arrow Cross, more closely approached the specificity of fascism than regimes such as Salazar's. Like most authoritarian regimes in southern and eastern Europe, Salazarism was decisively influenced by Italian fascism, but was affected neither by the specificity of the "movement" nor by the more totalitarian turn of the late 1930s. In other words, as noted by one Portuguese researcher, the comparison would have to focus on the institutions and the workings of the political system. A segment of the Portuguese authoritarian elite would come to believe in the Mussolini of the 1920s, who disciplined the Fascist party, reconciled with the Catholic Church, and was an apologist for "order", the "authoritarian" dictator of compromise with the Italian reactionary right. Yet even so, Salazarism and the core of its political elite did not identify with Mussolini as a charismatic leader, and even less so in his party.

Salazarism, like other similar regimes, sent study missions to Italy and adopted models which it changed and adapted. The statutes of corporatism, Propaganda, and the official organization of youth and women are some examples of the institutions set up along Fascist lines. They implied the adoption of certain requisites of mass politics by essentially reactionary regimes. These institutions, however, were limited and co-existed with others, not aiming for exclusive domination; they also did not experience the control of the fascist party. Although all the dictatorships of the period share elements of the Fascist model and were, in some cases, inspired by it when creating some of their institutions, they are still different in this one essential aspect.

It is not suprising therefore that the Salazarist example was often cited by contemporary dictators or radical right wing movements as an example. There are multiple quotes that show this, many of them previously quoted, such as those of General Pétain's Vichy and *Action Française*, of Eastern European intellectuals such as Manoilescu as well as of Hungarian reactionaries. In Italy itself it was the monarchists and the Catholics who looked to the Portuguese example. Even General Metaxas referred to Salazar as a close example, with one diplomat saying that "Portugal under Dr. Salazar, not the Germany of Hitler or the Italy of Mussolini, provided the nearest analogy" with his regime[97] .

---

[97] See John Kofas, *Op. Cit.*, p. 186.

Bibliography

Reference to most of the sources (namely from public archives in Lisbon and Rome) and works consulted in the preparation of this book can be found in the footnotes to the text.

The bibliography is divided into three sections: (1) general studies dealing with political theory and comparative politics that the author found particularly useful; (2) general studies and essays on Fascism and Authoritarianism; (3) studies dealing with the *Estado Novo* and the Salazar era.

1- General Studies

Almond, Gabriel A., and G. B. Powell, *Comparative Politics. A Developmental Approach* (Boston: 1966).

Arendt, H., *The Origins of Totalitarianism* (New York: 1951).

Aron, Raymond, *Sociologie des Sociétés Industrielles. Esquisse d'une théorie des régimes politiques* (Paris: 1958).

Berg-Schlosser, Dirk, and Mitchell, Jeremy (Edited by), *Crises, Compromise, Collapse. Conditions for Democracy in Interwar Europe* (London: Forthcoming).

Friedrich, Carl J., and Zbigniew K. Brzezinski, *Totalitarian Dictatorship and Autocracy* (Cambridge: 1956).

Hermet, Guy, *Aux Frontières de la Démocratie* (Paris: 1983).

Huntington, Samuel P., and Clement H. Moore (Edited by), *Authoritarian Politics in Modern Society* (New York: 1970).

Linz, Juan J., and Alfred Stepan (Edited by), *The Breakdown of Democratic Regimes* (Baltimore: 1978).

Lipset, Seymour M., *Political Man: the social bases of politics* (New York: 1959).

Menze, Ernst A., (Edited by), *Totalitarianism Reconsidered* (Port Washington: 1981).

Moore Jr., Barrington, *Social Origins of Dictatorship and Democracy: Lord and Peasant in the Making of the Modern World* (Boston: 1966).

Moore, Clement H., "The Single Party as Source of Legitimacy" in Samuel P. Huntington and Clement H. Moore (Edited by), *Op. Cit.*, (New York: 1970), pp. 49-72.

Morlino, Leonardo, *Come cambiano i regime politici. Strumenti di analisi* (Milano: 1980).

Mouzelis, Nicos, *Politics in the Semi-Periphery. Early Parliamentarism and Late Industrialization in the Balkans and Latin America* (London: 1986).

O'Donnell, Guillermo, *Modernization and Bureaucratic-Authoritarianism* (Berkeley: 1973).

Organski, A. F. K., *The Stages of Political Development* (New York: 1965).

Sartori, Giovanni, *Parties and Party Systems-A framework for analysis* (Cambridge: 1976).

——, *The Theory of Democracy Revisited* (Chatham, New Jersey: 1987).

Schmitter, Philippe C., Et Alli (Edited by), *Transitions From Authoritarian Rule. Southern Europe* (Baltimore and London:1986).

Williamson, Peter, *Corporatism in Perspective. An introductory guide to corporatist theory* (London: 1989).

2- Studies on Fascism and Authoritarianism

AA VV, *Historikerstreit* (München: 1987).

Aquarone, Alberto, *L'Organizzazione dello Stato Totalitario* (Torino: 1965).

Ayçoberry, Pierre, *La Question Nazie. Les interprétations du National Socialisme.1922-1975* (Paris: 1979).

Azéma, Jean-Pierre et Bédarida, François, (Sous la direction de), *Vichy et les Français* (Paris: 1992).

Beetham, David, *Marxists in Face of Fascism* (Manchester: 1983).

Blinkhorn, Martin, (Edited by), *Fascists and the Conservatives* (London: 1990).

Borejsza, Jerzy W., *Il Fascismo e L'Europa Orientale. Dalla propaganda all'aggressione* (Roma-Bari: 1981).

Botz, Gerhard, *Krisenzonen einer Demokratie. Gewalt, Streit und Konfliktunterdrückung in Österreich seit 1918* (Frankfurt:1987).

Bourderon, Roger, *Le Fascisme. Idéologie et pratiques. Essai d'analyse comparée* (Paris: 1979).

Bracher, Karl Dietrich, *The German Dictatorship* (Harmonsdsworth: 1978).

——, e Valani, Leo, (A Cura Di), *Fascismo e Nacional Socialismo* (Bologna: 1986).

Brooker, Paul, *The Faces of Fraternalism. Nazi Germany, Fascist Italy, and Imperial Japan* (Oxford: 1991).

Burrin, Philippe, *La Dérive Fasciste. Doriot, Déat, Bergery, 1933-1945* (Paris: 1986).

Carstein, F. L., *The Rise of Fascism* (Berkeley: 1967).

Collotti, Enzo, *Fascismo, Fascismi* (Firenze: 1989).

Delzell, Charles F., *Mediterranean Fascism. 1919-1945* (New York: 1970).

De Felice, Renzo, *Mussolini. Il revoluzionario, 1883-1920* (Torino: 1965).

——, *Le Interpretazioni del Fascismo* (Bari: 1969).

——, *Intrevista sul fascismo*, a cura di M. A. Ledeen (Bari: 1975).

——, *Il Fascismo. Le interpretazioni dei contemporanei e degli storici* (Bari: 1970).

De Grazia, Victoria, *The Culture of Consent: Mass organization of Leisure in Fascist Italy* (Cambridge: 1981).

Dobkowski, Michael N., and Wallimann, Isidor, (Ed. by), *Radical Perspectives on the Rise of Fascism in Germany, 1919-1945* (New York: 1989).

Dobry, Michel, "Février 1934 et la découverte de l'allergie de la société française à la "Révolution fasciste", *Revue Française de Sociologie*, XXX, 1989, pp. 511-533.

Eatwell, Roger, and O'Sullivan, Noël, *The Nature of the Right* (London: 1989).

——, "Towards a New Model of Genetic Fascism", *Journal of Theoretical Politics*, 4-1°, April 1992, pp. 1-68.

Gentile, Emilio, *Le Origini dell'Ideologia Fascista* (Bari: 1975).

——, *Il Mito dello Stato Nuovo dall'Antigiolittismo al Fascismo* (Bari:1982).

——, *Storia del partito fascista, 1919-1922. Movimento e milizia* (Bari: 1989).

——, *Il Culto del Littorio* (Bari: 1993).

Germani, Gino, *Autoritarismo, Fascismo e Classi Sociali* (Bologna: 1975).

Gregor, A. James, *The Fascist Persuasion in Radical Politics* (Princeton: 1974).

Griffin, Roger, *The Nature of Fascism* (London: 1991).

Jaccobelli, Jader, (a cura di), *Il fascismo e gli storici oggi* (Bari: 1988).

Kershow, Irwin, *The Nazi Dictatorship. Problems of Interpretation* (London: 1985).

Kofas, John V., *Authoritarianism in Greece. The Metaxas Regime* (Boulder: 1983).

Laqueur, Walter, (Edited by), *Fascism. A Reader's Guide. Analyses, Interpretations, Bibliography* (Berkeley: 1976).

Larsen, Stein U., et alli (Edited by), *Who Were the Fascists. Social Roots of European Fascism* (Bergen:1980).

——, et alli (Edited by), *Fascism and European Literature* (Bern and New York: 1991).

——, et alli (Edited by), *Modern Europe after Fascism* (New York: Forthcoming).

Ledeen, M. A., *Universal Fascism* (New York: 1972).

Lee, Stephen J., *The European Dictatorships. 1918-1945* (London: 1988).

Levine, R., *The Vargas Regime: The Critical Years, 1934-1938* (New York: 1970).

Linz, Juan J., "An Authoritarian Regime: Spain" Erik Allardt and Stein Rokkan (Edited by), *Mass Politics. Studies in Political Sociology* (New York: 1970), pp. 251-283.

——, "Totalitarian and Authoritarian Regimes" in F. Greenstein and N. Polsby (Edited by), *Handbook of Political Science* (Reading, Mas.: 1975), vol. 3, pp.175-411.

—— , "Some notes toward a Comparative Study of Fascism in Sociological Historical Perspective", in Walter Laqueur (Edited by), *Op. Cit.,* (Berkeley: 1976), pp. 3-121.

—— , "Political Space and Fascism as a Late-Comer", in Stein Ugelvik Larsen et alli (Edited by), *Op. Cit.*, pp. 153-189.

—— , *Fascism, Breakdown of Democracy, Authoritarian and Totalitarian Regimes: Coincidences and Distinctions*, Mimeo., 1986.

Milza, Pierre, *Les Fascismes* (Paris: 1985).

—— , *Le Fascisme Français. Passé et Présent* (Paris: 1987).

Mosse, George L., *The Crises of German Ideology: Intellectual origins of the Third Reich* (New York: 1964).

—— , *The Nationalization of the Masses* (New York: 1975).

—— , (Edited by), *International Fascism. New Thoughts and New Approaches* (London: 1979).

—— , *Masses and Man. Nationalist and fascist perceptions of reality* (New York: 1980).

Mülgruber, Detlef, (Edited by), *The Social Bases of European Fascist Movements* (London: 1987).

Nolte, Ernst, *Three Faces of Fascism* (New York: 1964).

—— , *Les Mouvements Fascistes. L'Europe de 1919 à 1945* (Paris: 1969).

Payne, Stanley G., *Fascism, comparison and definition* (Madison: 1980).

—— , *The Franco Regime, 1936-1975* (Madison: 1987).

—— , *História del Fascismo* (Madrid: Forthcoming).

Paxton, Robert O., *Vichy France. Old Guard and New Order* (New York: 1972).

Pinto, António Costa, "Fascist Ideology Revisited: Zeev Sternhell and His Critics", *European History Quarterly*, Vol. 19 (1986), pp. 465-483.

Polonsky, Anthony, *The Little Dictators. The History of Eastern Europe since 1918* (London and Boston: 1975).

Poulantzas, Nicos, *Fascisme et Dictature: La Troisième Internationale face au Fascisme* (Paris: 1970).

—— , *La Crise des Dictatures* (Paris: 1975).

Preston, Paul, *Las Derechas Españolas en el Siglo XX: autoritarismo, fascismo, y golpismo* (Madrid: 1986).

Ramirez, Manuel, *España.1939-1975. Régimen Político e Ideologia* (Barcelona: 1978).

Rémond, René, *Les Droites en France*, 4° ed. (Paris: 1982).

Rogger, Hans, and Eugen Weber (Edited by), *The European Right. A historical profile* (Berkeley: 1965).

Sirinelli, Jean-François, *Histoire des Droites en France*, Vol. 1-*Politique*, (Paris: 1992).

Soucy, Robert, *French Fascism. The First Wave* (New Haven and London: 1986).

Sternhell, Zeev, *La Droite Radicale. Les origines françaises du fascisme.1885-1914* (Paris: 1978).

——, *Ni Droite ni Gauche. L'idéologie fasciste en France* (Paris: 1983).

——, et alli, *Naissance de L'idéologie Fasciste* (Paris: 1989).

Sugar, Peter, (Edited by), *Native Fascism in the Sucessor States. 1918-1945* (Santa Barbara: 1971).

Trindade, Hélgio, *O Integralismo. O fascismo brasileiro na década de 30*, 2ª edição, (São Paulo: 1979).

Turner, Jr., Henri A., "Fascism and modernization" in Henri A. Turner Jr. (Edited by), *Reappraisals of Fascism* (New York: 1975).

Tusell, Javier, *La dictadura de Franco* (Madrid: 1988).

Vajda, Mihaly, *Fascism as a Mass Movement* (London: 1976).

Weber, Eugen, *Varieties of Fascism* (New York: 1964).

Woolf, S. J., (Edited by), *European Fascism* (London: 1968).

——, (Edited by), *The Nature of Fascism* (New York: 1968).

——, "Movimenti e regimi di tipo fascista in Europa", in Nicola Tranfaglia e Massimo Firpo (a cura di), *La Storia. I grandi problemi dal Medioevo all'Età Contemporanea*, Vol. 9, (Torino: 1986).

Wynot, Edward D., *Polish Politics in Transition. The Camp of National Unity anf the Struggle for Power, 1935-39 (Athens: 1974).*

Zarnowski, Janusz, (Editor), *Dictatorships in East-Central Europe. 1918-1939*, Polish Historical Library n° 4, (Wroclaw: 1983).

3 - Studies on the Portuguese *Estado Novo*

AA. VV., *O Fascismo em Portugal* (Lisboa: 1982).

AA.VV., *O Estado Novo - Das origens ao fim da autarcia, 1926-1959*, 2 Vol., (Lisboa: 1987).

AA. VV., *Salazar e o Salazarismo* (Lisboa:1989).

AA.VV., *Portugal na Segunda Guerra Mundial. Contributos para uma reavaliação* (Lisboa: 1989).

Albonico, A., *Breve Storia del Portogallo Contemporaneo* (Napoli: 1977).

Baptista, Fernando Oliveira, *A Política Agrária do Estado Novo* (Porto: 1993).

Brito, José Maria Brandão de, *A Industrialização Portuguêsa no Pós-guerra (1948-1965). O condicionamento industrial* (Lisboa: 1989).

Bruneau, Thomas C., "Church and State in Portugal: Crises of Cross and Sword", *Journal of Church and State*, Vol. 18, n° 3, Autumn 1976, pp. 463-490.

——, *Politics and Nationhood. Post-revolutionary Portugal* (New York: 1984).

Cabral, Manuel Villaverde, "Sobre o Fascismo e o seu advento em Portugal: ensaio de interpretação a pretexto de alguns livros recentes", *Análise Social*, Vol. XII (48), 1976, pp. 873-915.

——, "A Grande Guerra e o Sidonismo. Esboço interpretativo", *Análise Social*, Vol. XV(58), 1979, pp. 327-392.

——, "O Fascismo Português numa Perspectiva Comparada" in AA.VV., *O Fascismo em Portugal* (Lisboa: 1982), pp.19-30.

Caldeira, Arlindo Manuel, "O partido de Salazar: antecedentes, organização e funções da União Nacional (1926-34)", *Análise Social*, vol. XXII (94), 1986, pp. 943-977.

Campinos, Jorge, *Ideologia política do Estado Salazarista* (Lisboa: 1975).

——, *A Ditadura Militar: 1926-1933* (Lisboa: 1975).

Carrilho, Maria, *Forças Armadas e Mudança Política em Portugal no Séc. XX. Para uma explicação sociológica do papel dos militares* (Lisboa: 1985).

Cerqueira, Silas, "L'Église catholique et la dictature corporatiste portugaise", *Revue Française de Sciences Politiques*, vol. XXIII, n° 3, Juin 1973, pp. 473-513.

Cocco, Nuccio, "Salazarismo", in Nicola Tranfaglia et alli, *Storia d'Europa,* vol. 3, (Firenze:1980).

Cruz, Manuel Braga da, *As Origens da Democracia Cristã e o Salazarismo* (Lisboa: 1980).

——, *Monárquicos e Republicanos sob o Estado Novo* (Lisboa: 1987).

——, *O Partido e o Estado no Salazarismo* (Lisboa: 1988).

————, "As Elites católicas nos Primórdios do Salazarismo", *Análise Social*, vol. XXVII(116-117), 1992, pp. 547-574.

Ferreira, José Medeiros, *O Comportamento Político dos Militares. Forças armadas e regimes políticos em Portugal no séc. XX* (Lisboa: 1992).

Gallagher, Tom, *Portugal. A twentieth-century interpretation* (Manchester: 1983).

Georgel, Jacques, *Le Salazarisme. Histoire et Bilan, 1926-1974* (Paris: 1981).

Giannotti, P., e Privato, S., *Il Portogallo dalla prima alla seconda Republica, 1910-1975* (Urbino: 1978).

Goméz, Hipólito de la Torre, *La Relación Peninsular en la Antecamara de la Guerra Civil de España, 1931-36* (Mérida: 1989).

Graham, Lawrence S., "Portugal: The Bureaucracy of Empire", *LADS Occasional Papers*, Series 2, N° 9, (Austin: 1973).

————, "Portugal: The Decline and Collapse of an Authoritarian Order", *Contemporary Political Sociological Series* (Beverly Hills: 1975).

Kuin, Simon, "Fascist Italy and Salazar's Portugal, 1926-1936", *Yearbook of European Studies*, 3-Italy-Europe, (Amsterdam: 1990), pp.101-118.

————, "Mocidade Portuguesa nos Anos Trinta: a instauração de uma organização paramilitar de juventude", *Análise Social*, 122, 1993, pp. 555-588.

————, "O Braço Longo de Mussolini: os C.A.U.R. em Portugal (1933-1937)", *Penélope*, n° 11, 1993, pp. 7-20.

Leeds, Elizabeth, "Salazar's 'modelo Económico': The Consequences of Planned Constraint", *in* T. C. Bruneau, Victor M. P. da Rosa, and Alex Macleod (Edited by), *Portugal in Development: emigration, industrialization, the European Community* (Ottawa: 1984).

Lewis, Paul H., "Salazar's Ministerial Elite, 1932-1968", *Journal of Politics*, 40, August 1978, pp. 622-647.

Lucena, Manuel, *A Evolução do Sistema Corporativo Português*, Vol. I - *O Salazarismo* (Lisboa: 1976).

————, "The evolution of portuguese corporatism under Salazar and Caetano" in Lawrence S. Graham and Harry M. Makler, *Contemporary Portugal. The Revolution and its Antecedents* (Austin: 1979), pp. 65-66.

————, "Interpretações do Salazarismo: notas de leitura crítica -I", *Análise Social*, Vol. XX (83), 1984-4°, pp. 423-451.

Machado, Diamantino P., *The Structure of Portuguese society. The failure of Fascism* (New York: 1991).

Margarido, Alfredo "La comparaison de L'incomparable: Les solutions dictatoriales portugaise (1926-1974) et brésilienne (1930-1945)", AAVV, *Portugal, Brésil, France. Histoire et Culture* (Paris: 1988), pp. 57-87.

Marques, Alfredo, *Política Económica e Desenvolvimento Económico em Portugal, 1926-1959* (Lisboa: 1988).

Marques, A. H. Oliveira, *História de Portugal*, Vol. III, (Lisboa: 1982).

——, "the Portuguese 1920s: a general survey", *Revista de História Económica e Social*, n° 1, Janeiro-Junho 1978, pp. 87-103.

——, and Serrão, Joel, (Direção de), *Nova História de Portugal*, Vol. XII-*Portugal e o Estado Novo* (Coord. de Fernando Rosas), (Lisboa: 1992).

Martins, Herminio, "Portugal", Stuart Woolf (Edited by), *European Fascism* (New York: 1969), pp. 302-336.

——, "Opposition in Portugal", *Government and Opposition*, Vol. 4, N° 2, Spring 1969, pp. 250-263.

——, "The Breakdown of the Portuguese Democratic Republic", Mimio., Seventh World Congress of Sociology, Varna,1970.

——, "Portugal", Margaret Scotford Archer and Salvador Giner (Edited by), *Contemporary Europe: class, status and power* (London: 1971), pp. 60-89.

Medina, João, *Salazar em França (Lisboa: 1977)*.

——, *Salazar e os fascistas. Salazarismo e Nacional-Sindicalismo. A história de um conflito, 1932-1935 (Lisboa: 1977)*.

Mónica, Maria Filomena, *Educação e Sociedade no Portugal de Salazar — A escola primária salazarista,1926-1939 (Lisboa: 1978)*.

Oliveira, César, *A preparação do 28 de Maio. António Ferro e a propaganda do fascismo:1920-1926* (Lisboa: 1980).

——, *Portugal e a Segunda República de Espanha, 1931-1936* (Lisboa: 1987).

——, *O Salazarismo e a Guerra Civil de Espanha* (Lisboa: 1988).

——, *Salazar e o seu tempo* (Lisboa: 1991).

Opello Jr., Walter C., *Portugal's Political Development. A comparative approach* (Boulder: 1985).

Pais, José Machado, *As "Forças Vivas" e a Queda do Regime Liberal Republicano*, Madrid, Unpublished Dissertation, 1983.

——, "A crise do regime liberal republicano: algumas hipóteses explicativas", AA VV, *O Estado Novo — das origens...*, pp.129-144.

Patriarca, Fátima, *Processo de implantação e Lógica e Dinâmica de funcionamento do Corporativismo em Portugal. Os primeiros anos do Salazarismo* (Lisboa: Forthcoming).

Payne, Stanley G., "Fascism in Western Europe" in Walter Laqueur (Edited by), *Op. Cit ,* (Berkeley: 1976), pp. 295-311.

——, "Salazarism: "fascism" or "bureaucratic authoritarianism" ?", AA VV, *Estudos de História de Portugal. Homenagem a A. H. Oliveira Marques*, vol. II-sécs. XVI-XX, (Lisboa: 1983), pp. 523-53.

——, "Fascism and Right Authoritarianism in the Iberian World: the last Twenty Years", *Journal of Contemporary History*, vol. 21(1986), pp. 163-177.

——, "La oposición a las dictaduras en la Europa occidental: una perspectiva comparativa" in Javier Tusell et alii, *La Oposición al Régimen de Franco*, 3 vols., (Madrid: 1990), pp. 51-64.

——, "Authoritarianism in the Smaller States of Southern Europe", H. E. Chehabi and Alfred Stepan (Edited by), *Politics, Society and Democracy. Comparative Studies (essays in honor of Juan J. Linz)* (Boulder: Forthcoming).

Pinto, António Costa, and Ribeiro, Nuno, *A Acção Escolar Vanguarda (1933-1936). A juventude nacionalista nos primórdios do Estado Novo* (Lisboa: 1980).

——, "The Radical Right and the Military Dictatorship: The National May League (1928-1933)", *Luso-Brazilian Review*, Vol. 23, n° 1, Summer 1986, pp.1-15.

——, "The Radical Right in Contemporary Portugal", Luciano Cheles et alli (Edited by), *Neo-Fascism in Europe* (London and New York: 1991), pp. 167-190.

——, "L''Etat Nouveau' de Salazar et le Régime de Vichy", Jean-Pierre Azéma et François Bédarida, (Sous la direction de), *Op. Cit.*, (Paris: 1992), pp. 664-688.

——, "The Literary Aspirations of Portuguese Fascism", Stein U. Larsen and B. Sandberg (Edited by), *Fascism and European Literature* (Bern: 1991), pp. 238-253.

——, "As elites Políticas e a Consolidação do Salazarismo: O Nacional Sindicalismo e a União Nacional", *Análise Social*, vol. XXVII (116-117), 1992, pp. 575-613.

——, *O Salazarismo e o Fascismo Europeu. Problemas de interpretação nas Ciências Sociais* (Lisboa: 1992).

——, "Lo 'stato nuovo' di Salazar e il fascismo europeo. Problemi e prospettivi interpretative", *Stória Contemporanea,* Vol. XXIII, n° 3, giugno 1992, pp. 469-524.

——, "The 'New State' of Salazar-An overview", Richard Herr (Edited by), *Portugal, Democracy and Europe* (Berkeley: 1993), pp. 73-106.

——, *Os Camisas Azuis. Ideologias, elites e movimentos fascistas em Portugal, 1914-1945* (Lisboa: 1994).

——, et Cova, Anne, "Femmes et Salazarisme", Christine Fauré (Sous la dir. de), *Encyclopédie politique et historique des femmes* (Paris: forthcoming).

Portela, Artur, *Salazarismo e artes plásticas* (Lisboa:1982).

Raby, Dawn Linda, *Fascism and Resistence in Portugal. Communists, liberals and military dissidents in the opposition to Salazar, 1941-1974* (Manchester: 1988).

Ramos, Rui, "O Estado Novo perante os poderes periféricos: o governo de Assis Gonçalves em Vila Real (1934-39)", *Análise Social*, vol. XXII (90), 1986, pp.109-135.

Robinson, Richard A. H., "The Religious Question and the Catholic Revival in Portugal, 1900-30", *Journal of Contemporary History*, 12 (1977), pp. 345-362.

——, *Contemporary Portugal. A history* (London: 1979).

Rodrigues, Luís Nuno, "A Legião Portuguesa no Espectro Político Nacional (1936-1939)", *Penélope*, 11, 1993, pp. 21-36.

Rosas, Fernando, "Cinco pontos em torno do estudo comparado do fascismo", *Vértice*, 13, Abril de 1989, pp. 21-29.

——, *O Estado Novo nos anos trinta. Elementos para o estudo da natureza económica e social do Salazarismo,1928-1938* (Lisboa: 1986).

——, *O Salazarismo e a Aliança Luso-Británica* (Lisboa: 1988).

——, *Portugal entre a Guerra e a Paz* (Lisboa: 1990).

Santarelli, Enzo, "Il caso porthogese: radici e premesse di una rivoluzione", *Critica Marxista*, n°4, Luglio-Agosto 1975, pp. 41-59.

Schmitter, Philippe C., "Corporatism and Public Policy in Authoritarian Portugal", *Contemporary Political Sociological Series*, Sage Professional Series, Vol.I, (London: 1975).

——, "Liberation by *Golpe*: Retrospective Thoughts on the Demise of Authoritarian Rule in Portugal", *Armed Forces and Society*, vol. II, n°1, November 1975, pp. 5-33.

——, "The Impact and Meaning of "Non-competitive, Non-Free and Insignificant" Elections in Authoritarian Portugal. 1933-74", Guy Hermet, Richard Rose and Alain Rouquié (Edited by), *Elections Without Choice* (London: 1978), pp. 145-168.

———, "The 'Régime d'Exception' That Became the Rule: Forty-Eight Years of Authoritarian Domination in Portugal", Lawrence S. Graham and Harry Makler (Edited by), *Contemporary Portugal. The Revolution and Its Antecedents* (Austin: 1979), pp. 2-46.

Schwartzman, Katheen C., *The Social Origins of the Democratic Collapse. The First Portuguese Republic in the Global Economy* (Lawrence, Kansas: 1989).

Serra, João B. and Matos, Luís Salgado de, "Intervenções Militares na Vida Política", *Análise Social*, (72-73-74), I° vol., 1982, pp. 1165-1195.

Telo, António José, *Decadência e Queda da I República Portuguesa*, 2 vols., (Lisboa: 1980 e 1984).

———, *Propaganda e Guerra Secreta em Portugal, 1939-45* (Lisboa: 1990).

———, *Portugal na Segunda Guerra, 1941-45*, 2 vols., (Lisboa: 1991).

Torgal, Luís Reis, (Org.), *Ideologia, Cultura e Mentalidade no Estado Novo. Ensaios sobre a Universidade de Coimbra* (Coimbra: 1992).

Torre, Hipólito de la, (coord.), *Portugal y España en el cambio político,1958-1978 (Mérida: 1989).*

Wheeler, Douglas L., "The Military and the Portuguese Dictatorship, 1926-1974: 'The Honor of the Army'", Lawrence S. Graham and Harry M. Makler (Edited by), *Op. Cit.*, pp. 191-219.

———, "In the Service of Order: The Portuguese Political Police and the British, German and Spanish Intelligence, 1932-1945", *Journal of Contemporary History*, Vol. 18 (1983), pp. 1-25.

———, *A Ditadura Militar Portuguesa, 1926-1933* (Lisboa: 1988).

Wiarda, Howard J., *Corporatism and Development. The Portuguese Experience* (Amherst: 1977).

Index

Economy, 88-90, 183-7
Education, 81-2, 197-9
Eisenstadt, S., 55
Elections: during First Republic, 93, 96, 101, 110, 136-8; during Salazarism, 79-80, 179. *See also* electoral laws
Electoral Laws, 93, 96-101, 136, 166
Eliassem, K., 157n
Elley, Geoff, 21
Ellwood, Sheelagh, 174n
Emigration, 91, 92, 135, 193
Empire, 55, 88, 192-3. *See also* colonialism
Employers Confederation (CP), 95
England, 19, 72, 74, 86-7, 90, 96, 106
Espada, João Carlos, viii
Estatuto do Trabalho Nacional (ETN), 62, 182, 183. *See also* corporatism
ETN. *See Estatuto do Trabalho Nacional* (ETN)
European University Institute, vii
Evolutionist Party, 99, 100, 102, 107, 136-7

Faisceau, Le, 120
Falange. *See* FET de las JONS
Fátima, miracle of, 66, 203
Faure, Christian, 195n
Fauré, Christine, 198n
Felice, Renzo De, 2, 4n, 5, 6, 22, 24, 57
Fernandes, Castro, 135
Fernandes, Vasco da Gama, 162n
Ferraz, General Ivens, 75
Ferreira, José Medeiros, 74n, 76n, 140n, 167n
Ferro, António, 119, 161, 187, 195
FET de las JONS, 5, 11, 174, 191. *See also* Franco; Spain
Filipe, Prince, 103
Firpo, Massimo, 36n
First Republic: socio-economic constraints, 88-92; party system of, 96-

101, 136-7; cabinet instability during, 101-2; political violence during, 103-4; elections, 97-101; interest groups and, 94-6; radical right and, 110-35; Army intervention, 139-42; breakdown of, 45-9, 142-6
First World War. *See* World War I
Fischer-Galati, Stephen, viii, 35n
Flanders, 167
Florence, vii, viii
France, v, 26-9, 111, 120. *See also Action Française;* Maurras, Charles; Vichy
Franco, Francisco, 1, 8, 9, 10, 17-8, 24-6, 36, 73, 164, 170, 173, 200-1, 205, 207. *See also* Spain; Spanish Civil War; Spanish Popular Front
Freire, João, 80n, 94n
Freitas, General Vicente de, 75, 151
Friedrich, Carl J., 1n
Futurism, 119, 195

Galicia, 105
Gallagher, Tom, 76n
General Confederation of Labor (CGT), 94-5, 138
Gentile, Emilio, viii, 7, 22n, 123n, 179n, 191n
Georgel, Jacques, 30
Germani, Gino, 13, 15
Germany, 2, 4, 15-8, 25, 31, 35, 36, 50-1, 57-8, 67, 71, 73, 85, 105, 164, 175, 181, 194, 206, 208
Giannotti, P., 22n
Giner, Salvador, 25, 39n, 87n
GNR. *See* National Republican Guard (GNR)
Gomes, Teixeira, 132
Gonçalves, Assis, 79n
Governamentais, 136-7
Grazia, Victoria De, 183n, 199n
Graham, Lawrence S., 50n, 51n, 55, 59, 76n, 82n
Great Britain. *See* England